Footsteps

Old Testament, Volume 2

Revised Edition

God *Provides for Us*

by

Bernice Claire Jordan

BCM
INTERNATIONAL

BCM International, Inc.

201 Granite Run Drive, Suite 260, Lancaster, PA 17601
70 Melvin Avenue, Hamilton, Ontario L8H 2J5 Canada
P.O Box 688, Weston-super-Mare, N. Somerset BS23 9PP England

Footsteps of Faith is BCM's primary Bible teaching curriculum for children's Bible Clubs. This unique series has been revised for teaching God's Word in other settings, such as Sunday school, children's church, Christian school, and home schooling.

Revision Committee
Revised by Pamela Rowntree
Edited by Donna Culver
David and Lois Haas
Richard Winters
Patricia Black

Cover design & book layout:
Bert VandenBos
Fran Lines

Copyright © 2001, 2020
BCM International, Inc. All rights reserved.

ISBN 978-0-86508-168-0

CONTENTS

Course Overview iv

Introduction v

    Understand Your Children vi

    Prepare Yourself to Be God's Channel vii

    Prepare Your Lesson viii

    Prepare Your Visual x

    Manage Your Class Effectively ix

    Lead Your Children to Christ x

    Keep in Touch xi

    Important Information xii

Lesson 1   God Protects Baby Moses 1

Lesson 2   Moses Leaves Egypt 13

Lesson 3   God Calls Through a Burning Bush 22

Lesson 4   Moses Confronts Pharaoh 33

Lesson 5   God Sends Plagues Against Egypt 42

Lesson 6   God Sends the Final Plague 54

Lesson 7   Israel Crosses the Red Sea 63

Lesson 8   God Supplies Manna & Quail 73

Lesson 9   God Helps Israel at Rephidim 82

Lesson 10   God Gives the Law 90

Lesson 11   The People Worship a Gold Calf 98

Lesson 12   Israel Builds the Tabernacle 108

Lesson 13   The Priests Offer Sacrifices 119

Lesson 14   Israel Fails to Trust God

               The People Complain About Manna *(Part 1)* 130

               The People Turn Back *(Part 2)* 139

Lesson 15   Moses Makes a Brass Snake 148

Lesson 16   Moses Goes to Heaven 156

Resource Section 167

Teaching Materials & Supplies 180

God Provides for Us
Course Overview

No.	Title	Theme God Provides for Us...	Scripture	Verse
1	God Protects Baby Moses	Wisdom	Exodus 1:1–2:9	James 1:5
2	Moses Leaves Egypt	Guidance	Exodus 2:9-25	Isaiah 58:11
3	God Calls Through a Burning Bush	Purpose	Exodus 2:23–4:28	Philippians 2:13
4	Moses Confronts Pharaoh	Courage	Exodus 4:29–7:5	Deuteronomy 31:6
5	God Sends Plagues Against Egypt	Power	Exodus 7–10	2 Samuel 22:33
6	God Sends the Final Plague	Faith	Exodus 10:28–12:36	Ephesians 2:8
7	Israel Crosses the Red Sea	Deliverance	Exodus 12:37-42; 13:17–15:21	Daniel 3:17
8	God Supplies Manna & Quail	Food	Exodus 15:22–16:36	Matthew 6:11
9	God Helps Israel at Rephidim	Help	Exodus 17	Psalm 46:1
10	God Gives the Law	Rules	Exodus 18:1–20:26	Psalm 40:8
11	The People Worship a Gold Calf	Correction	Exodus 24:12-18; 31:18; 32:1-35; 34:1-32	Proverbs 3:11, 12
12	Israel Builds the Tabernacle	Fellowship	Exodus 25–31; 35:4–40:38	1 John 1:3
13	The Priests Offer Sacrifices	Cleansing	Exodus 28	1 John 1:9
14-1	The People Complain About Manna	Thankfulness	Numbers 11–12	Ephesians 5:20
14-2	The People Turn Back	Thankfulness	Numbers 13–14; 20:1-13	Ephesians 5:20
15	Moses Makes a Brass Snake	Salvation	Numbers 20:1, 23-29; 21:4-9	John 3:17
16	Moses Goes to Heaven	Hope	Numbers 26–27 Deuteronomy 1:1-5; 6:4-9; 31; 32; 34	Titus 2:13

INTRODUCTION

Footsteps of Faith is an eight-volume Bible teaching curriculum that covers the Bible in basically chronological order. Its overall aim is to help children respond to the love of God in Christ and learn to walk in the footsteps of faith and obedience.

Each volume is complete in itself and centers around a theme that is carried through every lesson in that volume to provide for consistent learning as well as continual review and application of the Bible truth.

The course is non-graded and undated, written for teaching children ages 6-12, but adaptable to different age groups and many teaching situations. It has been used effectively in Bible Clubs, children's church programs, vacation Bible schools, and Sunday school classes, as well as in Christian schools and home school classes.

The series
- shows God at work in the world. The Old Testament points ahead to Christ's coming, revealing man's fall into sin, God's promise of a Savior, and his program for accomplishing this. The New Testament records the actual fulfillment of God's program in the birth of Christ, his life and death and resurrection, the birth of the Church, the establishing of a missionary program, and the yet-to-be-fulfilled promise of Christ's return!
- teaches Bible doctrine and history along with the principles of Christian living. emphasizes Scripture memorization and provides Bible Study Helps, which are coordinated with the lessons and may be used as work sheets or take-home devotionals.
- is both evangelistic and Christian-growth oriented, clearly presenting the plan of salvation and emphasizing practical Christian living.

The lessons
- emphasize specific Bible truths.include practical, hands-on application of those truths for both Christian and non-Christian children.
- are structured with a teaching aim designed to help the teacher present the Bible truth and encourage the children to relate and apply that truth to their daily lives.

A unique review system
- is built into each volume and visualizes the main theme of that course and the complementary lesson themes.
- relates the lessons logically to each other and to the central theme of the course.
- provides a framework for remembering biblical truth so that the children can apply it in their daily lives.
- enables the teacher to review and reinforce previous lessons and memory verses quickly, regularly and in an interesting way.
- stimulates the children to *see, hear, verbalize* and *do*, thus involving them in the learning process.

Correlated visual aids enhance learning

- The Visual CD contains the following PowerPoint presentation for two tracks (KJV and NIV): the Review Chart, the Memory Verses, and the Bible Lessons. The PowerPoint presentation can be displayed on a computer screen or with a video projector. The CD is suitable for all PCs capable of running PowerPoint 97 or higher. A copy of PowerPoint 97 player is included with the CD. The disk contains a set of files in Adobe Acrobat format for use in printing full-colored flashcards. A copy of Adobe Acrobat is also included in the disk.
- The *Resource CD* contains the following, all of which can be downloaded and printed:
  - *Creative Idea Menus* provide a wealth of ideas to reinforce and extend learning in programs and learning centers.
  - *Visualized Memory Verses* (available in both KJV and NIV) furnishes visual pieces for teaching every memory verse in the course.
  - *Student Memory Verse Tokens and Holders* (adapted from the Review Chart and available in both KJV and NIV) are colorful take-home review aids that encourage children to memorize the verses and help to build links from week to week.
  - *Student Bible Study Helps* are take-home devotional guides that include daily Bible reading portions, questions to answer, and a weekly activity.
- Full-color *Felt Visuals*
  - The *Figures* focus attention and encourage children to visualize scenes as you tell the Bible story.
  - The *Review Chart* provides a structured system for introducing and reviewing lessons.
  - The *Felt Backgrounds* provide a scenic backdrop for the figures and can be used as an alternative to PowerPoint or flashcard visuals on the Visual CD.

God Provides for Us, Old Testament, Volume 2, of the *Footsteps of Faith* series covers the book of Exodus and selected portions of Leviticus through Deuteronomy. It tells the amazing story of God's remarkable love and care for his chosen people, Israel, as he freed them from slavery in Egypt and guided them on their journey to the Promised Land. Moses, their leader, demonstrates the power of a life lived by faith in God and obedience to his commands and challenges us to follow his example.

The course draws a parallel between Israel's wilderness journey and the children's journey through life. It aims to show that God is as faithful to his own character and to believers today as he was to his ancient people; that their deliverance was by faith in God, and that our salvation and deliverance from sin is by faith in Jesus Christ.

The Review Chart for *God Provides for Us* is a door which represents "God's Supply Room and a suitcase into which the children "pack" the provisions God makes for them. Whether using the Review Chart on a computer or on the felt board you will be able to take advantage of its flexibility to introduce and review Bible facts and truths as well as Bible memory verses.

Understand Your Children

Children, influenced by fast changing technology,
- access the world through computers and the internet.
- are used to a fast-paced, "instant everything" society.
- are bright, eager to learn, and well informed.
- receive much of their information in "sound bytes" (capsulized reports).
- are accustomed to seeing most problems solved within a 30- or 60-minute time slot in a television schedule; consequently, have short attention spans.
- expect great variety in all they see and hear.
- can be impatient with sitting still, being quiet or waiting.

Children, growing up in an unstable, immoral, and pluralistic world, are sometimes
- feeling a deep need for someone to love them, to care about them, to give them a reason to hope.
- being exposed by the media to too much too early.
- being conditioned to accept materialism, deteriorating moral standards, and a secular world view as the norm.
- being assaulted by violence in the media and in their homes and neighborhoods.
- being traumatized by broken homes, tragedies, or incurable diseases.
- being left to solve problems on their own.
- being bombarded with moral and belief systems that contradict the Word of God.
- lacking a biblical world view to help them sift conflicting information.

Children learn in many different ways.
- Some learn best by *seeing* what they're learning.
- Others learn best by *talking* about it.
- Still others learn best by *moving* or *doing*—being actively involved or making things.
- Some process information globally—by seeing "the big picture."
- Others are analytic thinkers and want all the details.

Remember these things when preparing to teach. Try a variety of the teaching methods and options suggested in the text, even if they do not all appeal to you. They will help you incorporate variety in methods and visuals and capsulize important points in "sound bites" the children can see and hear over and over. You will soon know which are most effective with your class members.

What a privilege—and what a sobering responsibility—to take to them the wonderful news that God loves them, that he has provided salvation for them and that he has a plan for their lives! There is hope in him!

For *GOD never changes*! His truth is timeless! God's eternal Word is a guidebook for living a life that pleases God in any age. His miracle provision of a dry path through the Red Sea, food, and water for 2,000,000 people in the wilderness, and clothes and shoes that never wore out encourage us to believe that he will provide for us, too. Knowing him and walking in the footsteps of faith and obedience provide security and stability in an uncertain world.

Therefore, it is essential to take time to get to know your students and understand their needs, so that you can demonstrate Christ's love to them and lead them to security in him amid their insecure world.

Prepare Yourself to Be God's channel

You, the teacher, are the living link between God's truth and the children in your class. You channel Christ's love to them. You teach them God's Word so that they may understand his truth and receive Christ as Savior, then follow him in loving obedience. You model how to practice in daily life the truth they are learning. And you are their guide to discovering truth for themselves and attaining their greatest potential for serving God.

- Submit yourself to God that you may be a Spirit-empowered teacher.
- Expect God to speak to you personally as you study your lesson each week, then to guide you as you prepare to teach.
- Realize that you are a tool in God's hands. As you depend on him, he will work through you and in the hearts of the children to draw them to himself.
- Enjoy your class! Be enthusiastic; enter into activities with the children so they see you not only as teacher but as a friend.
- Encourage the children to bring their Bibles, and plan ways for them to use them every week. Teach them how to find passages in Scripture. Frequently have them follow along in their Bibles as you teach the lesson. As you instruct boys and girls to love and respect God's Word and show them how to use it correctly and inspire them to obey it, you give them an invaluable gift that will go with them throughout life. (If some don't have Bibles, look for a place to get them inexpensively—a Bible society or an organization that distributes free ones.)
- REVIEW, REVIEW, REVIEW! Without reviewing the lessons, the children will probably forget to apply many essential Bible truths you are teaching them.
- Avoid using many questions that can be answered with a simple yes or no.
- Use the questions suggested in the lesson, or others you devise yourself, to involve the children in the learning process and find out what they have or have not learned. Then you will have the opportunity to correct faulty understanding, and they will learn more because they are thinking and interacting.
- Avoid calling on students who find it difficult or embarrassing to read aloud or answer questions publicly. Find other ways to involve them until they feel safe enough to interact.

Remember that your effectiveness in class often depends upon the relationship that you have established with students outside of class.

- Find ways to spend time with students, such as attending some of their school or neighborhood activities and visiting at least some of their homes.
- Learn their names and show a real interest in them.
- Listen when they talk about their families, their friends, and their struggles. Listening shows the child that you care and helps you learn how to apply Scripture effectively.
- Notice individual's strengths and affirm them regularly.
- Compliment those you see practicing what they're learning.
- Seek to discern the spiritual progress of individual students and help them to grow in Christlikeness
- Don't be afraid to be explicit when dealing with the issues that surround them. They are exposed to life experiences and life styles far beyond what they should be. They need to know what God has to say and how to live for him in the midst of their life situations. Ask God to guide you and make you sensitive to their needs and his direction.
- Pray for them.
- Make the brief time they spend with you each week a happy time, a safe place—a refuge.

Prepare Your Lesson
Pray that God will speak to you through the Scripture passage, then guide you as you prepare to teach.

- Follow the plan in the teacher's text or use it as a pattern to write your own. A lesson plan will keep you on track, by helping you use your time wisely and accomplish the purpose God lays on your heart for the lesson.
- Study the Scripture passage thoroughly, making notes of points that seem important to you. Look for answers to six important questions: *Who* was involved? *What* was happening? *Where* were they? *When* did it happen? *How* did it happen? *Why* did it happen? or *Why* did he say that?
- Make simple outline notes to use as a guide when teaching. Put them in your Bible so that the children will see you teaching from God's Word, not the teacher's text.
- Read the printed lesson, thinking it through with your children in mind. Each part of the lesson has a specific purpose.
  The **Aim** is the statement of what you want to accomplish—with God's help—as you present the lesson.
  The **Introduction** is a plan for getting the students' attention and directing their thinking in preparation for the Bible story.
  The **Bible Content** is the Bible story and the Bible truth it illustrates and reinforces.
  The **Conclusion** is a plan for completing the lesson by showing the children how to apply the Bible truth and providing a way for them to respond to it in daily life.

Prepare Your Visuals
When using the Visual CD:
- Become familiar with how the visual CD is programmed. Learn how to access the Review Chart and to work with the memory verse. Become familiar with accessing the lesson and coordinating the PowerPoint visuals with the teacher's text.
- To show the PowerPoint slides on a screen, connect your computer to a video projector.
- Practice as many times as necessary to become proficient in using the PowerPoint visuals with the lesson.
- To prepare flashcards to visualize the lesson, click on the print icon on the title page of the PowerPoint lesson. Print the scenes on the size paper you want and laminate them to increase their continued use.

When using the Felt Visuals:
- Sort out the figures you will need and stack them in the order you will use them.
- Put the Review Chart and the backgrounds on the felt board in the order they will be used, with the last one on the bottom. Secure them to the top of the board with large binder clips.
- Use the sketches in the lesson as guides for placing figures on the scenes. Practice placing them as you stand at the side of the board. Check from the front to see if they are straight and in their proper places. Sometimes it is helpful to put some of the figures on the backgrounds ahead of time so that you just add the main figure(s) while telling the story.
- Practice telling the story aloud as you put the figures in place until you can do it comfortably and without interruption.
- When you teach, be careful to always work from the side of your board so you don't block a student's view. Maintain eye contact with the children and don't turn your back on them.

Manage Your Class Effectively

A well-managed classroom honors God by creating an atmosphere for learning, providing a secure refuge for students, making learning enjoyable, and preventing many behavior and discipline problems. A well-managed classroom requires three elements.

A prepared teacher
- yielded to God in mind, heart, and spirit
- ready with both lesson and program
- knowing each student's name, characteristics, needs, and interests
- praying for each student
- planning behavioral goals for the children
- arriving early to prepare the room before the children arrive

A prepared environment
- visuals and equipment set up and in working order
- appropriate seating arranged so all can see and hear
- comfortable temperature and adequate lighting
- minimal distractions (e.g., clutter, noise, activities)

Prepared students
- knowing class rules: for example, where to put their coats, where to say their verses, how to answer or ask questions, enter and leave class, or take bathroom breaks
- aware that you expect them to obey class rules, that you appreciate good behavior and will praise them for it, and that there will be consequences for inappropriate behavior

The ultimate purpose of managing your class well is to create an environment in which God the Holy Spirit is able to work through the Word of God to bring about change in the children's lives.

Lead Your Children to Christ

Leading children to receive Jesus Christ as their Savior is a glorious privilege and an awesome responsibility. It is our deep conviction that to adequately carry out this responsibility the teacher must do four things:
- Present salvation truth frequently.
- Give students opportunities to respond to the truth.
- Speak privately with those who respond.
- Follow up on those who make a profession of faith.

In class
- *Present salvation truth.*
  "God is holy. We are sinners, deserving punishment. We must believe the Lord Jesus Christ died for us and receive him as our personal Savior."
  Use the salvation ABCs:
  - ADMIT I am a sinner: I've done wrong things, displeased God (Romans 3:23).
  - BELIEVE that Jesus Christ is God, that he died on the cross for me, and that he rose again (Romans 5:8).
  - CHOOSE to receive Christ as Savior (Romans 10:9).
- *Invite the children to respond.*
  "Perhaps you have never received Christ as your Savior and would like to do that today. If so, I'd like to talk with you after class and show you how."

After class
Talk individually with those who respond, being careful to have the door open and a helper nearby.
- *Find out if they understand why they came.*
  - "Is there a special reason you came to talk to me?"
  - "Have you ever received Jesus as your Savior before?"
- *Review basic facts about Christ.*
  - Who Jesus is (both God and man) John 3:16; 1 John 5:20
  - What Jesus did (died on the cross to take the punishment for our sins; rose again to be our living Savior) 1 Corinthians 15:3, 4
  - Why they need Jesus ("You are a sinner deserving punishment for your sins. Jesus can make you right with God and give you eternal life in heaven"). Romans 3:10; 6:23
- *Review the ABCs of salvation listed above.*
  - Say, "Jesus wants to be your Savior right now. Will you receive him?" John 1:12
  - If they say yes, ask them to pray aloud. Let them use their own words, but guide them if necessary ("I admit I am a sinner; I'm sorry for my sins and want to be free from them. I believe you died for me, and I receive you as my living Savior.")
  - Be sure they base their salvation on God's Word, not on their feelings! Show them Scriptures (Romans 10:9; John 1:12; 1 John 5:11-13) that indicate salvation is by faith, believing what God says.
- *Follow up.*
  Give them the tract entitled *"How to Become a Child of God,"* as a reminder of what they have done. Read through it with them. Then use it as a guide for Christian growth in the weeks ahead.

Keep in Touch

Use Mailbox Bible Club correspondence lessons to keep in touch after the series is finished. When the children return their completed lessons (either by mail or in person) to be checked and to receive the next lesson, you have an excellent opportunity to answer questions and provide continuing guided help for their walk with the Lord. *(See the Teaching Materials & Supplies list on page 180 for information on ordering materials and obtaining a lesson sample.)*

**Do you have suggestions or questions? Do you need help or training?
Contact us at**

BCM INTERNATIONAL, INC.
201 Granite Run Drive, Suite 260, Lancaster PA 17601
Toll-free: 1-888-226-4685; FAX: 1-717-560-9607
email: publications@bcmintl.org

70 Melvin Avenue, Hamilton, ON L8H 2J5 CANADA
Phone: 1-905-549-9810; FAX: 1-905-549-7664
email: mission@bcmintl.ca

P.O. Box 688, Weston-super-Mare, N. Somerset BS23 9PP ENGLAND
Phone: 1934-413484; email: office@bcm.org.uk

Important Information
About the Teaching Materials for This Course

Listed below are general visual aids you should have available before you begin teaching the course, along with instructions for preparing some teaching aids that are used in most lessons. Check the "Materials to Gather" section in each lesson for items to collect for that lesson. Choose from the Options those learning activities that are appropriate for the various learning styles in your group.

PowerPoint visuals available on the Visual CD (FO2VCD)

Use a computer or a video projector to display the Lesson, Memory Verse, and Review Chart visuals. If you do not have PowerPoint 97 or higher in your computer, install it free by following the directions on page 5 of the guidebook that comes with the Visual CD. The visuals are programmed to follow the sequence of the lesson in the text. Click on the right arrow of the computer to add or remove figures and to change sketches when the lesson text tells you to place, add, or remove the figures. You can use colored flashcards to teach the lessons by clicking on the "Print icon" on each lesson's title slide.

Visualized memory verses available on the Resource CD (FO2RCD)

Print the visuals on heavy paper and cut them out. Place each verse in a separate file folder.

Memory verse tokens & token holders available on the Resource CD

Use these as an incentive to memorize weekly Bible verses (available in KJV and NIV). Print the holders on card stock. Print the colored tokens and cut them out before class. When the students can say a verse correctly, have them paste its token on their token holders. Or, paste all tokens on the token holders; then let those who say the verse correctly put a small sticker on their token. (Prepare an extra set of tokens if you want to give a token to each child after class to practice the verse at home.) Send the token holders home at the end of the course.

Bible Study Helps available on the Resource CD

To encourage daily Bible reading, print and give out one lesson at a time to each student to take home. Have the children bring their completed sheets the next week for you to check.

Felt Figures

Cut out the figures and file them in numerical order in file folders labelled 1-10, 11-19, etc. Provide an additional folder for carrying the figures to class.

Felt Backgrounds

Order from BCM or use your own flannelgraph backgrounds (the *Felt Figures* will adhere to the flannel).

Patterns & Maps: Use a copier to enlarge and print the patterns and map indicated. Attach these visuals (or any chart you make) to the felt board with clips or loops of tape when indicated.

Bookmarks: Use a copier to duplicate the bookmarks on page 178 on colored heavy paper, if available. Cut them apart to give one to each child.

Word strips & cards: Word strips are available in the Felt Figure's packet. If you are not using the felt figures, use your computer to prepare and print word strips and cards specified for each lesson. Cut them apart and glue small pieces of double-faced flannel to the back of the strips so that they will adhere to the felt board. Or, print the words clearly on quality paper towel or construction paper strips, and use sandpaper to roughen the back of the construction paper strips.

Handouts: Use a copier to duplicate the pattern specified in Materials to Gather.

For information about ordering any of the above teaching materials see page 180.

God Protects Baby Moses
Theme: *Wisdom*

Lesson 1

❃ BEFORE YOU BEGIN...

We don't hear much talk about wisdom these days. Many reject the idea of absolutes; instead, they want to live by their own standard of what is good or "right."

But the eternal, all-wise God is the author of wisdom—the ability to both understand what is true or right in a situation and to choose the right way to act. He has given us the sourcebook of wisdom, his Word, the Bible. Our children need to know him, to become familiar with his Word and learn to draw wisdom from it for their daily life situations.

Jochebed is an outstanding example of one who needed wisdom. When faced with a government that would kill her baby, she went to God for wisdom and he gave it—a daring, unorthodox idea! Teach your children that God is the one who can give them wisdom to know and do the right thing, even in tough situations. Help them recognize that the Bible has answers for life's daily problems. Encourage them to form the habit of turning to God and his Word in *every* situation so that their lives will honor him and be a witness to others. *"For the Lord gives wisdom; from His mouth come knowledge and understanding" (Proverbs 2:6, NKJV).*

☞ AIM:

That the children may

- Know that God gives his children wisdom based on his Word when they ask him for it.
- Respond by becoming God's child; by studying God's Word and asking him for wisdom in difficult situations.

📖 SCRIPTURE: Exodus 1:1-2:9; 6:20; Hebrews 11:23

♥ MEMORY VERSE: James 1:5

If any of you lack wisdom, let him ask of God...and it shall be given him. (KJV)
If any of you lacks wisdom, he should ask God...and it will be given to him. (NIV)

1

▲ Option #1

Make word strips: GENESIS, EXODUS, LEVITICUS, NUMBERS, DEUTERONOMY. Place GENESIS on the board as you review its content; then add EXODUS. You will use the others in later lessons.

▲ Option #2

Display a world map or globe; help the children locate present-day Israel and where their own country is in relation to it.

Wisdom

1   James 1:5

▲ Option #3

Definition word card:
Exodus = out of (exit).

Print the word on one side of a flash card; the definition, on the reverse.

📁 MATERIALS TO GATHER

Memory verse visual for James 1:5 (see page xii)
Backgrounds: Review Chart, Plain Background, Palace, City Wall, Plain Interior, River
Figures: R1, 1, 2, 3, 4, 5, 6, 7, 8, 9, 10, 11, 12, 13, 14, 15, 16(2), 103
Token holders & Memory verse tokens (see page xii) for James 1:5
Bible Study Helps for Lesson 1 (see page xii)
Special:
- *For Review Chart:* "God Provides for Us" bookmarks, Wilderness Map
- *Bible content 1:* Wilderness Map
- *For Review Chart & Bible Content 1:* Wilderness Map
- *For Memory Verse:* Newsprint & marker or chalkboard & chalk
- *For Conclusion:* Word strips WISDOM, GOD, OWN
- *For Application:* Newsprint & marker or chalkboard & chalk; word strips ADMIT, BELIEVE, CHOOSE
- *For Options:* Materials for any options you choose to use
- *Note: Follow the instructions on page xii to prepare the "God Provides for Us" bookmarks, the Wilderness Map (pattern P-1 on page 168) and the word strips.*

💼 REVIEW CHART

Display the Wilderness Map. Have the "God Provides for Us" bookmarks ready to distribute and the Review Chart with R1 placed behind God's Supply Room ready to display when indicated.

Who can tell me the name of the first book of the Bible? *(Response)* Yes, it is Genesis and it means *beginnings*. Let's find it in our Bibles. *(Help any who need assistance.)* ▲#1

In Genesis we can read about the beginning of many things. For example, we learn that God created the world and everything in it, including people. We also read that God chose a man named Abraham and his descendants (his family who came after him) to be God's own special people. He wanted to make himself known to them and through them to the other nations of the world. In the Bible they are called Israelites, children of Israel, Hebrews and Jews. Today we call them Jewish people. Many of them live in the country of Israel, but Jewish people also live in many other countries of the world. 📖(1)

God promised his people that he would give them a special land to be their own. When we first read about it in the Bible, it is called Canaan *(indicate Canaan and Egypt on the map)*. Later it would be called Israel. Abraham and his descendants lived in Canaan for many years before the family moved to Egypt. During the years that the Israelites lived in Egypt, God was preparing them for the land he had promised. He was also preparing the land for them. ▲#2

In our Bible lessons we are going to learn how the Israelites left Egypt and went back to Canaan. We will hear some exciting stories about how God freed them from slavery and provided everything they needed while they were traveling. We can find the story of this trip in the second book of the Bible. Who can tell me its name? *(Response)* Yes, it's Exodus. *(Distribute the "God Provides for Us" bookmarks.)* Find Exodus 1:1 in your Bible and place your bookmark there.

The word *exodus* is related to the word *exit* which we see over doors in public buildings. What does the word *exit* tell you when you see it over a door? *(Response)* Yes, it means this is the way out of the building. And the book of Exodus tells us how God took his people out of one land and into another. ▲#3 ▲#4

Have you ever gone on a long trip, maybe a vacation with your parents or to camp for part of the summer? What were some of the things you had to do to get ready? *(Encourage response.)* Probably one of the most important things you did was to pack things in your suitcase or duffel bag. What kinds of things did you pack? *(Allow for response.)*

The trip the Israelites were about to make would be very long and often difficult. *(Indicate on the map.)* They would travel through desert or wilderness country much of the time and face many problems. They would live in tents which they could pack up and move. They would pack what they thought they would need, but when they ran out or needed something they did not have, what would they do? Would they be able to supply it for themselves? Could they go to a store? No, they would have to learn to trust God to supply their needs and help them; there was no one else.

In some ways you and I are like the Israelites. They were traveling from Egypt to Canaan; we are traveling on a journey through life. This journey began when we were born and will end when our lives are over. Then, if we have trusted Jesus as Savior, we will "arrive" in heaven to live with God forever. But while we are on this earthly trip we have needs and problems each day, just as the Israelites did. God is the same today as he was then. He made us and the world. He has all power and can do anything, so he is able to meet all our needs. He is wise and knows all things, so he can help us solve our problems.

In our Bible lessons we are going to learn about some of the things God provided for his people as they traveled through the desert. *(Display the Review Chart.)* This door *(indicate God's Supply Room)* is the entrance to a place called God's Supply Room. We all have seen supply rooms or closets, perhaps where the teacher or your parents keep the things they need. God's Supply Room is far bigger than any room or closet we have ever seen. This is just to remind us that God has everything we will ever need for our lives here on this earth, just as he had for the Israelites. He wants to supply our needs and help us solve our problems as we make this journey through life.

Each time we have a lesson we will take something new from God's Supply Room and "pack" it into our suitcase *(indicate on the Chart)*. Each thing we pack will be something God gave to his people as they traveled towards Canaan—things they needed to keep them alive or to help them on their trip. These are also the very things God wants to give us to help us as we travel through life. By the end of our lessons, we will have packed our suitcase full of many good things from God. Let's see

▲ **Option #4**

Show an actual "exit" sign and/or find exit signs in the building where your class meets.

◨ **Note (1)**

Several names are used in the Bible for the people of God.

Israelites, in the Old Testament, is the most common designation for the descendants of Jacob, whose name was changed to Israel by the angel of the Lord in Genesis 32.

Jews referred originally to those who lived in the territory of Judah, the southern kingdom, during the Exilic and post-Exilic periods in the Old Testament. It is the most common designation for the Israelites in the New Testament, where it takes on political and religious significance during the first century A.D.

Hebrews is the least-used term. The Babylonians and Egyptians originally used it to refer with contempt to foreigners. It later became an ethnic term for the Jewish people. The word is used quite often in the book of Exodus—more times than in any other book of the Bible.

For clarity's sake, we have chosen to use the term *Israelites* to refer to God's chosen people in this series of lessons, even though they are frequently called Hebrews in the book of Exodus.

⌂ Note (2)

In this lesson we view wisdom as God's enabling to make choices based on his values and perspectives as revealed in his Word. Thus God's Word is the test for all human ideas and counsel. The better people know God's Word, the more able they are to make wise decisions.

> If any of you lack wisdom, let him ask of God, and it shall be given him. James 1:5

▲ Option #5

Definition word card:
Wisdom = understanding what is true or right; common sense.

⌂ Note (3)

If you choose to display the memory verse on the Felt Board, put it on a plain background throughout this volume.

▲ Option #6

Print Romans 3:23 and 6:23; John 1:12 and 3:16 on newsprint so all the children can see and read them together as you teach this section. Or, as time permits, have the children look them up in their Bibles.

---

what the first one is. *(Have a student take R1 from God's Supply Room and read what it says.)* It's *Wisdom!* (Place it on the suitcase.) ⌂(2)

Perhaps you have said, "I don't know what to do! How can I know what is the right thing to do?" *(Have children share experiences.)* That's when we need wisdom. What is wisdom? The dictionary says that wisdom is understanding what is true or right and having common sense—knowing how to use what we know. So to have wisdom is to understand what is true or right in a situation and be able to decide the right way to act. Our memory verse will help us understand how we can get this wisdom from God. ▲#5

♥ MEMORY VERSE

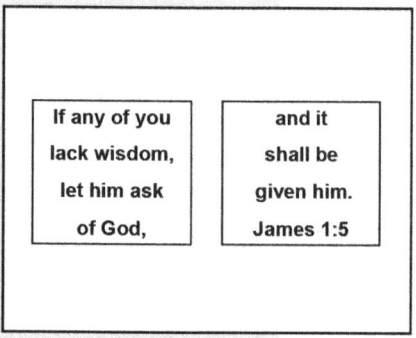

Display the visual to teach James 1:5. Have newsprint & marker or chalkboard & chalk ready to use when indicated. ⌂(3)

Our memory verse is from God's Word; let's read it together. *(Read it aloud together.)* It tells us what we should do when we *lack* wisdom. To *lack* something means to be without it or to need it. Can you think of a time when you lacked something? *(Response)* Maybe it was friends to play with or money to buy something you really wanted. Our verse says we can lack wisdom. We may not know what is true or right in a situation or we may not be able to decide the right way to act.

Do you need God's wisdom for some situation today? *(List the children's responses on newsprint or chalkboard. If necessary, suggest some examples to stimulate thinking, such as how to help a friend who is in trouble, or choosing the right thing to do or say when others want you to do a wrong thing.)*

What does our verse tell us to do when we need wisdom—when we don't know what is right or what we should do? Yes, we should pray, asking God to give us wisdom. How does God give us this wisdom? As we read God's Word, we become more aware of what pleases him and how he wants us to live. With his help we can apply what God's Word says to specific situations. God also uses people who have lived longer and have learned from experience to share their advice.

What does our verse say will happen when we ask God for wisdom? *(Response)* Yes, he will give it to us. Does everyone have the right to ask God for his wisdom? No! Only those who belong to his family have the right to ask him for anything. Only children have the right to ask their father for what they need. That is true of God's family, too.

If you are not sure that you are part of God's family, here are some things you need to know. *First,* God is holy and righteous; he has never done anything wrong. *Second,* you are not like God. The Bible says we all have done wrong things and deserve to be punished for what we have done (Romans 3:23). ▲#6 That punishment is death or being separated from God (Romans 6:23). *Third,* God loves you so much that he sent his only Son Jesus into the world to take the punishment for your sin and give you eternal life (John 3:16). And *fourth,* you must believe that Jesus did this for you and receive him as your Savior (John 1:12). When you do that, you will become his child. As his child you will belong to him forever and have the right to ask him for whatever you need, including wisdom.

God will give us wisdom whenever we need it if we ask him for it. We study the Bible here in our class, so we will know how God wants us to live. Then we can depend on God to help us know what to do and how to do it in *every* situation we face when we trust him. That's why it is also important for Christians to study their Bibles at home and at church. *(Work on memorizing the verse.)* ▲#7

▲ Option #7

Memorizing the verse: Have the children read the verse aloud together several times. Then divide them into two groups and the verse into three phrases. Have the groups alternate in saying the phrases, but all say the reference together. Gradually remove the visual pieces as you drill the verse. Finally, "conduct" the two groups as a choir, having them follow your lead as to which group should say which part. Vary the parts to make the activity interesting and challenging.

BIBLE LESSON OUTLINE

God Protects Baby Moses

■ Introduction

Joe needs wisdom

■ Bible Content

1. God's people multiply in Egypt.
2. Pharaoh tries to destroy God's people.
    a. By making them work hard.
    b. By killing boy babies.
3. A family trusts God.
4. A family asks God for wisdom.
5. A princess rescues the baby.

■ Conclusion

Summary

Application
Learning how to get God's wisdom

Response Activity
Asking God for wisdom to handle a difficult situation

BIBLE LESSON

■ Introduction

Joe needs wisdom

Joe didn't know what to do! A gang of older boys had been teasing and bullying some young children in the neighborhood and trying to get

▲ **Option #8**

Have two boys act out what they think might have happened when Joe confronted Nate.

▲ **Option #9**

Mural Time Line: Have the children create an on-going mural time line for this series of lessons, either as an activity time immediately after the lesson or as a pre-session or review activity the following week.

Before class, tape single sheets of white paper together (one sheet for each drawing) or prepare lengths of newsprint or white shelf paper by marking them into segments for each drawing.

In class, explain to the children that they will be illustrating key parts from each lesson to make a picture story of what they are learning. Provide crayons or washable markers for them to do the drawing at the end of each lesson or in your pre-session or review time of the following lesson. Use masking tape to display the mural on the wall where it will become an unconscious means of constant review.

Have the children illustrate key scenes that are marked as Mural Options or others that you choose.

If you choose to use this Option, be sure to use the Mural as a review tool. The visual reminder will give the children a bird's-eye view of God's working for his people that they will not forget.

money from them. This afternoon he had accidentally discovered that his older brother Nate was part of the gang! He knew his parents didn't know what was happening; neither did the children's parents. All the children were afraid to tell for fear they would be beaten up by the gang.

Joe was scared, too! If he reported his brother and friends, what would happen to his brother? And what would happen to him? But if he didn't report what he knew, how much longer would the children be terrorized by the older boys? He knew it was right to tell someone what he knew, but he needed wisdom about how to do it. Because he had trusted Jesus as his Savior and was part of God's family, he prayed, asking God for wisdom to know the right thing to do.

The next day Joe was playing ball with his friend. As he caught sight of the older boys tormenting the little children again, he could see that his brother was not enjoying what they were doing. Then God reminded Joe of a part of a verse he had learned in Sunday school: "Love one another as I have loved you" (John 13:34). Right then Joe knew what to do. He thought, "I'll talk to Nate tonight and tell him what I know before I tell anyone else."

That night Joe prayed that God would give him the right words to say. When he spoke to his brother, God answered his prayer. Nate seemed relieved! He decided he would not be a part of that bad activity anymore. Together the brothers decided they would talk to their parents. They would know the right thing to do to solve the problem. ▲#8

What Joe did wasn't easy, but many children were helped because he trusted God and relied on his wisdom in a tough situation.

Today we will learn about one Israelite family who needed God's wisdom in a dangerous situation and how God showed them what to do when they prayed and trusted him.

■ **Bible Content**

1. God's people multiply in Egypt. ▲#9
   (Exodus 1:1-7)

(Wilderness Map)

We have already said that the Israelites, God's special people, began with a man named Abraham. He and his family lived in tents in this land of Canaan *(indicate on the map)* for many years. ▲#10

Abraham's great-grandson Joseph was sold by his brothers to foreign merchants who took him to the land of Egypt where he became a slave. That was hard for Joseph, but it was all part of God's plan. Joseph eventually became a great ruler in Egypt because God gave him wisdom to help save the world from a terrible famine. At that time Joseph moved his father Jacob and his entire family—70 people in all—to Egypt. Pharaoh [fer'o or fa'ro] (the title for the Egyptian king) gave them a special place to live and raise their sheep and cattle in the land of Goshen *(indicate on the map)*. ▲#11

2. Pharaoh tries to destroy God's people.
(Exodus 1:8-22)

(Pharaoh 1, servants 2, 3, 4)
As the years passed, Joseph, his brothers and all his generation died, but his children and his grandchildren married and had more children. From the 70 people who had come to Egypt with Jacob they grew into a great nation of about two million people living in a land where there were only about seven million Egyptians. During this time different Egyptian pharaohs came to the throne. Eventually a man became king *(place 1 on the board)* who hardly remembered Joseph and what he had done for Egypt. Instead he became very nervous about this huge group of foreign people living in his country.

One day he said to his servants, *(add 2, 3, 4)*, "There are so many of these Israelites! If there should be a war, they might join with our enemies and fight against us. We can't allow that to happen!" So, he decided he must do something before the Israelites could become a danger to his country. Read Exodus 1:11 to find what he did. What did Pharaoh do? *(Response)*

Sketch 1 — Palace

▲ **Option #10**

Use teaching pictures and/or visuals from your own resources to briefly review the story of Joseph and the Israelites' background in Egypt. Allow children to share what they know about Joseph and/or illustrate a scene from his life.

a. By making them work hard.

(Slave master 5, slave 6)
Place 5, 6 on the board.
The first thing the king did was make the Israelites slaves. Instead of working for themselves and their families, looking after their animals and tending their gardens, they were forced to work very hard for the Egyptians. ▲#12

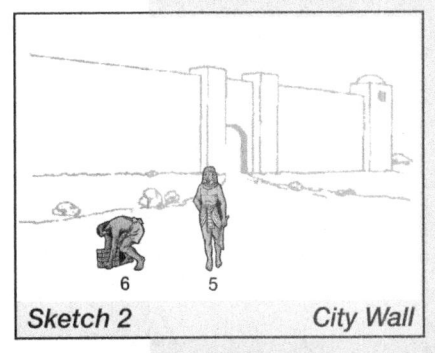

Some had to carry water to irrigate the farmlands, some had to make bricks for building and others used the bricks to build new cities where Pharaoh would store his treasures. They had no freedom. The slave masters were cruel and made life hard for the Israelites, beating them if they didn't work hard enough or fast enough. But God kept his people healthy, and many new babies were born every year. The Egyptians became more afraid and were even more cruel, making the slaves work harder and harder.

Sketch 2 — City Wall

Finally Pharaoh said, "This isn't working; what shall I do next?" Soon he had a very cruel plan.

b. By killing boy babies.

(Pharaoh 1, servant 3, Hebrew midwives 7, 8)
The king *(place 1, 3 on the board)* sent for two Israelite midwives. They were like nurses who helped the Israelite mothers when they gave birth to their babies. They must

Sketch 3 — Palace

L-1   7

▲ **Option #11**

Draw on newsprint or large poster board a floor map of Israel and Egypt connected by desert.

(Use the outline from pattern P-1 on page 168 as a guide.) Have children take the parts of Abraham, Joseph, Pharaoh and Joseph's family and move around the map according to the places mentioned in Part 1.

▲ **Option #12**

Mural scene.

Sketch 4 — Plain Interior

have been scared when Pharaoh called for them, but they trusted God to help them.

When the midwives *(add 7, 8)* appeared before the king, he said, "These are your orders. When a boy baby is born to an Israelite mother, kill him! When a girl baby is born, allow her to live." He knew that girls would not grow up to be soldiers and fight against them, so they were not included in his cruel plan.

The midwives believed in God and realized this was a very wicked order, but what could they do? If they obeyed the king and killed the baby boys, they would be disobeying God. If they obeyed God and didn't kill the babies, they would be disobeying the king. Read verse 17 to see what they did. *(Response)*

Even though they knew the king could have them put to death if they didn't follow his orders, they decided not to obey him. Instead, they chose to obey God and he gave them wisdom to answer when the king questioned them. And we read that because they obeyed God, God gave them large families of their own *(remove 7, 8)*.

When Pharaoh saw that this second plan had failed too, he gave a third order—this time to all the Egyptians: "Every boy baby that is born to the Israelites you must throw into the river, but you may let the girl babies live." The Israelites must have been very sad and afraid when they heard about the king's command. *(Discuss with the children what they might have done if they had been part of an Israelite family with a baby boy when this new order was given.)*

3. A family trusts God.
(Exodus 2:1, 2; 6:20; Hebrews 11:23)

(Amram 10, Jochebed 9, Miriam 11, Aaron 12, baby Moses 13, basket 16)

The Israelites had been in Egypt for a long time and many of them had forgotten that God had promised to one day bring them back into the land of Canaan. Some had even turned away from him to worship the false gods of Egypt (Joshua 24:14; Exodus 20:3-5). It was so hard being slaves that some became angry with God.

But others remembered the promises God had given to Abraham—that he would make them a great nation and give them the land of Canaan as their own. They also remembered that God had said they would have trouble in Egypt and serve there as slaves, but that God would deliver them and lead them back to the promised land.

Amram [Am'ram] *(place 10 on the board)* and his wife Jochebed [Jok'e bed] *(add 9)* loved God and trusted him. They knew God's promises and believed them. They taught their children to love and trust God, too. Amram probably had to work hard each day under one of the cruel Egyptian overseers. Perhaps he was beaten. Maybe this family wondered when God would deliver them and how he would do it, but they never stopped trusting him. ▲#13

Their daughter Miriam *(add 11)* was about 12 or 13 years old and their son Aaron *(add 12)*, about three when Jochebed gave birth to another baby boy *(add 13)*. I'm sure they wondered how long it would be before someone would discover their baby and throw him into the river as the king had commanded. However, they were not afraid of the king's order. Since they believed that God had a special plan for their baby, they hid him and trusted God to protect him. *(Leave all the figures on the board.)*

4. A family asks God for wisdom.
(Exodus 2:3, 4)

But the baby grew! When he was three months old, they knew they would have to do something else. He was bigger now and made more noise. Soon he would want to walk and talk. They must have prayed day after day, asking God for his wisdom. ▲#14

God answered their prayers and gave Jochebed the wisdom she needed—an idea for how to protect their baby boy. She went to the river and picked a big armful of the reeds that were growing along the bank. Jochebed wove these reeds into basket *(add 16)* big enough for a small baby. She also made a lid and painted the outside with some special mud to fill in the cracks and make it waterproof. On the inside she probably put something soft to make it warm and comfortable.

When the basket was ready, Jochebed must have kissed her tiny baby, given him one last hug, and then tucked him carefully into the little basket *(place 13 behind 16)*. Do you suppose she prayed before she closed the cover over him?

(Reeds 16, Jochebed 9, Miriam 11, basket 16)
Place reeds 16 on the board.

Can you guess what Jochebed did next? *(Have the children read Exodus 2:3b for the answer; allow for response.)* Yes, she put him *in* the river—just where the king said he should be! She and Miriam *(add 9, 11)* carried the small basket to the river bank and placed it among the reeds along the edge of the water *(place basket 16 behind reeds 16)*. ▲#15 Quickly Jochebed went home *(remove 9)* so that no one would see her, but Miriam *(remove 11)* hid nearby, watching to see what would happen to her baby brother.

How do you think Jochebed felt when she left her little baby in the river? *(Response)* It must have been hard, but she trusted God. He had given her wisdom to know what to do for her baby, and now she believed God would protect him. *(Leave 16(2) on the board.)*

▲ **Option #13**

Mural scene.

▲ **Option #14**

Have a teacher or child read Exodus 2:1-10 aloud as children mime the different character parts.

▲ **Option #15**

Mural scene.

Sketch 5   *River*

5. A princess rescues the baby.
(Exodus 2:5-9)

Sketch 6 — River

▲ Option #16

Mural scene.

(Princess 14, maid 15, baby 13, Miriam 11, Jochebed 9)
Soon Pharaoh's daughter *(add 14)* and her helpers *(add 15)* came to the river to take a bath. As they were walking along the bank, the princess noticed the basket among the reeds. "Oh, look at the basket," she said to her maids. "What could that be? Bring it here so we can see." One of the maids went to get it *(have 15 move 16 (basket) to 14)*.

Just as the princess lifted the cover, the baby began to cry *(place 13 on 16)*. "Oh," she said, "it's one of the Israelite babies." Do you think she felt sorry for him? Do you think she guessed someone was trying to save his life? We don't know exactly what she was thinking, but when Miriam *(add 11)* offered to get an Israelite woman to nurse the baby, the princess said, "Let's do that." She decided they would call the baby Moses. It means "pulled out of the water." *(Remove 11.)* ▲#16

Where did Miriam go? Look in verse 8. *(Response)* Yes, she ran straight home and brought her own mother back! *(Add 11, 9)*. Pharaoh's daughter said to Jochebed, "Take this baby home with you and nurse him, and I will pay you for taking care of him." *(Move 13 to the arms of 9)*. Can you imagine how happy and thankful and excited Jochebed must have been as she carried her very own baby back home? Now the princess of Egypt was going to protect him! Can you imagine Amram's joy when he came home and discovered what had happened?

The family must have had a special time of praising God and thanking him that night. Their baby was home with them, at least for a while. They had trusted God for wisdom and God had done something even more wonderful than they could have imagined!

■ Conclusion

Summary

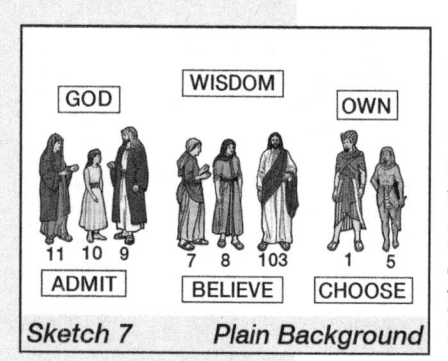

Sketch 7 — Plain Background

(Word strips WISDOM, GOD OWN; Pharaoh 1, slave master 5, midwives 7, 8, Jochebed 9, Amram 10, Miriam 11)
Who can remember what this word wisdom means? *(Place WISDOM on the board; allow for response throughout.)* Yes, it means to understand what is true or right in a situation and be able to decide the right way to act. Our lesson reminds us how important it is to seek God's wisdom rather than rely on our own. *(Add GOD, OWN.)* Let's see if we can decide what kind of wisdom these people from our lesson used. *(Add 1, 5, 7, 8, 9, 10, 11 as the children, one at a time, choose a figure, tell which kind of wisdom he or she used, and then place the figure under GOD or OWN. Note: Pharaoh and slave master should be placed under OWN; all others, under GOD.)*

How did Jochebed and the others get God's wisdom? Yes, they trusted God and he gave it to them. To whom does God promise to give wisdom? Yes, God promises to give us wisdom when we ask for it. Let's say our memory verse together. *(Do so.)*

Application

(Jesus 103; word strips ADMIT, BELIEVE, CHOOSE)

The first step to getting wisdom from God is making sure that you are one of his children by receiving the Lord Jesus as your Savior. Then you will have the right, as his child, to ask him for wisdom when you need it.

If you have not yet received Jesus as your Savior, you must believe what the Bible says about all of us—that we are sinners and cannot go into heaven to be with God with our sin. Then, you must believe what the Bible says about God's Son, Jesus Christ *(add 103)*—that he is God and that he died on the cross for you and rose again. Finally, you must *do* what the Bible says: ADMIT *(add ADMIT)* that you are a sinner, BELIEVE *(add BELIEVE)* that Jesus is God and died for you and rose again, and CHOOSE *(add CHOOSE)* to receive him as Savior and Lord. When you do that you will become part of God's family and you, too, will have the right to pray to God and ask for his wisdom.

The next step to getting wisdom from God is reading the Bible every day to learn what he says. There we learn how God wants us to live. God is interested in every part of your life just as he cared about all the things that were happening to Jochebed and the Israelites. Let's think about how this works in everyday life. ▲#17

Read aloud one or more of the following situations and have the class identify the need for wisdom in each. Then read the Bible verse and talk about how to apply it in the situation.

1. Sue sees her best friend cheat on a test. She knows she should do something about this, but doesn't want Sue to get in trouble or be mad at her. Galatians 6:1
2. Janelle's two friends won't speak to each other because they had an argument. They both want her to play with them only. John 13:34, 35
3. Carlos is new at school. Some fellows invited him to a party at Lisa's. No adult will be at home. 2 Timothy 2:22

Response Activity

Invite unsaved children to receive Jesus as Savior. Encourage them to come and talk with you or a helper so that you can talk and pray with them.

Recite the memory verse together. Have the saved children think about a difficult situation they know they will soon be facing and pray quietly, asking God for wisdom in that situation.

▲ **Option #17**

Ask children ahead of time to prepare to act out one or more of these situations.

⌂ Note (4)

Because regular Bible reading is so necessary to the spiritual health and growth of believers, we urge you to use the Bible Study Helps and to encourage your children week by week to develop this important habit.

To obtain inexpensive Bibles, contact:
American Bible Society
http://americanbiblesociety.org

✍ TAKE HOME ITEMS

Distribute **memory verse tokens for James 1:5** and **Bible Study Helps for Lesson 1**. Encourage the children to take ten minutes each day to read the assigned Scripture verses in the Bible Study Helps, answer the questions, and pray, asking God to help them obey what they have read. Explain that it is more effective to do the reading one day at a time than to do it all at once. Next week ask if they read the Bible passages and if they have any questions about what they read. ⌂(4)

Moses Leaves Egypt
Theme: Guidance

Lesson 2

❋ BEFORE YOU BEGIN...

"I'll do it my way" is a phrase familiar to us all. We like to be in control; most of us resent being told what to do. Most of us have also experienced the mess we can make of things when we forge ahead without seeking God's guidance and help. Everyone of us, including the children we teach, faces the same decision: Will I let God be my guide and follow his leading? Or will I go my own way, making my own decisions according to my own wisdom? The world says, *I can do anything I want to do if I just try hard enough and get the right breaks.* But believers need to recognize that God has a perfect plan for each of his children and even controls the "breaks." He is the perfect guide!

Through this lesson help your children see how Moses got into trouble because he didn't ask God to guide him. his heart desires were right (and God knew that), but he tried to solve the problem in his own strength and with his own wisdom. Encourage your children to choose God as their guide for life. Help them study his Word to learn how God wants them to live and to apply its principles to their daily life situations. *"For this is God, our God forever and ever; He will be our guide even to death" (Psalm 48:14, NKJV).*

☞ AIM:

That the children may

- Understand that God guides his children by his Word, by his Spirit, and by wise people.

- Respond by seeking God's guidance for choices they need to make.

📖 SCRIPTURE: Exodus 2:9-25; Acts 7:21-29; Hebrews 11:24-27

♥ MEMORY VERSE: Isaiah 58:11

The Lord shall guide thee continually. (KJV)
The Lord will guide you always. (NIV)

▲ Option #1

Show or demonstrate various "guides": a ruler, a road map, a compass, a pattern for sewing. Allow the children to examine them and tell how they guide us. Encourage the children to give their own examples.

🔼 Note (1)

Carefully distinguish between having a "spirit guide" that New Agers talk about and having the living and true God as our guide. The former is Satan's deceptive counterfeit for the real thing.

Guidance
2 — Isaiah 58:11

🔼 Note (2)

To give basic teaching about the Trinity, show pictures or real objects that have three parts but are one object (a triangle, a tricycle, a hardboiled egg in the shell), a word strip for TRINITY, and a circle you have divided into three parts and labeled FATHER, SON, HOLY SPIRIT.

Each of these things (show pictures or objects) has three parts but is only one object *(demonstrate)*. God is something like this. He

(continued on page 15)

📁 MATERIALS TO GATHER

Memory verse visual for Isaiah 58:11
Backgrounds: Review Chart, Plain Background, Plain Interior, Palace, General Outdoor, City Street, Wilderness
Figures: R1, R2, 5, 6, 9, 10, 11, 12, 13, 14, 17, 18, 19, 20, 21, 22, 23, 24(4), 98, 99(2), 103, 104, 114, 115
Token holders & memory verse tokens for Isaiah 58:11
Bible Study Helps for Lesson 2
Special:
- *For Introduction:* Blindfolds, large word card GUIDE with cord attached for hanging around the neck
- *For Response Activity:* "I Choose God to Be My Guide" handouts, pencils
- *For Options:* Materials for any options you choose to use
- *Note:* Follow the instructions on page xii to prepare "I Choose God to Be My Guide" handouts, (pattern P-3 on page 170).

💼 REVIEW CHART

Display the Review Chart with R2 inside God's Supply Room; have R1 ready to use where indicated. Use the following questions to review Lesson 1.

1. In what country were the Israelites living as slaves? *(Egypt)*
2. Why had they become slaves? *(Pharaoh was afraid because there were so many Israelites and they might fight on the side of his enemies in a war.)*
3. How did Pharaoh try to control the growth of God's people? *(By making them slaves and forcing them to work hard, by having baby boys killed at birth, by throwing baby boys into the river)*
4. What wise idea did God give Jochebed for saving her baby? *(God gave her the idea to hide him in the river.)*
5. What special person did God send to protect the baby? *(Pharaoh's daughter)*
6. What wonderful thing did God do for Jochebed and her family? *(He saved Moses from death and gave him back to them to raise.)*
7. How can we get God's wisdom today? *(Place R1 on the Review Chart as you repeat James 1:5.)*

Let's look at the next thing God will provide for his people from his supply. *(Have a child remove R2 from God's Supply Room and place it on the Chart.)* God wants to give us *Guidance*. Let's say it together. *(Do so.)*

We can see another word in the word Guidance. What is it? *(Response)* Yes, it is *guide*. What does it mean to guide someone?

(Response) That's right, it means to show that person the way by leading or directing or advising him. We all need guidance sometimes. ▲#1

♥ MEMORY VERSE

Display the visual to teach Isaiah 58:11.

Today's verse is a promise from God. Let's read it together. *(Do so.)* What is the promise? *(Encourage response throughout.)* Yes, God will guide us. *(Explain that the word* thee *means you.)* He will show us the right way to live or the next thing to do.

Is it important to be able to trust the one who is guiding us? Yes, it is. We need to be able to depend on our guide to lead us in the right way and get us where we want to go. Why is the Lord the best guide to have? That's right; he knows everything. He loves us, and he will always do what is best for us, even in hard times. △(1)

> The Lord will guide thee continually.
> Isaiah 58:11

The first way God wants to guide us is to show us that we need to trust in his Son, Jesus, as our Savior. He tells us in the Bible that everyone is a sinner—that we naturally think and act in ways that go against his Word (Romans 3:23). He also tells us that the wages of (or punishment for) our sin is death or separation from him forever (Romans 6:23). But God loves us, so he made a way for us to be in his family and escape that punishment. That way is through Jesus who died to take the punishment for our sin and rose again to give us life (John 14:6). When we believe Jesus died for us and receive him as our Savior, God forgives us and makes us his children. The Holy Spirit comes to live in us and promises that we will someday have a home in heaven with him (John 14:2, 3). △(2)

After we trust Jesus as Savior, God wants to guide us through our lives here on earth. He wants to show us the very best way to go and how to make choices that please him. Can you think of some ways God might do that? *(If necessary, suggest ideas such as reminding us of Bible verses when we are tempted to sin or become confused, helping us choose the right friends, showing us how to tell someone about Jesus or guiding us to a person who can help us with a problem we have at home or school.)*

Sometimes God guides us through what we read day by day in his Word while trusting him to help us understand what the best thing to do is. At other times he may guide us through people who love God and can help us solve our problems. God will not force us to follow him, but he is always ready to guide us when we choose to follow him.

What word in our verse tells us *when* God will guide us? Yes, the word *continually (always)*? Let's say that word together. *(Do so.)* What does it mean to do something *continually (always)*? Yes, it means to do it without stopping. Isn't it wonderful that God will never stop guiding us? He is always ready to show us the right way when we ask him and keep on reading his Word to find out how he wants us to live. *(Work on memorizing the verse.)* ▲#2

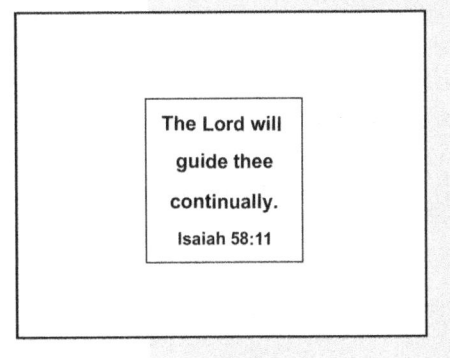

(continued from page 14)

is the one true and living God *(place circle on board)*, yet He is also three distinct persons: Father, Son and Holy Spirit. God the Father created our world; God the Son (or Jesus) came to earth as a man to die on the cross; and God the Holy Spirit comes to live within us when we receive Jesus as our Savior. We use the word Trinity *(add TRINITY)* to express this "3-in-1" truth about God.

▲ Option #2

Memorizing the verse: Read verse and reference aloud together. Have the children choose partners. Give each pair some time to practice saying the verse to each other without looking. Then ask for volunteer pairs to stand and say the verse together. Have that pair choose another pair to do the same. Continue until all pairs have said the verse.

📖 BIBLE LESSON OUTLINE

Moses Leaves Egypt

■ Introduction

Why we need a guide

■ Bible Content

1. Moses lives with his family.
2. Moses goes to live in the palace.
3. Moses chooses his own people.
4. Moses tries to help his people.
5. Moses goes to live in Midian.

■ Conclusion

Summary

Application
    Choosing to follow God's way

Response Activity
    Seeking God's guidance for making choices

📖 BIBLE LESSON

■ Introduction

Why we need a guide

(Blindfolds, GUIDE word card)
Depending on the size of your class, blindfold two to four children and spin them around gently. Instruct the rest of the class to watch what happens. Tell one or two of the blindfolded children to find their way around the room and back to their seats on their own. Then hang the GUIDE sign around your neck and lead the other blindfolded children around the room, helping them miss tables, chairs, etc., and back to their places. Then ask the class what they observed.

What problem did the first two children have? Why? *(Allow for response throughout.)* What made the difference for the last two children? Yes, they had someone to guide them. How did the guide make the difference? Yes, the guide could see the way and lead them around the obstacles so they would not run into things and perhaps get hurt.

Where else might you need a guide? ▲#3 Perhaps on a trail you've never hiked before or in a big new school or in a new neighborhood. We need a guide through life, too. God gave us our parents and teachers to guide and help us while we are growing up, but they will not always be there. Aren't you glad that God has promised he will guide us continually? Let's say our memory verse again. *(Do so.)*

▲ Option #3

Have the children draw a picture, describe or act out a situation where they really needed a guide.

▲ Option #4

Mural scene.

Today we will see how baby Moses grew up and learned to trust God to guide him and show him how to help his people the Israelites.

■ Bible Content

1. Moses lives with his family.
(Exodus 2:9)

(Amram 10, Jochebed 9, Miriam 11, Aaron 12, baby Moses 13)
Place all the figures on the board.

Jochebed and Amram were very thankful to have baby Moses at home with Miriam and Aaron. He was safe from Pharaoh's terrible order because the princess had rescued him and protected him. They knew they would have him for only a few years, just until he was old enough go live in the palace with the princess where he would become her son.

The Bible doesn't tell us what happened during those years. ▲#4 Did Jochebed take him to visit the princess? Did the princess send him gifts? We don't know. But we do know that his parents taught him to love and trust the one true God, the one they worshiped instead of the gods of the Egyptians. They taught him how God had promised Abraham, Isaac, and Jacob that he would give them and their descendants their own special land to live in—and how Joseph and their people had been brought to Egypt and finally become slaves. They also taught him that God had promised to someday take his people back to the promised land called Canaan. They must have told him who he really was and how God had protected him when his mother asked God for wisdom.

2. Moses goes to live in the palace.
(Exodus 2:10; Acts 7:21-22) △(3)

(Jochebed 9, Moses 17, princess 14)
Place all the figures on the board.

Moses was probably four or five when he went to live at the palace with the princess. The whole family must have been very sad as they kissed him goodbye, maybe wondering if they would ever see him again *(remove 9)*. How empty the house must have seemed without him, but they prayed for him and trusted God to watch over him.

The princess adopted him as her son. Everyone treated him like a prince. He wore fancy clothing, ate good food, and had servants to wait on him. When he went out into the streets, the people bowed down to him, even though he was just a boy. He was part of the strongest (or greatest) empire in the world at that time. ▲#5

The Bible tells us that Moses was taught in *all* the wisdom of the Egyptians (Acts 7:22), who were very intelligent and educated people. He was trained to be a prince. He learned to read and write the Egyptian

---

△ **Note (3)**

For younger children: Omit many of the details in Parts 2 and 4 to keep the story line simple.

Sketch 8 — Plain Interior

▲ **Option #5**

From an encyclopedia or the Internet, collect information about and pictures of Egyptian hieroglyphics, architecture, medical achievements, the people's dress and daily activities at that time to help your children visualize the things that Moses experienced.

Sketch 9 — Palace

⌂ Note (4)

The Jewish historian Josephus wrote that Moses was trained to be a great soldier. While still a young man living in the palace he was put in charge of Pharaoh's armies and won a great victory over an invading army.

Sketch 10   General Outdoor

▲ Option #6

Mural scene.

Sketch 11   General Outdoor

picture alphabet called hieroglyphics. He probably studied mathematics, astronomy, history, art and music and was active in sports. He learned to throw a spear and drive a chariot and he became a military leader. ⌂(4)

He also learned about all the idols the Egyptians worshiped day and night in the palace and throughout the whole country. All the Egyptians knew who Moses was and that someday he might be one of the rulers of Egypt next to Pharaoh.

3. Moses chooses his own people. (Hebrews 11:24-26)

(Moses 18, slave 5, slave master 6)
While Moses *(place 18 on the board)* was living the life of an Egyptian prince, he never forgot the things his parents had taught him as a young boy. As he grew up, he knew he could not worship the gods of Egypt. He was an Israelite and must worship the one true God. It must have been difficult for him; surely he loved his Egyptian family, too.

When he became a man, Moses would ride through the land in his chariot. He would see Israelite slaves *(add 5)* everywhere working in the hot sun with their slave masters *(add 6)* standing ready to beat them if they did not work hard enough or fast enough. They had barely enough food to eat. Their children could not go to school. How do you suppose that made him feel? ▲#6

More and more Moses must have realized what it meant to be an Israelite. These suffering people were *his* people. Finally, he knew he could no longer be known as the son of Pharaoh's daughter. No matter what it cost, he must admit that he was an Israelite—and let other people know it, too! He wanted to help his people.

We read in the New Testament that Moses made this choice *by faith*. He chose to believe God and obey him, even though he couldn't see what was ahead. He was 40 years old at the time. Was he remembering that God had promised to send a deliverer who would lead his people out of Egypt and back to Canaan? Did he believe that God had prepared him to be that deliverer? We don't know the answers to these questions, but Moses thought he knew what to do.

4. Moses tries to help his people. (Exodus 2:11-15; Acts 7:23-29)

(Moses 18, slaves 19)
One day Moses was watching some of the Israelites at work. Read Exodus 2:11 to find out what he saw. *(Encourage response; have them put their "God Provides for Us" bookmarks in place.)* That's right; he noticed one of the Egyptian slave masters cruelly beating one of the slaves. Moses was furious! "I must help him," he said to himself, and he tried to defend the slave. Now he was openly showing the

choice he had made, but in his anger he did a foolish thing. He hit the Egyptian so hard that he died. "Now what?" he must have thought. "Did anyone see me?" It was a very dangerous thing to kill an Egyptian. He looked around, but no one seemed to have noticed. So, he buried the Egyptian's body in the sand.

The next day Moses *(place 18 on the board)* went back among his people. When he saw two slaves fighting *(add 19)*, Moses asked them, "Why do you want to hurt each other? You're both Israelites."

One of them answered, "Who gave you the right to tell us what to do? Are you going to kill me like you did the Egyptian yesterday?" Obviously they didn't understand who Moses really was or why he had done this thing.

Then Moses was afraid. He thought, "Everyone must know what I did." ▲#7 Pharaoh soon heard what Moses had done. He realized that Moses was taking sides with the Israelite slaves. Maybe it dawned on him what Moses' name really meant. He became very angry and put out an order that Moses should be killed. What do you think Moses did then? Read verse 15. *(Response)* Yes, he ran away into the desert. Suddenly he was running for his life instead of helping his people! Can you imagine what he must have been thinking out there alone? *(Response)* He had only wanted to serve God and help his people, but everything had gone wrong!

Why had it gone wrong? Did he let God be his guide? Or did he lose his temper and do what he thought was right? *(Response)* That's right; Moses chose to do things his own way instead of God's way. He let his anger control him and it got him into trouble. ▲#8 It was God's plan for Moses to deliver his people from Egypt, but it wasn't God's time yet. Moses tried to do what he thought was right without asking God to guide him. But God was still in control and would work out his plan for Moses and his people. Later Moses would understand that God had many more lessons for him to learn before he would be ready to deliver his people.

5. Moses goes to live in Midian.
(Exodus 2:15-22; Hebrews 11:27)

(Well 23, Moses 18, Jethro's daughters 20, sheep 24[4], shepherds 21, 22)

Place 23 on the board.

Moses *(add 18)* had to travel many miles to the country of Midian, which was desert or wilderness land *(indicate on the map)*. When he came to a well one day, he sat down to rest. ▲#9 Living in that wilderness land was a man named Jethro who had seven daughters. Every day they would bring their father's sheep to the well to drink. ▲#10

As Moses sat by the well that day, he saw the girls *(add 20, 24[4])* coming to get water for their animals. Then he saw some other shepherds *(add 21, 22)* trying to push the girls and their sheep away from the well. "That's not right!" he

▲ **Option #7**

Mural scene.

▲ **Option #8**

If the opportunity presents itself, discuss with the children the consequences of uncontrolled anger. Allow them to tell from their own experience about how letting their anger control them has led to bad consequences.

▲ **Option #9**

Mural scene.

▲ **Option #10**

Have the children dramatize this section as a narrator reads Exodus 2:16-22 or from the teacher's text.

Sketch 12   *Wilderness*

thought to himself, and he forced the shepherds to leave *(remove 21, 22)*. Afterward he drew water from the well for the girls' sheep.

Later at home Jethro asked his daughters, "Why have you come home so early today?"

The girls must have been excited. "An Egyptian man helped us! He rescued us from the shepherds and then drew water from the well for the sheep!" they answered.

"And you didn't bring him home for supper?" Jethro said. "Go find him and invite him to come have something to eat. We must thank him!" Moses agreed to have supper with them. Then Jethro invited him to stay with them and help take care of the sheep.

After a while, Moses married Zipporah, one of Jethro's daughters. They were very happy when God gave them a baby son and, later, a second little boy. Moses named his sons Gershom and Eliezer (Exodus 18:4).

Moses lived happily with his family in Midian for many years. He learned to know the desert very well as he led the sheep from place to place to find water and food. He did not know it then, but this was the very country through which he would later lead the Israelites on their way to Canaan. But God knew. And even though Moses had tried to serve God his own way and failed, God knew Moses really did want to please him. God was guiding him and preparing him to be the leader for his people.

■ Conclusion

Summary

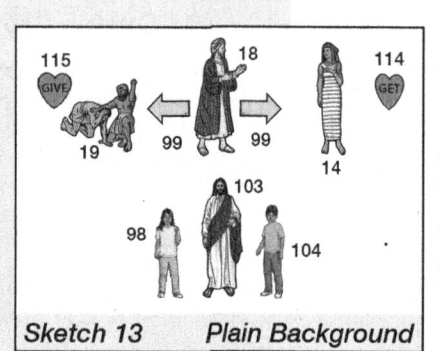

Sketch 13   Plain Background

(Moses 18, Pharaoh's daughter 14, Israelites fighting 19, arrows 99[2], hearts 114, 115)

Let's think about the choice Moses *(place 18 on the board)* had to make. What were the two possibilities and what results would there be in his life? *(Allow for response throughout.)* Yes, he could choose to continue being known as the son of Pharaoh's daughter *(add 14)* or he could choose to let everyone know he was an Israelite *(add 19)* so he could help his people.

If he chose to remain the son of Pharaoh's daughter, what would be the result? *(Add 99[1].)* He could *get (add 114)* many things—stay at the palace, be part of Pharaoh's family and have great riches and position in Egypt. He would never need anything in this world, but his people would remain slaves.

If he said, "No, I can't do that, I am an Israelite—one of God's people," what would be the result? *(Add 99[1].)* That's right; he would *give (add 115)* up many things. He could no longer be one of the Egyptian rulers, living in the palace, having servants and riches and everything he wanted, but he might be able to help his people to be free and to go to live in the promised land. He would be *giving* himself to God and *giving* help to his people.

What did Moses do? He chose to trust God and become known as an Israelite *(remove 14, 114)*. Do you think it was an easy choice? *(Discuss)*

What did God then do for Moses? Yes, God became his guide and took care of him even when he made mistakes. God was preparing him to lead the Israelites when he took them out of Egypt.

Application

(Girl 98, boy 104, Christ 103)

We *(add 98, 104)* must choose to let God be *our* guide or to go our own way. How can we let God be our guide? *(Response)* We must first trust his Son Jesus as our Savior. Then we are born into God's family and can depend on him to guide us in every decision we need to make.

Moses did not have the Bible, but we do. God guides us as we read his Word and learn how he wants us to live. That's how we learn to make choices that please God. He also guides us through other people (like parents and teachers) who help us learn what is right and wrong. And he guides us by the Holy Spirit who lives in our hearts and reminds us of what God wants and then helps us do it. But we must *choose* to let him guide us each day. We need to say, "Lord, I want to do your will; I want to obey your Word." Have you decided who will be your guide? Are you already part of God's family? Will you choose to let Jesus *(add 103)* be your guide and help you make right choices in every situation? Will you read the Bible to learn how God wants you to live and then ask him to help you obey what you learn?

If you have never received Jesus as your Savior, will you choose to accept him as your Savior and guide before you go home?

Response Activity

Invite the children to come after class to talk with you about their choice. Be sure you have people available to help those who want to trust Jesus as their Savior. Challenge those who already know Christ as Savior to seek God's guidance for any choices they may be facing now.

*Distribute the **"I Choose God to Be My Guide" handouts** and pencils. Encourage the children to print in the CHOICE column a tough choice they had to make this week (discuss some examples together), check whether they chose God or themselves to be their guide, and then print what happened. Have them bring their handouts back next week and give them an opportunity to share their experiences.*

✎ TAKE HOME ITEMS

Distribute **memory verse tokens for Isaiah 58:11** and **Bible Study Helps for Lesson 2.**

God Calls Through a Burning Bush
Theme: Purpose

Lesson 3

❋ BEFORE YOU BEGIN...

What is God's purpose for your life? For the children in your class? Most children are wondering things like, *How can I know what I should be when I grow up?* Or, *Why should I work hard in school when I don't like it?* In a world of many dysfunctional families, crumbling moral standards, a fluctuating economic climate, and little job security, even adults are asking, *Is there purpose to life? How do I find it?*

What a privilege to say, *Yes, there is purpose in life! God has a purpose—a plan—for every one of his children! He knew it before you were born!* Moses is a great example of this truth. Though he didn't understand what was happening, God was weaving together all the experiences of his life—both good and bad—to prepare him to lead his people out of Egypt.

Use this lesson to teach your children that God has an individual plan for everyone who has trusted Jesus as Savior. Encourage them to seek God's purpose for their lives and to devote themselves to preparing to fulfill that purpose. *"For we are His workmanship, created in Christ Jesus for good works, which God prepared beforehand that we should walk in them"* (Ephesians 2:10, NKJV).

☞ AIM:

That the children may

- Recognize that God has a special purpose for each believer's life.
- Respond by committing themselves to seek God's plan and prepare themselves for it.

📖 SCRIPTURE: Exodus 2:23–4:28; Acts 7:30-35

♥ MEMORY VERSE: Philippians 2:13

For it is God which worketh in you both to will and to do of his good pleasure. (KJV).

For it is God who works in you to will and to act according to his good purpose. (NIV)

📁 MATERIALS TO GATHER

Memory verse visual for Philippians 2:13
Backgrounds: Review Chart, Plain Background, Wilderness, Plain with Tree
Figures: R1-R3, 24(4), 25, 26, 27, 28, 29, 30, 32, 34, 116, 117, 118, 119
Token holders & memory verse tokens for Philippians 2:13
Bible Study Helps for Lesson 3
Special:
- *For Bible Content 1 & 2:* Wilderness Map from Lesson 1
- *For Bible Content 4 & Summary:* God's Promises word strips: 1. I will be with you. 2. I AM God. 3. Miracle: Snake /Leprosy. 4. I will help you speak.
- *For Application:* "Lessons I Am Learning" chart; marker or chalk
- *For Response Activity:* "Prayer of Commitment" handouts, pencils
- *For Options:* Materials for any options you choose to use
- *Note:* Follow the instructions on page xii to prepare the word strips and the "Prayer of Commitment" handouts (pattern P-4 on page 170).
  To prepare the "Lessons I Am Learning" chart, print LESSONS I AM LEARNING across the top of newsprint or chalkboard. Draw a line down the middle. On one side print HEAD; on the other side, HEART.

💼 REVIEW CHART

Display the Review Chart with R1 and R2 in place and R3 in God's Supply Room. Have individual children choose R1 or R2, tell how God provided it for the Israelites and recite the corresponding memory verse. Use the following WHO AM I? questions to review Lessons 1 and 2.

1. We grew to a nation of two million people while living in Egypt. Who are we? *(Israelites)*
2. I gave an order to have the Israelite baby boys killed. Who am I? *(Pharaoh)*
3. I watched over my brother when he was in a basket among the reeds in the river. Who am I? *(Miriam)*
4. I rescued and protected an Israelite baby boy. Who am I? *(The princess or Pharaoh's daughter)*
5. I was taught in all the wisdom of the Egyptians. Who am I? *(Moses)*
6. We taught our son about the one, true God. Who are we? *(Amram and Jochebed or Moses' parents)*
7. I chose not to be known as the son of Pharaoh's daughter. Who am I? *(Moses)*

Let's look in God's Supply Room to find the next thing God provides for his people. *(Have a child remove R3 from its place, read the word on it, and place it on the Chart.)* Yes, God provides *Purpose!*

What is a purpose? *(Response)* That's right; it's something you intend to do or get. Today it was your purpose to come here to this Bible class. When you leave here it will probably be your purpose to go home and get something to eat, or even to do your homework!

God has a purpose for you, too. The Bible says that he has a plan for every one of his children (Jeremiah 29:11), and that he has planned good works for all of us to do (Ephesians 2:10). Our memory verse tells us how God will accomplish his purpose for us.

♥ MEMORY VERSE

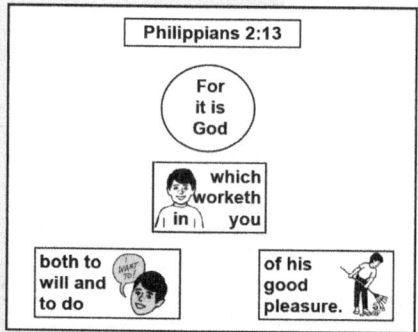

Use the visual to teach Philippians 2:13 when indicated.

Did anyone ever give you a big or a difficult job and then walk away without helping you or giving you the special instructions you needed to do it? *(Allow for response throughout.)* How did it make you feel? You probably felt frustrated or like a failure or even like giving up and never doing that job again. Sometimes people do things like that to us, but God does not! When he tells us in his Word to do something, he also promises to give us the help we need to do it.

Today's memory verse *(display the verse visual)* tells us how God does this for all those who belong to his family through believing in Jesus. Let's read it together. *(Do so.)* What does our verse say God does? Yes, he works in you! He doesn't go away and leave you; he is right there working in you to help you.

What's the first thing he works in you? That's right; he works in you to "will" or to *want* "his good pleasure (purpose)." God helps us to have the right attitude so we will want to please and obey him.

What's the second thing God works in us? Yes, he actually helps us to *do* what he wants us to do. "his good pleasure" is his purpose for our lives at that time. For example, if you read in the Bible, "Children, obey your parents," but really don't want to obey at that time, God will help you to *will* (or want) to obey—if you are willing—and then he will help you to *do* it, even though it's hard. God may even allow very difficult things to come into your life. When he does, he will also help you to trust him through those times. This is good practice and training for doing God's special purpose for you in the future.

As we said before, God has a plan for each of his children and work he wants to do through us someday. He might want you to be a missionary or a pastor or a doctor or a mechanic or a stay-at-home mom or any one of many other things. All the things you are learning now, through the easy times or the hard times, whether at home or in school, are preparing you for the great work he has planned for you to do in the future. *(Work on memorizing the verse.)* ▲#1

▲ **Option #1**

Memorizing the Verse: Have the class read the verse from the board. Allow children, one at a time, to remove a piece of the verse visual. Each time have the class or individuals repeat the verse until the group can say it without any visual reminder. Then have several children replace the pieces in correct order. Finally, have the group say the verse once more together.

📖 BIBLE LESSON OUTLINE

God Calls Through a Burning Bush

Introduction

Sam learns to paint

Bible Content

1. God's people suffer in Egypt.
2. Moses learns from God in the desert.
3. God calls Moses to work for him.
4. Moses makes excuses to God.
5. Moses returns to Egypt.

Conclusion

Summary

Application
Preparing to carry out God's purpose

Response Activity
Making a commitment to follow God's plan for their lives

📖 BIBLE LESSON

Introduction

Sam learns to paint

Sam spent many Saturdays one spring helping his dad paint the outside of their house. He learned how to scrape off the old paint that was peeling and put on the new. Though he often wished he could be hanging out with his friends, it did make him feel good to see the house look so much nicer.

"Sam," his dad insisted, "always be careful and do the best job you can. Clean up when you're finished and put all your tools away before you quit. The day will come when you will be very glad you've learned how to do this." Sometimes Sam grumbled, but he tried to do what his dad said.

That summer Mrs. Conley, the older lady who lived alone next door, saw him outside and called him over. "Sam," she asked, "would you paint my fence? I've seen you helping your dad and I think you could do it."

Sam looked at the fence. It needed a lot of work! It was long and would take a long time to paint! But he liked Mrs. Conley, so he said he would. Each morning he worked hard. It took several days just to get the old fence ready to paint, and even more days to paint it—but Sam didn't quit. When he was finished each day, he cleaned up and put his tools away, just as his dad had taught him. Sometimes Mrs. Conley brought him a cold drink and a cookie. Sometimes they talked for a few minutes.

When Sam had finished the fence, Mrs. Conley said, "Sam, I'm really impressed by the good job you've done, especially since you're just a boy. I've seen your friends stop by and ask you to go off with them, but you didn't go. How were you able to do such a good job and not quit part way through?"

Sam was embarrassed, but he said, "Well, I just tried to do what my dad taught me—and I asked God to help me."

"You asked God to help you?" said Mrs. Conley. "Why would you do that?"

That gave Sam an opportunity to tell her how he had received Jesus as his Savior and really wanted to please him. Mrs. Conley seemed surprised, so Sam said, "Would you like to go to church with us on Sunday?"

"Yes, I would," she answered, "and I also want to pay you for doing such good work!"

"Wow!," thought Sam. "Now I have the money for those new skates I've been wanting, and Mrs. Conley is going to church with us—all because I tried to do the best work I could on her fence!" Sam learned an important lesson that day. It's important to do whatever God puts before you the best way you can, because he may use it in ways you never dreamed! God has a purpose for everything he allows to come into your life.

Today we will see how God used everything that had happened in Moses' life to prepare him to accomplish God's purpose for him. Find Exodus 2 in your Bible and place your bookmark there.

■ Bible Content

1. God's people suffer in Egypt. (Exodus 2:23-25)

(Wilderness Map)
Moses lived in the desert *(indicate the area surrounding Mt. Sinai on the map)* for 40 years. During all that time the Israelites continued to be slaves to the Egyptians. It must have been discouraging. They didn't have the Bible like we do to encourage and help them. The older ones told the younger ones what they had been taught by their fathers, but many had forgotten about the living God and were worshiping the gods of Egypt. Perhaps some even thought that God had forgotten them.

But as their suffering and sadness increased, they began to pray to God for help. Let's read Exodus 2:24 to learn what God did then. *(Do so; wait for response.)* Yes, God remembered the promise he had made to Abraham to bring the people to a special land of their own and to bless them. The Bible says that he was concerned for his people and so he put a plan into action to help them.

2. Moses learns from God in the desert.
(Exodus 3:1)

(Moses 25, rod 34, sheep 24[4], HEAD 27, books 28, heart 29, HEART 30; Wilderness Map)

God had been preparing Moses *(place 25, 34 on the board)* all along to lead his people out of Egypt. Of course, Moses didn't really know what the Lord was doing. Sometimes he would be away from home for many days at a time, trying to find grass for the sheep *(add 24[4])* to eat and water for them to drink in the desert *(indicate the area surrounding Mt. Sinai on the map)*. Day after day the sheep were his only company. The sun beat down on him and the desert sands were hot under his feet. his work didn't seem very important or satisfying. But God was teaching him what he needed to know before he could be trusted to be the leader and shepherd of his people.

In Egypt Moses had gained much "head" knowledge *(add 27, 28)*. As the son of the princess, he received a good education. Now he was a student in God's special "school of the desert." After 40 years of taking care of the sheep, he knew the desert well—where to find whatever water and food were available, how to get from one place to another, and all about the different groups of people who lived there.

He was also learning some things God wanted him to know in his heart *(add 29, 30)*—that part of us where we have feelings and make choices to obey or disobey God. What do you think those "heart" lessons might have been? *(Response)* ▲#2

Moses must have learned not to be afraid when he was alone, because God was with him. he must have learned, as he looked every day for water and pasture for the sheep, that he could trust God to provide. And while traveling slowly across the desert sands with his sheep, he must have learned not to rush into things too quickly. As he daily looked at the vast desert and sky and thought about the God who made him and everything he could see, he must have learned that he was not as important as he once thought he was—but that God is very great and wonderful and powerful. God was preparing Moses to be the leader of his people, the Israelites. God had a plan (or purpose) for Moses' life and for delivering his people from Egypt. *(Remove 27, 28, 29, 30.)*

Sketch 14 — Wilderness

▲ Option #2
Ask the class to suggest lessons Moses might have learned from living in the desert. List them on newsprint or chalkboard as the children respond. Use this list again in the Summary.

3. God calls Moses to work for him.
(Exodus 3:1-10; Acts 7:30-35)

(Burning bush 26)

One day while Moses was in the desert with the sheep *(place 25, 34 and 24 on the board)*, he saw a bush catch fire *(add 26)*. He probably had seen something like that before. It was very hot and sometimes fires started on their own. But this

Sketch 15 — Wilderness

▲ **Option #3**

Have the children dramatize Part 3 of the lesson (Exodus 3:1-10). Choose one child to read the story and another to take the part of Moses and do appropriate actions. Or, choose one child to be the narrator and other children to read the lines for God and Moses. Construct a paper "burning bush" to make it more authentic.

▲ **Option #4**

Mural scene.

▲ **Option #5**

Continue the dramatization through this section, using the verses noted in the parentheses.

Or, have individual children read aloud God's answer to each of Moses' excuses as you place the visuals on the board.

Sketch 16   Wilderness

---

bush kept burning—it didn't burn up and turn to ashes! Moses thought that was strange and walked over to take a closer look. Read Exodus 3:2 to see what happened. *(Wait for response.)* ▲#3

The Bible says that the Angel of the Lord (another name for God) was in the bush. He called out, "Moses! Moses!" That must have been a startling experience. Maybe Moses felt like running, but he knew something unusual was about to happen. ▲#4

Moses answered, "Here I am."

Then God said, "Don't come any closer. Take off your shoes, for the place where you are standing is holy ground." God wanted Moses to know that this was a special conversation. In that day people removed their shoes to show reverence or respect to God. Moses took off his shoes.

Then God spoke again: "I am the God of your father, the God of Abraham, Isaac, and Jacob." He wanted Moses to know that he had been watching over his people all along. He had a purpose for them and wanted to use Moses to help them find it.

At once Moses hid his face because he was afraid. There was so much he didn't understand. ◮(1)

God said, "I have seen how miserable my people are in Egypt. I have heard them crying out because of their slave drivers. I am concerned about their suffering. So I am going to rescue them and bring them out of Egypt to their own good land—the land I promised to Abraham."

That must have been wonderful news to Moses! It was just what he'd wanted to happen for many years! But then God said, "Get ready now because I have a special plan. I will send you to Pharaoh to lead my people out of Egypt."

That must have been quite a shock! Moses wanted his people to be free, but he had already tried to help them and failed. How could he go back now? What would Pharaoh do? How would the people react? What about his family and his life in Midian? Surely God must have made a mistake. he wasn't the right man. He wasn't prepared. Immediately he began to make excuses. *(Leave all the figures on the board.)*

4. **Moses makes excuses to God.** ▲#5
   (Exodus 3:11–4:17)

(WHO AM I? 116, WHAT SHALL I SAY? 117, THEY WILL NOT BELIEVE ME 118, I CANNOT SPEAK 119; God's Promises word strips 1-4)

"Who am I?" asked Moses, "that I should go to Pharaoh and lead my people out of Egypt?" *(Add 116.)* Perhaps he thought, "I'm only a shepherd in the desert." Read verse 12 to see how God answered this excuse. *(Wait for response.)* Yes, Go)d said, "I will be with you." *(Add 1. I WILL BE WITH YOU.)* If God went with him, Moses would not have to be afraid and he would not have to depend on himself to know what to do.

"But what if the people ask me your name?" asked Moses. "What shall I tell them?" *(Add 117.)* He was probably thinking that he didn't know enough. Look in verse 14 to find God's answer. *(Wait for response.)*

That's right; God said, "Tell them my name is I AM, and that I have sent you. *(Add 2. I AM GOD.)* I AM the God of their fathers, and this is my name forever." He wanted his people to know that he never changes; he is always the same.

God said, "Tell the leaders of my people that I have seen what is happening to them and I am going to deliver them. They will listen to you. Then go to Pharaoh and say, 'The Lord God wants you to let us go into the wilderness and sacrifice to him.' At first he will not listen to you, but I will strike his people with my wonders (or miracles) until he lets you go."

"But what if the people don't believe me or won't listen to me?" asked Moses *(add 118)*. He was really scared and perhaps a bit confused.

This time the Lord said, "What do you have in your hand?"

"A staff (or a rod)," Moses answered. It was probably the shepherd's staff he used with the sheep.

"Throw it on the ground," said God. So Moses threw it on the ground. It became a snake and he ran away from it. *(Add 3. MIRACLE: SNAKE/LEPROSY.)*

"Pick it up by the tail," was the Lord's next command. Is that a good way to pick up a snake? No, it's not and Moses must have known that. But Moses trusted God, so he did what God said and as soon as he picked it up, it turned back into a staff.

Then the Lord said, "Do this sign so the people will believe that I have appeared to you." Only God can make life out of a stick.

Then, just in case the people still didn't believe, the Lord said, "Moses, put your hand inside your cloak." When Moses did and pulled it out again, it was all white and covered with the sores of leprosy, a disease that attacks the skin, the flesh, and the nerves. It was one of the worst things that could happen to a person and was almost always incurable. Moses must have gasped! What a terrible thing to happen!

"Now put it back inside your cloak," said the Lord. Again, Moses obeyed and when he looked at his hand again, the leprosy was all gone! Only God could cure leprosy! Surely the people would believe when they saw this. ▲#6

Then the Lord said to Moses, "If they do not believe the sign of the staff, they may believe the sign of your hand. If they don't believe either one, then pour some water from the river on the dry ground and it will turn to blood before their eyes." That would get your attention, wouldn't it?

"But Lord," said Moses, "I am not a good speaker; sometimes I stutter and it's hard for me to find the right words. Choose somebody else." *(Add 119.)* He didn't think that he had the abilities necessary to fulfill God's plan (or purpose).

God answered patiently, "Who made your mouth, Moses? I did. Now go and I will help you when you have to speak and I will teach you what to say." *(Add 4. I WILL HELP YOU.)*

⌂ Note (1)

Normally, human beings cannot see God because:
1. He is a spirit and is invisible to the human eye (John 4:24).
2. He is so holy and pure that when sinful people get near his glory, they die) Exodus 33:20).

There are only two ways that human beings have seen God:
1. When God took on the form of an angel or a human being to speak to people in the Old Testament (Judges 6:11 ff).
2. When God revealed himself through Jesus Christ, his incarnate Son, in the New Testament (John 1:18; 14:9).

▲ Option #6

Have the children illustrate either of two scenes: the staff becoming a snake or Moses' hand becoming leprous.

Still Moses hesitated. Finally God said to Moses, "Your brother Aaron speaks well. He will be glad to see you and he can go with you to do the talking. I will teach you both what to say. Now take this staff in your hand and go." God didn't want to hear any more excuses. He had prepared Moses in every way to accomplish his purpose and he wanted him to get started.

5. Moses returns to Egypt. (Exodus 4:18-28)

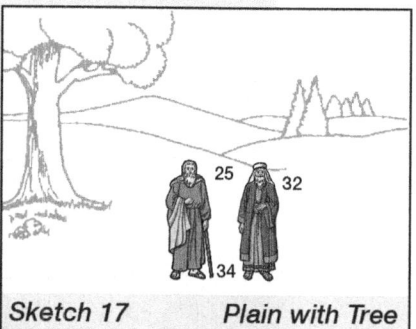

(Moses 25, rod 34, Aaron 32)

Moses *(place 25, 34 on the board)* had a lot to think about as he herded the sheep home that night. Maybe he didn't know how to explain all this to his wife and to Jethro his father-in-law. He just said, "Let me go back to Egypt to see if any of my family is still alive after all this time."

Jethro said, "Go, and I hope you find them well."

At the same time, the Lord spoke to Aaron in Egypt: "Moses is coming back. Go meet him in the desert." What exciting news! What a joyful reunion! *(Add 32.)* It must have taken them a long time to catch up on the 40 years they had been apart. Moses wanted to hear from Aaron all about his family and his people. Aaron wanted to know where Moses had been and what he had been doing.

Finally, Moses told Aaron about the special plan that God had for them. He told him what they were supposed to say and about the wonderful signs God had commanded him to perform. It must have been exciting for them to know that God had a special work for them to do, just as it is exciting for us to know that God has a special purpose or plan for every one of us. ▲#7

Sketch 17 — Plain with Tree

▲ **Option #7**
Mural scene.

■ Conclusion

Summary

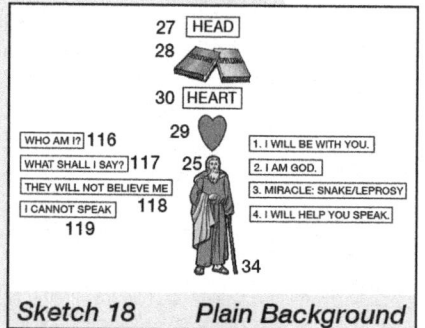

(Moses 25, rod 34, HEAD 27, books 28, heart 29, HEART 30; WHO AM I? 116, WHAT SHALL I SAY? 117, THEY WILL NOT BELIEVE ME 118, I CANNOT SPEAK 119; God's Promises word strips: 1-4)

What was the God's special purpose for Moses? *(Place 25, 34 on the board; allow for response throughout.)* Yes, it was to lead God's people out of Egypt. How did God prepare Moses to carry out this purpose?

He gave Moses a good education in the palace. He gained much "head" knowledge *(add 27, 28)*.

Then he put Moses out in the desert to take care of sheep for 40 years. There he learned to know God and trust him. We could call these "heart" lessons *(add 29, 30)*. Can you remember

Sketch 18 — Plain Background

what they were? That's right; he learned to be alone and unafraid because God was with him, to be patient and not rush into things, that God would provide what he needed, that he was not so important, but that God is very great, powerful and wonderful.

God knew exactly what Moses needed to learn so he would be prepared for the special purpose God had for him.

How did God help Moses to obey when he was afraid and making excuses to God? Yes, he answered every one of his fearful excuses *(add 116-119)* with a wonderful promise. Let's review them together. *(Add the God's Promises word strips 1-4.)*

▲ Option #8

Show pictures of various occupations. Have younger children illustrate what they think they might like to do in the future.

Application

("Lessons I Am Learning" chart; marker or chalk)
Have you ever thought about what you want to be or do when you grow up? *(Encourage response.)* ▲#8

It's fun to think about. And it's wonderful to know that God has a special purpose for your life, just as he did for Moses'. Even though you do not yet know what that purpose is, God knows exactly what you need to learn to be prepared for it.

What are some things you are learning or jobs you are doing right now? *(List responses under "Head" on the "Lessons I Am Learning" chart. Include the following if necessary: studying specific subjects at school, doing homework; studying the Bible to learn how God wants you to live; doing chores such as feeding animals and keeping them clean, washing dishes, cleaning your room, raking leaves, baby sitting for your parents; practicing and participating in team sports.)*

What "heart" lessons are you learning? *(List responses under Heart. Include the following if necessary: being patient with your brothers and sisters, trusting God for help in difficult situations—a family breakup or illness, faithfully completing jobs without complaining, learning how to get along with all kinds of people, choosing your friends wisely.)*

If you have trusted the Lord Jesus as your Savior, God wants you to do good work in all these lessons you are learning so you will be ready to fulfill his purpose for you in the future. He wants you to study your Bible now and live the way it tells you to. He promises he will help you whenever you ask. He will let you know what he wants you to do in the future when it is time.

If you have not received the Lord Jesus into your life, that is the first thing you need to do to be prepared for the purpose God has for your life.

Response Activity

*Distribute the **"Prayer of Commitment"** handouts and pencils. Read the prayer aloud together. As the children bow their heads,*

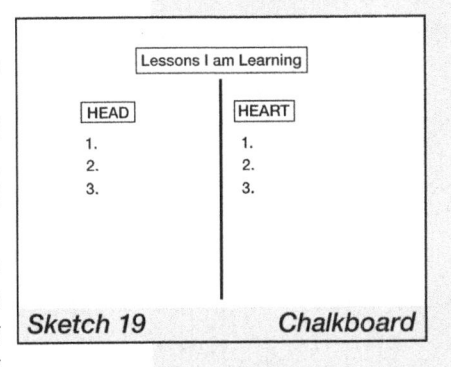

Sketch 19 — Chalkboard

Lessons I am Learning

HEAD	HEART
1.	1.
2.	2.
3.	3.

encourage all who have trusted Jesus as Savior to think seriously about making this commitment. Invite any who have never received Jesus to come talk with you or a helper after class. Allow time for all who are ready to commit their lives to Christ to pray the prayer silently and then sign the Commitment. Ask the children to let you know before they leave if they have made this commitment to the Lord.

TAKE HOME ITEMS

Distribute **memory verse tokens for Philippians 2:13 and Bible Study Helps for Lesson 3**.

Moses Confronts Pharoah
Theme: Courage

Lesson 4

❊ BEFORE YOU BEGIN...

Courage, according to one dictionary, is "the attitude of facing and dealing with anything recognized as dangerous, difficult or painful, instead of withdrawing from it." A big order for any of us, especially for children. But how they need it as they constantly face influences and temptations unknown a few short years ago—pornography on the internet, violence and sex on TV, inexpensive drugs available in the school yard, and "politically correct" attitudes that run contrary to biblical values. Coming from broken or dysfunctional families, many feel a great need to "belong," which often leads them into friendships that tempt them to sin. They need to learn how to courageously stand against sin and speak up for what they believe because God is with them.

Moses' example, standing courageously before Pharaoh and all the so-called gods of Egypt because he believed God's promise, "I will be with you," can help you teach this. Encourage them to believe that God's promise is for them, too, when they choose to speak up for him and do what is right. *"Wait on the Lord; be of good courage, and He shall strengthen your heart" (Psalm 27:14, NKJV).*

☞ AIM:

That the children may

- Know that God is with them to give the courage to speak up for him when they trust and obey.
- Respond by counting on God's presence and trusting him for courage to speak up for him.

📖 SCRIPTURE: Exodus 4:29–7:5

♥ MEMORY VERSE: Deuteronomy 31:6

Be strong and of a good courage, fear not nor be afraid of them; for the Lord thy God, he it is that doth go with thee; he will not fail thee, nor forsake thee. (KJV)

Be strong and courageous. Do not be afraid or terrified because of them, for the Lord your God goes with you; he will never leave you nor forsake you. (NIV)

📂 MATERIALS TO GATHER

Memory verse visual for Deuteronomy 31:6
Backgrounds: Review Chart, Plain Background, General Outdoor, Palace
Figures: R1-R4, 1, 2, 3, 4, 5, 7, 8, 9, 11, 25, 31, 32, 34
Token holders & Memory verse visuals for Deuteronomy 31:6
Bible Study Helps for Lesson 4
Special:
- **For Introduction:** Newsprint & marker or chalkboard & chalk
- **For Summary:** Word strip COURAGE
- **For Response Activity:** "Courage Card" handouts, pencils
- **For Options:** Materials for any options you choose to use
- **Note:** Follow the instructions on page xii to prepare the word strip and Courage Card" handouts (pattern P-5 on page 171.

💼 REVIEW CHART

Display the Review Chart with R4 in God's Supply Room. Place R1-R3 on the Chart as you review each theme and have individual children give the corresponding verses. Use the following questions to review Lesson 3.

1. What special work did God give Moses to do for him? *(To free the Israelites from slavery in Egypt)*
2. How did God tell Moses what he wanted him to do? *(The angel of the Lord spoke to him from a burning bush.)*
3. Give two of Moses' excuses for not obeying God. *("Who am I?," "What shall I say?," "They will not believe me," "I cannot speak.")*
4. Whom did God send to help Moses speak to his people and to Pharaoh? *(Aaron, his brother)*
5. What two miracles (or signs) did God give Moses to convince the people that God had sent him? *(The staff [or rod] turning into a snake and his hand being covered with leprosy)*

Do you ever feel afraid? What are some things that make you fearful? *(Allow for response throughout; lead the children to discuss being afraid to do something they know is the right thing to do.)* Perhaps you have been fearful of giving a report in class at school or needing to admit what you did when Mom or Dad wanted to know who broke the window, or wanting to disagree when someone bigger or mean says something bad about a friend or teacher. We all feel afraid sometimes, but today we will discover something in God's Supply Room that can help us when we feel this way. *(Have a child remove R4 from God's Supply Room and place it on the Chart.)* What is it? Yes, it is *Courage*. Our memory verse today will help us understand how we can have courage.

♥ MEMORY VERSE

Use the visual to teach Deuteronomy 31:6 when indicated.
What is courage? Does having courage mean you never feel afraid? *(Allow for response throughout.)* No. Does having courage make a job or situation easy? Not necessarily. Courage is an attitude, a way of thinking. It says, "I will face this thing, or I will do this thing even if it is difficult or it hurts—even if I am afraid. I will not run away from it." Having courage is not showing off or taking a dare to do something dangerous just to prove that you are brave or to impress someone. Real courage is about doing the things that please God.

God knew that his people would need courage when they left Egypt to go to their new land. It would be a hard journey; they would meet many enemies and difficult situations. So God gave them some commands. Who can tell me what a command is? That's right; it's an order—something we are told to do. *(Have some children give examples of simple commands, such as "sit up" or "stand up.")*

Our memory verse today gives several commands that God gave to his people. *(Display the first half of the memory verse up to the word them.)* Let's read our verse aloud together and see if we can identify them. *(Do so.)* God wanted his people to be strong, to have courage and not be afraid of the enemies they were going to meet in the new land.

Having courage is not easy, so God gave them some promises *(display the remainder of the visual)* to help them obey his commands. Let's read it together. *(Do so.)* How many promises are there? Yes, there are three. What are they? That's right; he would go with them, he would not fail them, and he would not forsake them. They could have courage to start off on their long journey through strange country to a land they had never seen. Why? Because God, who knows everything and has all power, promised to go with them and help them. He would give them the courage they needed. What a wonderful promise!

All of us who have received Jesus as Savior from sin have God the Holy Spirit living in us. He has promised he will never leave us, and he will always help us when we need it. When we are in a hard situation, we need to remember that he is with us and trust him for strength so we can face the situation with courage. What wonderful promises these are for us. *(Work on memorizing the verse.)* ▲#1

📖 BIBLE LESSON OUTLINE

Moses Confronts Pharaoh

■ Introduction

Exchanging our fear for God's courage

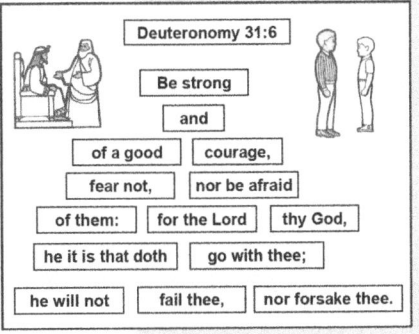

▲ Option #1

Memorizing the verse: After the children have studied the verse for a few minutes, place all visual pieces in a basket or paper bag. Have the children take turns drawing out pieces and placing them on the board in correct order. Allow class members to make corrections as needed. Finally, say the verse aloud together with all pieces in place, and then once more after the pieces are removed.

■ **Bible Content**

1. Moses and Aaron meet the leaders of Israel.
2. Moses and Aaron go to Pharaoh.
3. Pharaoh increases the work load.
4. God encourages Moses.

■ **Conclusion**

Summary

Application

Choosing to speak up for God in a specific situation

Response Activity

Asking God for courage to speak up for him this week

📖 **BIBLE LESSON**

■ **Introduction**

Exchanging our fear for God's courage

(Newsprint & marker or chalkboard & chalk)
When do you need courage? ▲#2 Do you ever find yourself in a situation in which you know the right thing to do, but it's hard to do or you're afraid of what will happen if you do it? *(Print responses on newsprint or chalkboard. If necessary, suggest saying no to sharing homework answers or doing drugs, telling the truth regardless of the consequences, showing kindness when others are being mean.)*

It is not always easy to do what we know God wants us to do. Moses and Aaron must have learned that when God asked them to do some hard things and speak up for him. If you listen carefully to the lesson, you will learn how to be brave when you face difficult situations.

■ **Bible Content**

1. Moses and Aaron meet the leaders of Israel. (Exodus 4:29-31)

(Moses 25, leaders 31, Aaron 32, rod 34)
Place all the figures on the board.
Soon after Moses and Aaron returned to Egypt they met with the leaders of the Israelite people, just as God had told them to do. These leaders already knew Aaron because he had lived among them for years, but most of them knew Moses only by the stories they had heard—how he had been raised in the palace, but had run away 40 years before. Find Exodus 4:29-31 in your Bible and place your bookmark there.

▲ **Option #2**

Put the children in small groups to act out situations in which they would need courage to do the right thing.

Sketch 20   General Outdoor

Read verse 30 to see what Aaron did. *(Response)* Yes, he told the leaders all that the Lord had said to Moses and then he performed the signs God had given to Moses. How do you think the leaders felt when they saw Moses' staff (or rod) turn into a snake and then back into a staff? Or when they saw Moses' hand suddenly covered with leprosy and then healed? ▲#3

▲ **Option #3**

Mural scene.

Read verse 31. What did the leaders do when they saw the signs God had sent? *(Response)* Yes, they believed and they bowed their heads and worshiped. How thankful they were to know that God had not forgotten them and that he had sent someone to deliver them! That was good news to take home to their families!

2. **Moses and Aaron go to Pharaoh. Exodus 5:1-5)**

(Pharaoh 1, servants 2, 3, Moses 25, Aaron 32)
Place all the figures on the board.

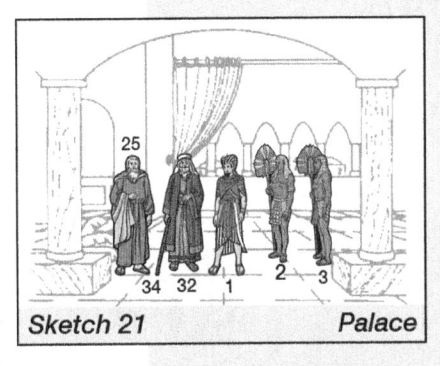

Later Moses and Aaron went to the palace to meet with Pharaoh. This Pharaoh (or king of Egypt) was the son of the Pharaoh who had ordered the deaths of the Israelite baby boys many years before when the princess rescued Moses. Moses had probably played with him and studied with him when they were growing up in the palace. Now he ruled the greatest nation in the world!

Sketch 21 — Palace

Pharaoh could do anything he wanted; his word was law (Genesis 41:13, 44). his people worshiped him as a god; in fact, they worshiped many gods—the sun and many different animals and even the Nile river where they got water for all their needs. But they didn't know about the living and true and all-powerful God. Was it scary for Moses to go there? Perhaps. This was a different king from when he left. He knew he was taking his life in his own hands; he had killed an Egyptian.

But Moses and Aaron knew that God had sent them and had promised to go with them. That gave them courage. They spoke boldly: "This is what the Lord, the God of Israel, says: 'Let my people go into the desert so they can hold a feast and worship me there.'"

Pharaoh must have been very surprised that anyone would dare to speak to him the way these men did. Probably he thought that the god of the slaves could not be very powerful. What did he have to fear? He said, "Who is the Lord, that I should obey *him*? I've never even heard of this "god" you are talking about and I will not let the people go!" ▲#4

▲ **Option #4**

Mural scene.

Moses and Aaron did not give up. "Our God," they said, "has given us clear instructions. Let us go for three days into the desert to offer sacrifices to him. If we don't go, we may get sick." If they were sick, they wouldn't be able to do any work. They probably thought that would get his attention.

But Pharaoh only became angry. "Why are you taking the people away from their labor? You are just confusing and distracting my slaves!"

he shouted. "Get back to work!" And he forced them to leave. *(Remove 25, 32, 34.)*

3. Pharaoh increases the work load. (Exodus 5:6-21)

(Slave masters 4, 5)

Later that day Pharaoh sent for the slave masters *(add 4, 5)* who were in charge of the Israelites. "These slaves must not have enough to do if they have time to think about going off into the desert," he thundered! "Make them work harder. Don't give them straw anymore; make them find it for themselves. But insist that they still make the same number of bricks as before." To make bricks the slaves mixed straw with clay (the straw made the bricks stronger), shaped the mixture into bricks and let them dry in the hot sun.

Sketch 22   Palace

(Slave masters 4, 5, foremen 31)

The slave masters *(place 4, 5 on the board)* announced to the people *(add 31)*, "Pharaoh says we will not give you any more straw, but you must still make the same number of bricks every day. Go get your own straw wherever you can find it! Now get back to work, everyone!"

What a sad day that was! The people scattered throughout all the countryside trying to find enough straw for the bricks they had to make. They must have worked even harder and for many more hours every day. But hard as they tried, they could not meet their quota. The slave masters demanded, "Why didn't you meet your quota yesterday and today?" And they beat the foremen.

Sketch 23   General Outdoor

When they couldn't stand it any longer, the Israelite foremen went to Pharaoh and said, "Why are you treating us this way? It's not our fault we can't meet the quota. Your people are not giving us any straw!"

"You're just lazy," Pharaoh answered. "That's why you keep saying, 'Let us go sacrifice to our God.' Get back to work! No one is going to give you straw and you are still required to make the same number of bricks!" *(Remove 4, 5.)*

(Moses 25, Aaron 32, rod 34)

Then the foremen realized they were really in trouble. Pharaoh was not going to change his mind and no one was going to help them. They found Moses and Aaron *(add 25, 32, 34)* waiting for them outside the palace. "Just look what you've done," they said. "You've made Pharaoh hate us. He'll work us to death and it's all your fault!" *(Remove 31, 32, 34; leave 25 in the center of the board.)*

Sketch 24   General Outdoor

38   L-4

4. God encourages Moses.
(Exodus 5:22–6:13; 6:28–7:5)

(Memory verse visual)

Moses must have felt terrible! He knew that he and Aaron had done exactly what God had told them to do. Why, then, were things only getting worse for his people? However, Moses knew what to do; he went right to God. "Why have you brought such trouble on the people?" he prayed. "Did you send me here only to make it harder for them? Ever since I did what you told me to do, Pharaoh has only increased their labor, and you haven't done anything about it!"

God knew how Moses felt. He spoke encouraging words to him. Look in chapter 6, verse 1 to see what he said. (Response) Yes, he said that he would do things so that Pharaoh would not only let the people go, but would make them go in a hurry. ▲#5

Then God said to Moses, "I am the Lord, the one who spoke to Abraham, Isaac, and Jacob. I have heard the people groaning and I have remembered my promise. Tell the people I will free them from being slaves to the Egyptians by my great power and I will bring them into the land I promised to Abraham and they will be my people." ▲#6

Do you think these words encouraged Moses? Yes, they did. They gave him courage to obey God. Our memory verse says some of the same things that God told Moses then. Let's say it together. *(Display the visual as the class says the verse together.)*

Hearing God's words gave Moses courage to go back to the Israelite leaders and tell them what God had promised. But by that time the leaders were discouraged by the cruel treatment and would not listen. So God spoke to Moses again: "Go back to Pharaoh and tell him to let the Israelites go out of his country."

"But Lord," Moses objected, "even my own people will not listen to me now. How can I expect Pharaoh to listen?"

Surprisingly, God agreed with Moses then. "You are right," he said. "Pharaoh will not let the people go because his heart is hardened against me. He has turned his back on what I have told him. But I will do many signs and wonders in the land and then I will bring my people out of this land. And the Egyptians will know that I am the Lord."

Moses was encouraged by God's promises even though he could not see what would happen next. He was willing to obey God and speak up for him even when it was hard and frightening and no one else was on his side.

■ Conclusion

Summary

(Word strip COURAGE; Moses 25, Aaron 32, rod 34, midwives 7, 8, Jochebed 9, Miriam 11)

▲ **Option #5**

Before class, print Exodus 6:1 on newsprint. Have the class read it together now.

▲ **Option #6**

Read Exodus 6:6-8 aloud as the children listen and count how many times God says "I will. . . ."

Sketch 25   Plain Background

▲ **Option #7**

Print the names listed on individual flash cards, punch two holes at the top of each and attach a string so it can be hung around a child's neck. Have different children choose a card and put it on, then tell what difficult thing that person had to face and how God gave courage.

▲ **Option #8**

Have small groups or pairs of children choose or be assigned one of the situations on the list and act out how they could show courage by their actions and words as they obey God in that situation.

▲ **Option #9**

Provide newsprint and markers or crayons. Have the children draw a picture of one situation on the list, showing courageous obedience, and then share it with the class.

What is courage? *(Place COURAGE on the board; allow for response throughout.)* That's right; courage is an attitude or way of thinking. It is being brave or bold. When I have courage, then I can say, "I will do what needs to be done even if it is difficult and I feel afraid." Moses and Aaron needed a lot of courage to face Pharaoh and their own people *(add 25, 32, 34 under COURAGE)*. They remembered God's promise, "I will be with you." They trusted him and believed he would give them his help and strength to speak up to their own people and to Pharaoh, the mightiest king of their time.

In an earlier lesson we learned about some other people who did the right thing even when they were afraid. *(Place 7, 8, 9 and 11 in a group opposite the word COURAGE.)* As I mention their names, I want you to tell me what difficult thing they did to show courage with God's help. *(As you mention the names listed below, have the children volunteer to tell what the person or persons did to show courage and then place the figure on the board under the word COURAGE.)* ▲#7

Midwives (7, 8): Women who helped Israelite women when their babies were born, had to kill the boy babies or disobey Pharoah; God gave them courage to disobey the Pharaoh's order and keep the babies alive, even if it meant they would die.

Jochebed (9): Moses' mother, had to disobey Pharaoh to save her baby boy's life; God gave her courage to do it and then hide him in the river.

Miriam (11): Moses' sister, had to stand guard alone to protect her baby brother when he was in the river; God gave her courage to speak to the princess about the care of her brother.

Because all these people put their trust in the true and living God and obeyed him, he gave them the courage they needed to trust him and to keep on going through the most difficult situations in their lives.

Application

(Memory verse visual; list made during Introduction, marker or chalk)

Does God still help people to be courageous as he helped Moses and Aaron? *(Response)* Yes, he certainly does, and our Bible verse reminds us of his promises to do it. *(Display the verse visual and have everyone repeat the verse together.)*

Let's think about the times when you might need courage to speak up for God. *(Display the list from the Introduction. Add additional responses.)* ▲#8 ▲#9 Do you think you might need courage to speak up for God in one of these situations this week? Let's talk about how you might do that. *(Discuss)*

How can we have the courage to speak up for the Lord, to do what is right when others are doing wrong and even making fun of us? We can do what Moses did—obey God and trust him to give us courage. To do this, we first must receive Jesus as Savior so that we are part of

God's family. Then anytime we are in a difficult place, we have the right to pray for his help to act with courage, believing that he will help us. For he has promised he will always be with us!

Response Activity

Invite any who want to receive Jesus as Savior to speak with you after class.

Distribute the **"Courage Card" handouts** and pencils. Have the children print on the back of the card what they need courage to do in the situation they've been thinking about during the Application time. Encourage them to pray individually—either silently or aloud (as time and numbers permit)—asking God for his courage to speak up for him this week. Send the cards home with them as a reminder to pray daily for his help and think about God's promises in the verse. Give them opportunity next week to tell how God helped them.

TAKE HOME ITEMS

Distribute **memory verse tokens for Deuteronomy 31:6** and **Bible Study Helps for Lesson 4.**

God Sends Plagues Against Egypt
Theme: Power

Lesson 5

❋ BEFORE YOU BEGIN...

"You have the power within. Tap into it and you can achieve whatever you want." This satanic philosophy—that man is his own source of power—pervades our world, reaching boys and girls daily through the media, their school rooms, their toys, games and books. Most parents are unaware of its influence on their children, even the preschoolers. In fact, it is so subtle and sounds so good that many of us are unaware of its influence on our own thoughts and attitudes.

What is the antidote? TRUTH! The confrontation between the Lord God and Pharaoh with his false gods is a wonderful opportunity to teach the truth that God has all power and that he is the source of all power. Moses and Aaron standing before the most powerful monarch of their day, boldly proclaiming the Lord God's demands, demonstrate that God gives strength and power to his children when they trust him.

Draw the line clearly! Teach your children that there is but one true God, the Lord God of the Bible, and that his strength and power are available to every one of his children. *"Great is our Lord and mighty in power; His understanding is infinite" (Psalm 147:5, NKJV).*

☞ AIM:

That the children may

- Know that the God of the Bible is the only true God and he desires to show his power through their godly actions.
- Respond by allowing God's power to produce changes in their lives that will attract others to Christ.

📖 SCRIPTURE: Exodus 7–10

♥ MEMORY VERSE: 2 Samuel 22:33

God is my strength and power; and he maketh my way perfect. (KJV)
It is God who arms me with strength and makes my way perfect. (NIV)

📁 MATERIALS TO GATHER

Memory verse visual for 2 Samuel 22:33
Backgrounds: Review Chart, , Plain Background, Palace, River
Figures: R1-R5, 1, 2, 3, 4, 25, 32, 33, 34, 95(3), 106, 107, 108, 109, 110, 111, 112
Token holders & Memory verse tokens for 2 Samuel 22:33
Bible Study Helps for Lesson 5
Special:
- *For Review Chart:* Pictures or models showing man-made power (e.g., truck, train, plane, space craft) and God's power in nature (e.g., lightning, storms, sun, waterfall)
- *For Bible Content 2:* Wilderness Map; word strips THE TRUE GOD, FALSE GODS, RIVER, DARKNESS; Win/Lose markers
- *For Application:* Newsprint & marker or chalkboard & chalk
- *For Response Activity:* "God's Power" handouts, pencils
- *For Options:* Materials for any options you choose to use
- *Note: Follow the instructions on page xii to make the word strips (make RIVER and DARKNESS approximately 1" x 3" to match plague symbols) and the "God's Power" handouts (pattern P-13 on page 175).*

  To prepare the Win/Lose markers, use a small lid as a pattern. Trace and cut nine "Win" markers from one color of felt and nine "Lose" markers from another color. Use a felt marker to print a "W" on the "Win" markers and an "L" on the "Lose" markers.

■ REVIEW CHART

Display the Review Chart with R5 in God's Supply Room and place the R1-R4 tokens in random order on a table. Have pictures or models of God's power (windstorm, sun, waterfall, or lightning) and man-made power (truck, train, space craft or plane) ready to use when indicated. Choose individual children to state one of the lesson themes, choose its token, and place it on the Chart. Use the True or False questions to review Lesson 4. Have the children restate each false statement to make it a true one.

True or False?
1. Moses and Aaron met with the Israelite leaders before going to Pharaoh. (*True*)
2. Pharaoh was pleased when he learned that the Israelites wanted to leave Egypt. (*False; he was angry.*)
3. The Israelites had to make a lot more bricks after Moses met with Pharaoh. (*False; they had to get their own straw.*)
4. God gave Moses and Aaron courage to stand up to Pharaoh. (*True*)

▲ **Option #1**

Provide newsprint and markers or crayons. Have children—individually or in small groups—make drawings illustrating what power means to them.

▲ **Option #2**

Have children help you demonstrate our idea of strength by lifting objects of varying weights: e.g., a pencil, a stack of books, some rocks or hand weights. Be sure to do this safely.

▲ **Option #3**

As time permits, have each child draw his or her idea of God. Then allow them to explain their drawings to the class.

5. The Israelite leaders became angry and didn't want to listen to Moses. (*True*)
6. God told Moses he would never have to see Pharaoh again. (*False; God told Moses to go back to Pharaoh.*)

Let's look in God's Supply Room to see what we're going to talk about today. *(Have a child take R5 from God's Supply Room and place it on the Chart.)* What is it? *(Allow for response throughout.)* Yes, it's *Power*. When we say the word *power*, what do you think of? Let's name some things in our world that are very powerful. *(Display pictures/models of God's power and man-made power.)* ▲#1 ▲#2

We use these things to accomplish things we want to do. A train or a plane can move people or freight from one place to another or we can use a waterfall to generate electrical power. They are powerful, but our God—the one true and living God—has *all* power.

We learn about this all-powerful God in the Bible. Today we will see how he used his power to convince Pharaoh that the Lord God of Israel is the one true God and that he should be obeyed. Our memory verse tells us some important things about him.

♥ **MEMORY VERSE**

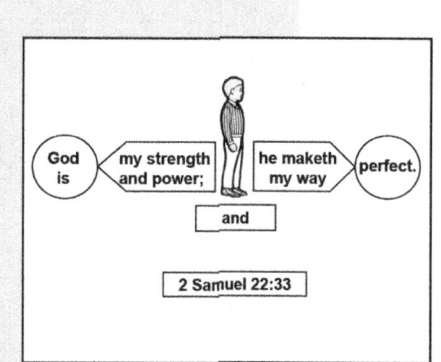

Use the visual to teach 2 Samuel 22:33 when indicated.

How would you describe God? *(Display the first visual piece. Discuss how their responses relate to who he is or what he is like. Then display the remaining visual pieces.)* ▲#3

Let's read our memory verse together. *(Do so.)* How is God described in the first part of the verse? *(Allow for response throughout.)* That's right; God is very strong and powerful. How has God shown his strength and power? Yes, the Bible tells us that he made the universe and our world and that he controls it all.

Many people think that they don't need God and that they can handle any situation that comes along—whether easy or hard—all by themselves. They say, "*I* am my strength and power." Others may say, "*Money* is my strength and power" or "*Being smart or popular* is my strength and power." *(Allow children to name other things that people trust in for power.)* ▲#4

King David, one of the greatest kings of Israel, wrote this verse to tell how he experienced God's great power in his everyday life. He knew how weak those other things are when big problems come. He had learned that God is able to give us the strength and power to do what is right and to please him.

Let's read the rest of the verse again. *(Do so.)* What does it say God will do for us? That's right; he will make our way perfect. When David wrote that God made his way perfect, he was saying that God worked in his life to remove the difficulties that could keep him from accomplishing God's plan for him. God's plan for your life is perfect and totally good.

When you allow him to work in your life you will be satisfied and God will be honored. God can help us no matter what our circumstances are. What a wonderful God we have! *(Work on memorizing the verse)* ▲#5

📖 BIBLE LESSON OUTLINE
God Sends Plagues Against Egypt

■ **Introduction**

God's power

■ **Bible Content**

1. Pharaoh refuses to let the Israelites go.
2. God judges Egypt with plagues.
   a. Water turned to blood
   b. Frogs
   c. Gnats (Lice)
   d. Flies
   e. Livestock disease
   f. Boils
   g. Hail storm
   h. Locusts
   i. Darkness

■ **Conclusion**

Summary

Application
   Thinking of ways to let others see God's power in your life

Response Activity
   Letting God help you make a specific change in your life

📖 BIBLE LESSON

■ **Introduction**

God's power

How does God show his power to people today? *(Response)* Yes, through things he has created. We see God's mighty power in hurricanes or tornadoes or floods. We also see it in our everyday world. Who put the sun in the sky? Who keeps it at just the right distance to give us life, but not burn up the earth? Who gives us just the right amount of light and darkness so that things will grow and we can live? Who set the boundaries for the oceans and keeps them from flowing over the continents? God did! The Bible tells us that God created all things and controls all things by his power. It also tells us that people can know God's power by looking at what he has made (Psalm 19:1, 2).

▲ Option #4

Before class, use a black marker to print POWER on newsprint or poster board.

In class, print "myself" and "money" on the poster as you teach. Have the children come and add their suggestions. *In conclusion*, use a red marker to print GOD across the entire poster.

▲ Option #5

Memorizing the verse: Have the children read the verse aloud together. Then have them do the following actions for each phrase of the verse (NIV in parenthesis)..

"God" (It is God) - *point upwards*;

"is my" (who arms me)- *point to self*;

"strength" (with strength) - *flex muscle on one arm and hold muscle with opposite hand*;

"and power" - *clasp hands firmly together*;

"and he" - *point upwards*;

"maketh my way" (and makes my way) - *point to self; then place palms together at chest and move them forward*.

"perfect" - *make a complete circle motion with hands and arms*.

▲ **Option #6**

Show pictures or drawings of Egyptian gods. (Pictures of the various gods and additional information about their worship may be found on the Internet, in encyclopedias or in Bible resource books).

⌂ **Note (1)**

The Pharaohs were believed to have descended from Ra, the sun god, which was Egypt's supreme god.

God's power is far greater than anything he has made or that man has made. He can do things that no human being can do or explain. We call these things miracles—things that only God can do!

Moses and the Israelites knew this, but Pharaoh and his people did not. They worshiped false gods that looked like cows or birds or other creatures. They believed that these false gods controlled everything from the weather to how many children they had. They also believed that Pharaoh was a god. Sometimes they worshiped him along with their idols. Pharaoh had no respect for the God of the Israelites. ▲#6 ⌂(1)

How could Pharaoh and the Egyptian people learn that the God of the Israelites was real, that he was any different from all the idols that they worshiped? They would see it when God used his mighty power to do miracles the Egyptian gods could not do. Today's exciting story tells how God used his mighty power to show Pharaoh and his people, *I AM GOD!* Try to imagine how you would have felt if you had been there. Find Exodus, chapter 7, in your Bible and place your bookmark there.

■ **Bible Content**

1. Pharaoh refuses to let the Israelites go. (Exodus 7:10-13)

(Pharaoh 1, servant 3, Moses 25, Aaron 32, rod 34, magicians 33, snakes 95[3], magicians 33)

Think back to the end of last week's lesson. How did Moses answer when God told him to go to Pharaoh once again and ask permission for God's people to leave the country of Egypt? *(Response)* Yes, he said to God, "My own people won't listen to me. How can I expect Pharaoh to listen?"

And what did God say then? *(Response)* "You're right, Moses. Pharaoh won't listen to you. his heart is hard (stubborn and unbelieving) against me. But I will do miracles and bring my people out of the land by mighty judgments. And the Egyptians will know that I am the only true God."

So, Moses and Aaron went back to the palace, as God had commanded them. They knew Pharaoh *(place 1, 3 on the board)* was a powerful man and could make life even more difficult for the Israelites, but they also knew that God has all power and would do what he had promised. So they decided to trust him and do what he told them. *(Add 25, 32, 34.)*

Once again they spoke God's words to Pharaoh: "Let my people go so they can worship me in the desert." Again Pharaoh refused. But God had given Moses and Aaron a plan, so they knew what to do. Read Exodus 7:10 to see what Aaron did. *(Response)* Yes, Aaron threw his staff down *(move 34 to the floor)* in front of Pharaoh and his servants and suddenly it became a snake *(replace 34 with one snake 95)*. You would think that would impress Pharaoh. It was a sign from God.

Sketch 26 — Palace

▲ **Option #7**

If necessary, shorten the explanation of each plague to: Moses' demand, Pharaoh's refusal, the plague itself and Pharaoh's response.

"Oh, that's nothing," said Pharaoh, "I have magicians who can do that, too." So he called for the magicians *(add 33)* and when they threw their staffs down, they also became snakes *(add 95[2])*. It appeared that their gods were just as powerful as the God of Israel. Read verse 12 to see how God showed that his power was greater. *(Response)* That's right! The snake that had been Aaron's rod swallowed up all the snakes that had been the magicians' staffs *(remove 95[3]; replace 34 in Aaron's hand)*. Still, Pharaoh's heart was hard and he refused to let the people go—just as God had said he would. The Lord would have to do something more dramatic to show that he was greater than the gods of Egypt.

2. God judges Egypt with plagues. ◻(2) ▲#7 ▲#8

a. Water turned to blood. (Exodus 7:14-25)

(Pharaoh 1, servants 2, 3, soldier 4, Moses 25, Aaron 32, rod 34; Wilderness Map)
Place all the figures on the board.
The Lord said to Moses, "Pharaoh's heart is still hard. Take Aaron with you to meet him on the river bank in the morning. Give him my message."

When Moses saw the king, he said, "You have not listened to the Lord God of the Israelites when he said, 'Let my people go so that they can worship me in the desert.' Now the Lord says: 'So that you will know that I am the Lord, I will strike the water in the Nile and it will turn to blood and so will the water in all the pools and streams in all the land. The fish will die, the river will stink, and the people will not be able to drink the water.'"

This was particularly embarrassing to Pharaoh because the Egyptians worshiped the Nile River as a god. It was supposed to give them life and help their crops to grow. Aaron struck the water of the Nile *(indicate on the map)* with his staff and immediately the water in the river and in all the pools and streams turned to blood. The fish died and the river smelled terrible. Where was the river god and his power now? The people had to dig in the ground just to find water to drink. ▲#9 ▲#10 ▲#11

However, Pharaoh's magicians used their magic arts to change some water into blood also, so he wouldn't listen. He just turned around and went back home, not even caring about how this would affect his people. The water remained dirty, stinking, and unusable for a whole week.

b. Frogs (Exodus 8:1-15)

(Win/lose markers; word strips THE TRUE GOD, FALSE GODS, RIVER, DARKNESS; Moses 25, Pharaoh 1, Aaron 32, rod 34, frog 106, magicians 33, gnat 107, fly 108, cow 109, Egyptian with boils 110, hail 111, locust 112

◻ Note (2)

According to Webster, a plague is a calamity or anything that afflicts or troubles—a contagious epidemic disease, a nuisance, an annoyance. In the Bible it is any of various calamities sent down as divine punishment. God said in Exodus 9:14 that he would send the plagues so that Pharaoh would know that there is no one like him in all the earth. (See also Exodus 11:1 and 12:13.)

Sketch 27 — River

▲ Option #8

Use one of the following verses from Exodus as a Bible Drill to introduce each plague: *Water to blood*: 7:20; *Frogs*: 8:2; *Gnats*: 8:16; *Flies*: 8:21; *Livestock*: 9:6; *Boils*: 9:10; *Hail*: 9:18; *Locusts*: 10:4; *Darkness*: 10:21. Have the first child to discover the name of the plague, come forward and print it on newsprint or chalkboard.

Or, print the names of the plagues on separate word strips and place them in random order on a table. Have children choose the one found in the verse and place it on the board.

Sketch 28   Plain Background

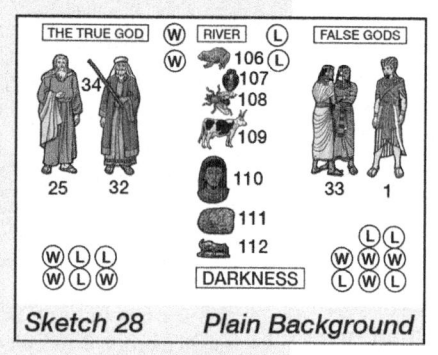

▲ **Option #9**

Fill a glass or plastic container with water. As you teach, add several drops of red food coloring to illustrate the water changing to blood.

Or, cut a red flannel or felt strip to match the shape of the river on your background; use it to cover the river at this point.

▲ **Option #10**

Mural scene.

▲ **Option #11**

Mural scene for plagues. Have the children add a drawing for each plague to the mural either as you teach, at the end of the lesson as a review, or the following week in pre-session time.

▲ **Option #12**

Prepare Sketch 28 on poster board. Print the headings as shown. Use small rolls of masking tape to attach figures, small word strips and Win/Lose markers.

Place nine Win/Lose markers in mixed-up-order on the bottom left corner of the board and nine in mixed-up order on the bottom right corner of the board and move them when indicated.

Next, God sent Moses to Pharaoh *(add 25, 1)* to say, "The Lord says, 'Let my people go so that they can worship me. If you refuse, I will send frogs to fill the land. They will come into your houses, into your beds and even into your mixing bowls and cupboards.'"

But Pharaoh again refused to listen, so Aaron *(add 32, 34)* stretched his rod over the river and frogs *(add 106)* came out of all the rivers and streams. They were everywhere! They covered the ground! They were in the houses—even the palace—in the beds, and on the chairs. They hopped onto the boards where the women mixed dough for bread. They even got into the ovens! It was terrible!

The Egyptians believed that frogs were sacred and had divine power. They imagined that a great goddess, who had a frog's head, took care of them, so they would never harm or kill a frog. But this goddess was not able to help them now.

Pharaoh's magicians *(add 33)* used their magic arts to make some frogs come out of the river, but they could not make them go away! Soon Pharaoh sent for Moses and Aaron and said, "If you pray that your God will make the frogs go away from me and my people, I will let your people go and worship the Lord."

"All right," said Moses. "When do you want the frogs to go away?"

"Tomorrow," answered Pharaoh.

Moses answered, "So that you will know there is no god like our God, the frogs will be gone tomorrow."

The next day the frogs suddenly died in the houses, the yards, and the fields. There were so many that the people shoveled them together in heaps and the smell was awful. The only living frogs left were those in the Nile River. But Pharaoh hardened his heart again and refused to let the people leave. *(Leave all the figures on the board.)*

c. **Gnats (Lice) (Exodus 8:16-19)** ▲#12 ◭(3)

This was a contest between the true God *(add THE TRUE GOD)* of the Israelites and Pharaoh and the false gods *(add FALSE GODS)* of Egypt. Who was winning? *(Response)* That's right; the true God was winning! He had defeated the river god *(add RIVER above 106)* and the goddess of the frogs. *(Move one Win marker to the left side of RIVER and one to the left of 106; move one Lose marker to the right side of RIVER and one to the right of 106.)* What would he do next? He simply said to Moses, "Tell Aaron to stretch out his rod and strike the dust of the ground. Throughout the land of Egypt the dust of the ground will become stinging gnats." Aaron did as God had said and soon flying, biting insects *(add 107)* covered all the people and the animals. There was no escape from the torture! God was winning the contest! *(Move one Win marker to the left of 107.)*

48   L-5

Once again Pharaoh called his magicians, but no matter how they tried, they could not produce the kind of gnats that God had sent. They said to Pharaoh, "This is really the work of God. You had better pay attention." *(Move one Lose marker to the right of 107.)* Still, Pharaoh's heart was hard and he would not let the people leave. He and his people were the losers.

d. Flies (Exodus 8:20-32)

So God sent Moses to meet Pharaoh at the river bank with his next message: "If you don't let my people go to worship me, I will send swarms of flies on you and your people. They will fill your houses and even cover the ground, but there will be no flies in the territory of Goshen where my people live *(indicate on the map)*. I want you to know that I AM THE LORD. This will happen tomorrow."

Pharaoh did not let them go, so dense swarms of flies filled the palace and all the homes of Egypt *(add 108)*. They swarmed over the Egyptians, including Pharaoh, all the time, even when they were eating or sleeping. But there were no flies where the Israelites lived! This was another miracle—more evidence that the Lord God was more powerful than the false gods of Egypt. *(Move one Win marker to the left of 108 and one Lose marker to the right of it.)*

Finally, Pharaoh sent for Moses and Aaron and said, "You can go sacrifice to your God, but you must do it here in Egypt." He was afraid that if he let them leave his country, they would not come back.

Moses answered boldly: "That would not be right. When we worship, we offer sheep and oxen as sacrifices to our God. The Egyptians worship these animals and if they see us killing them, they will kill us. We must do as the Lord our God commands us and go at least three days' journey into the wilderness to worship."

"All right," Pharaoh agreed, "you can go, but you must not go very far. Now pray that the flies will go away."

Moses promised that the flies would be gone the next day, and they were. But Pharaoh hardened his heart again and would not let the people leave.

e. Livestock Disease (Exodus 9:1-7)

Once again the Lord sent Moses back to the palace to announce to Pharaoh, "The Lord, the God of the Israelites, says: 'Let my people go so they can worship me. If you keep holding them here, I will send a terrible plague on all your livestock that are out in the field—your horses and camels and donkeys, your cattle and sheep and goats. But not one animal that belongs to my people will die.'"

Pharaoh did not let the people go, so the next day God's promise came true! All the livestock *(add 109)* the Egyptians left out in the field got sick and died. Many of these animals were sacred to the Egyptians; they even had gods that looked like bulls and cows. Pharaoh sent

Note (3)

Having these tiny biting, stinging creatures in their eyes and ears, down their throats, inside their clothes and homes—and even on their sacred animals must have been particularly difficult for the Egyptians, and especially the nobility, who were very careful to keep their bodies and clothes clean. The priests of their various gods also worked very hard at being clean and keeping their temples and all the sacred animals clean for their religious practices. The plague of flies must also have been very repulsive to them because the flies brought such filthiness.

his servants to Goshen *(indicate on the map)* to investigate and they discovered that not even one of the Israelites' animals had died, just as God had promised! *(Move one Win marker to the left of 109.)* Still, Pharaoh would not give in to God and would not let God's people go. He was losing the contest, but he wouldn't admit it. *(Move one Lose marker to the right of it.)*

f. Boils (Exodus 9:8-12)

Next God sent Moses and Aaron to Pharaoh with handfuls of ashes from a furnace. They threw the ashes into the air and the wind blew them out over the land. Moses told the king that the ashes would turn into terrible boils on the people and the animals. Boils are infected open sores that are very painful.

God's word came true. Soon people and animals all through Egypt were suffering from these terrible sores *(add 110)*. Even the magicians could not stand before the king because they were hurting so much.

The Egyptians were fearful of diseases and had several gods which supposedly had power to protect and heal them. But their gods had no power to stop the boils that came from the true God. *(Move one Win marker to the left of 110 and one Lose marker to the right of it.)*

g. Hailstorm (Exodus 9:13-35)

God spoke again. "Moses, go to Pharaoh early tomorrow and give him this message."

Moses obeyed. To Pharaoh he said, "The God of the Israelites, says: 'Let my people go so they can worship me. If you refuse, tomorrow I will send the worst hailstorm that has ever happened in all of Egypt's history. If you believe me, give the order now to bring all your livestock and servants into shelter. Any person or animal who is outside in the storm will die.'"

Pharaoh's officials heard the message, too. Those who feared the word of the Lord hurried to bring all their servants and animals inside for safety, but many ignored it and did nothing.

The next day the Lord sent thunder and hail *(add 111)* and lightning—the worst storm they had ever had. The hail struck everything in the field, killing people and animals, stripping the bark off all the trees and destroying the crops. But there was no hail in Goshen *(indicate on the map)* where the Israelites lived. *(Move one Win marker to the left of 111)*. The Egyptian god that was supposed to protect the crops and make them grow well could not save them from God's hail. *(Move one Lose marker to the right of 111.)*

The Egyptians—even Pharaoh—were very afraid. Pharaoh sent for Moses and Aaron and said, "This time I realize that I have sinned. God is right; I and my people are wrong. Please pray to the Lord; we have had enough of this terrible hail and thunder. I will let you and your people go."

So Moses left the city and prayed. Immediately the thunder and hail and rain stopped! But when Pharaoh saw that the storm was over, he hardened his heart and again refused to let the people leave.

h. Locusts (Exodus 10:1-20)

God did not give up. He wanted his people to be free and he wanted Pharaoh to know him as the one true and living God. He also wanted his people to know for sure that he is the Lord and he could take care of them because he has all power.

So he sent Moses and Aaron to Pharaoh again. Moses spoke God's message boldly: "If you refuse to let my people go, I will bring so many locusts into your land that they will cover the ground so it can't be seen; they will even fill your houses. And they will eat everything that was left after the hail storm."

When Moses had gone, Pharaoh's officials said to him, "How long is this man going to be a problem to us? Let them go and worship their God. Don't you realize that Egypt has been destroyed?" They knew that they had lost the contest with God. It was obvious their gods couldn't help them.

So Pharaoh sent for Moses and Aaron. "Go!" he said. "Worship the Lord your God—but take only the men. Leave the women and children behind. Now get out of my presence!" He knew that they would have to come back if they left their families behind.

Moses stretched out his rod and God sent a strong wind carrying swarms of locusts *(add 112)*. There were so many that they looked like a dark cloud; the noise they made sounded like an army. They covered the ground until it looked black and they ate everything that had been left in the fields by the hail. Not a green thing was left growing in the land of Egypt. What would the people eat? They had already lost the fish, their cattle had been killed in the storm, and now the green vegetables were all gone!

Pharaoh was frightened. Quickly he called for Moses and Aaron and said, "I have sinned against the Lord your God and against you. Please forgive my sin once more and pray to your God to take these terrible locusts away." Who had won? *(Response)* Yes, once more God had won and Pharaoh had lost. *(Move one Win marker to the left of 112 and one Lose marker to the right of it.)*

Moses prayed and the Lord took the locusts away. But, again Pharaoh refused to obey God and would not let the people go.

i. Darkness (Exodus 10:21-29)

Quickly and without warning God spoke again: "Moses, stretch your hand toward the sky and thick darkness will cover all of Egypt— darkness you can feel." Moses obeyed and darkness covered the whole land—except for where God's people lived. They had light as usual. The darkness lasted for three days *(add DARKNESS)*. It was so dark

> **◸ Note (4)**
>
> Ancient Egyptians loved light. Their buildings and clothing were made to reflect the sunlight (from the sun god Ra) to the maximum.

> **▲ Option #13**
>
> Mural scene.

that they couldn't see anything, not even a hand in front of their eyes. *(Darken the room or blindfold the children to help them understand.)* They couldn't see to cook or move around their houses or take care of their animals or work in the fields.

This was the worst thing so far. The Egyptians worshiped the sun and believed that it gave them energy and life. ◸**(4)** But the sun god was no match for the God of Israel. Once again God had demonstrated his power over the false gods of Egypt. *(Move one Win marker to the left of DARKNESS and one Lose marker to the right of it.)*

At the end of the three days Pharaoh sent for Moses. "Take your families and go worship your God. Just leave your flocks and herds behind." He thought that they would come back for their animals, and if they didn't, at least, the animals would be left.

"We can't do that," Moses answered. "We must take our livestock so that we can make sacrifices to our God."

Pharaoh was furious! "Just get out of my sight!" he thundered. "And don't come back! If you do, you will die!" He was a stubborn, rebellious man! He and his gods were defeated and he knew it. *(Remove all the figures.)* ▲#13

■ Conclusion

Summary

(Frog 106, gnat 107, fly 108, cow 109, Egyptian with boils 110, hail 111, locust 112, word strips RIVER, DARKNESS)
Place all the figures on a table.

Let's see if we can list all the plagues we've talked about today. *(Allow volunteers to place the corresponding figures on the board as the plagues are mentioned.)* God worked these mighty miracles through his servants Moses and Aaron to show his power to Pharaoh and his people. God could use Moses and Aaron because they trusted God and were willing to obey his commands.

God sent these plagues because he wanted to rescue his people from Egypt. Did he have to send plagues to do that? No, he could have done it some other way. He sent the plagues because he wanted Pharaoh to recognize him as the one true and living God who was more powerful than all the false gods of Egypt. But Pharaoh stubbornly refused to believe in God or obey him.

Application

(Newsprint & marker or chalkboard & chalk; memory verse visual)
God still wants people to recognize him as the one true and living God. He also wants them to believe in him and obey him. How does God show his power to people today? *(Response)* Yes, through the things he has created and by keeping our everyday world running. But also through the lives of people. When we trust his Son Jesus as Savior,

he forgives our sin. That is one of God's greatest and most powerful miracles. The Holy Spirit then comes to live in us to give us God's power to obey his Word and live to please him.

What are some ways we can show God's power in our lives each day? *(List the responses on newsprint or chalkboard. If necessary, suggest things like showing kindness, speaking the truth, not using swear words or saying hurtful things to others, or doing chores without complaining.* ▲#14

When we obey God and live as he wants us to, others will see that our lives are different. Some may even ask us about it. Then we can tell them about God and his Son Jesus, about his power to forgive sin and to help us obey him.

Some may be like Pharaoh, refusing to believe or laughing at us or ignoring us. But remember our memory verse. *(Display the verse visual and read it together with the class.)* God will give us the strength and power we need to obey him and live the way he wants us to.

Can you think of someone who needs to know that the Lord God is the only true and living God? Look at our list again. What could you trust God to help you change in your behavior so the person you're thinking of can see God's power at work in your life?

Response Activity

Distribute **"God's Power" handouts** *and pencils. Have each one print on the first line the name of the person whom they're thinking about. Then have them print on the next line what change they want to see in their own lives so that the person they're thinking of will see God's power at work in them. For example, "I want MOM to see God's power in me this week as I DO DISHES WITHOUT COMPLAINING."*

Remind them that if they have not received Christ as their Savior, they do not have God's power at work in them. Invite any who want to receive him to talk with you or a helper after class.

When everyone is finished, have them turn their circles over and read the memory verse together. Then give them time to pray silently for two things: 1. That God will be their strength and power to obey him in that thing this week, and 2. That the person they were thinking about will see God's power in them.

Close by praying that each one will trust God to be their strength this week so others will see God's power in their lives. Have them take their circles home and keep them as a prayer reminder. Next week give opportunity for them to tell how God helped them.

✍ TAKE HOME ITEMS

Distribute **memory verse tokens for 2 Samuel 22:33** *and* **Bible Study Helps for Lesson 5.**

▲ **Option #14**

Before class, put some children in pairs and assign each pair one of these situations. Ask them to prepare to act out its opposite. For example, if a pair is assigned "showing kindness," they should act out "being mean" or "leaving someone out."
In class, have them do their skits. Then discuss with the class how God's power could be shown in that situation and have them act out the positive suggestion.

God Sends the Final Plague
Theme: *Faith*

Lesson 6

✸ BEFORE YOU BEGIN...

What is faith? Hebrews says it is "the substance of things hoped for, the evidence of things not seen" (11:1). We have defined it in this lesson as "believing what God says, trusting him to do what he promised, and obeying him no matter what." This passover lesson is a good illustration of this. Though killing a lamb and putting its blood on their door frames may have seemed a ridiculous thing to do, the Israelites believed what God said, trusted him to keep his promise, and obeyed. The results? They were saved from death and freed from slavery.

Help your children to see the parallel in their own lives. Encourage them to believe what God says about the Lord Jesus Christ who loves them and gave his life for them; to trust God to keep his promise to forgive their sin and give them life eternal; and to obey by receiving Jesus as their own Savior. And then to have faith in him as the One who will always keep his word and is worthy of their trust; the One to whom they can go when problems come and they can't see a solution. *"So then faith comes by hearing, and hearing by the word of God" (Romans 10:17, NKJV).*

☞ AIM:

That the children may

- Know that God provides salvation as a gift that must be received by faith.
- Respond by trusting the Lord Jesus as their personal Savior.

SCRIPTURE: Exodus 10:28–12:36

MEMORY VERSE: Ephesians 2:8

For by grace are ye saved through faith; and that not of yourselves: it is the gift of God. (KJV)

For it is by grace you have been saved, through faith – and this not from yourselves, it is the gift of God. (NIV)

📁 MATERIALS TO GATHER

Memory verse visual for Ephesians 2:8
Backgrounds: Review Chart, Plain Background, Palace, City Street, Plain Interior
Figures: R1-R6, 1, 3, 4, 7, 10, 11, 12, 17, 24(1), 25, 31, 32, 35, 36, 37, 38(3), 39, 40, 41, 49, 69, 106, 107, 108, 109, 110, 111, 112
Token holders & memory verse tokens for Ephesians 2:8
Bible Study Helps for Lesson 6
Special:
- *For Response Activity:* "God's Gift" handouts & pencils
- *For Options:* Materials for any options you choose to use
- *Note:* Follow the instructions on page xii to prepare the "God's Gift" handouts (pattern P-14 on page 176).

💼 REVIEW CHART

Display the Review Chart with R6 in God's Supply Room and R1-R5 ready to use. Allow students to place the R1-R5 tokens on the Chart as they recite the related memory verse. Use one of the following suggestions to review Lesson 5. Through this review, help the children see that Pharaoh refused every opportunity to believe and each time God brought greater judgment.

1. Place figures 106-112 on a table in random order. Then have children come one at a time, choose a picture of a plague, place it on the board, tell why it was a terrible blow to Pharaoh and the Egyptians.
2. Have the children draw pictures of each plague.
3. Have volunteers briefly act out how Moses and Aaron appeared before Pharaoh to warn him about each of the plagues.

Who would like to see what's in God's Supply Room today? *(Choose one child to remove R6 from God's Supply Room and place it on the Chart.)* What is it? *(Allow for response throughout.)* Yes, it is *Faith*. Have you heard this word before? What do you think it means? Faith is believing what God says, trusting him to do what he promised, and obeying him no matter what. ▲#1 If we want to please God, we must learn to trust him and obey him every day—to walk in the footsteps of "trust and obey." ▲#2

♥ MEMORY VERSE

Display the visual to teach Ephesians 2:8.
Our memory verse tells us one reason why we need faith. See if you can find it as we read together. *(Do so.)* What is the reason? *(Allow for response throughout.)* Yes, we are saved *through faith*. We are saved from the punishment for our sins when we *believe* what the Bible says—that Jesus

▲ **Option #1**

Definition word card:: Faith = Believing what God says, trusting God to do what he promised, and obeying God no matter what.

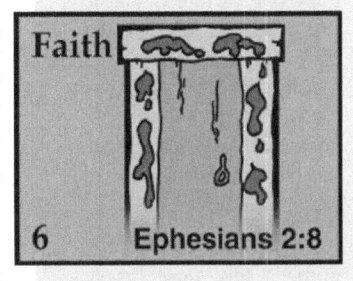

▲ **Option #2**

Teach the familiar chorus, "Trust and Obey."
Trace a pair of athletic shoes on poster board to make a set of large footprints (10" – 12"). Print TRUST on one and OBEY on the other. Use both the chorus and the footprints to reinforce this truth whenever it comes up in a lesson.

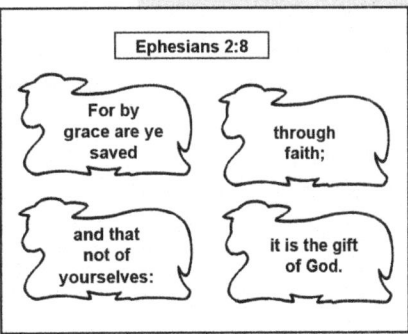

▲ **Option #3**

Definition word cards (one for each word):
Faith = Believing, trusting, obeying God, no matter what!
Grace = God's giving us what we do not deserve.
Salvation = Being rescued or saved from danger.

▲ **Option #4**

Memorizing the verse: Distribute the verse visual pieces to five children. Have them display their pieces in the proper order, with the class repeating the words aloud each time a piece is added. When the verse is completely displayed, have the class repeat the entire verse together.

After the class repeats the verse a few more times, distribute the visual pieces to another set of children. Have them, on a given signal, run to the front, arrange themselves in order and lead the class in repeating the verse. Continue with different groups until all have an opportunity to participate. Time each group to see which can do it the fastest.

died on the cross in our place—and *trust* God to forgive us for our sins. That is faith. ▲#3

Now what does our verse tell us about *how* we are saved? That's right; it says that God saves us *by grace*. This word *grace* means that he forgives us and gives us everlasting life even though we don't deserve it.

The verse tells us two more things about our salvation. What's one of them? Correct, it's *"not of yourselves."* We can't do anything to save ourselves. We can't be good enough or give enough money or go to church enough.

What is the second thing the verse tells us? Yes, *it is the gift of God*—so that no one can boast and say, "I was good enough to go to heaven all by myself." God gives us the gift of forgiveness and salvation when we accept it by *faith*; when we *believe* what his Word says—that Jesus died for our sin and came back to life again. *(Work on memorizing the verse.)* ▲#4 ▲#5

📖 BIBLE LESSON OUTLINE

God Sends the Final Plague

■ **Introduction**

A test of faith

■ **Bible Content**

1. Moses warns Pharaoh of the final plague.
2. The Israelites prepare to leave Egypt.
   a. They ask neighbors for gold and silver.
   b. They prepare their lambs.
   c. They prepare a meal and pack their belongings.
3. God strikes every Egyptian firstborn.

■ **Conclusion**

Summary

Application

We can be saved from sin through faith in Jesus.

Response Activity

Receiving Jesus as Savior

📖 BIBLE LESSON

■ **Introduction**

A test of faith

Ross and his little brother Tony were having a lot of fun playing in their neighbor's orchard after school. Ross was "teaching" Tony to climb some of the small trees and then jump down out of them. But while

Ross wasn't watching, Tony had climbed too high in one of the taller trees and now he was crying and would not move. It was getting late and Ross was scared. What was he going to do? He couldn't just leave his brother in the tree while he went for help.

Just then their dad came through the orchard searching for them since they had not come home for supper. Right away he saw the problem and stood under the tree, looking up at Tony. "What will Dad do?" Ross wondered. "Would he climb the tree, too? Tony was up really high."

But Dad didn't climb up. Instead, he called to Tony, "Jump down, Tony. I'll catch you."

"Wow!" thought Ross. "Will Tony really jump from way up there? I don't know if I could do that. It's scary!"

Tony was scared, too, and kept on crying. But his dad talked quietly and gently, saying, "Come on, Tony. Jump right down into my arms. I'll catch you and put you on the ground and you'll be just fine."

After what seemed like a long time, Tony fearfully slid off the branch and jumped into his father's arms. Ross couldn't bear to look. But, just as Dad had promised, he caught Tony and put him safely on the ground. Tony really needed faith in his father to get safely out of the tree. He had to believe his father would do what he said—catch him! And he had to do what his father told him to do—jump! ▲#6

Today we will see how Moses and Aaron and all the Israelites really needed faith in God if they were ever to get out of Egypt. They had to believe what he said, trust him to do what he promised and then obey—do what he told them to do. They showed their faith by obeying. Let's see what we can learn from them that will help us have faith in God and obey him. Find Exodus, chapter 11, in your Bible and place your bookmark there.

■ Bible Content

1. Moses warns Pharaoh of the final plague. (Exodus 10:28–11:1, 4-8)

(Pharaoh 1, servant 3, Moses 25)
Place all the figures on the board.

You'll remember from last week's lesson that Pharaoh sent for Moses one more time after the plague of darkness. What did he tell Moses that he and the Israelites could do? *(Allow for response throughout.)* Yes, he said they could go and worship the Lord, but they had to leave their livestock behind. When Moses told him that was not possible, what did Pharaoh then do? That's right; he still would not let them go. Instead he shouted angrily at Moses and told him not to return to the palace or he would die.

Before Moses left the palace, he spoke God's final words to Pharaoh saying, "The Lord has said that *he* will go out in the land of Egypt at

Sketch 29   Palace

▲ Option #5

An object lesson to show the meaning of faith:

Place a chair before the class. Have a child help test it as you examine its parts and design. Demonstrate its sturdiness by thumping it lightly on the floor.

This looks like a good chair. Nothing seems loose or broken. Would it hold me up if I sat on it? Yes, I believe it would. I have *faith* that it will hold me. But what must I do to prove I believe in the chair? Yes, I must sit on it. *(Do so.)*

Faith in God is like that. It's not just knowing about him or saying we believe in him. Faith confidently believes what he says, trusts him to do what he promises and obeys his commands—even when we can't see what he's doing or understand how he will keep his promise.

▲ Option #6

Have the children give examples of when they needed faith in another person. Or, have them draw pictures of their examples or work together to dramatize them.

◩ **Note (1)**

The Bible is not completely clear, but most scholars believe that the reference is to the oldest son in every family who was not himself a father.

midnight and the firstborn in every family will die, from the firstborn in the palace to the firstborn in the poorest home and even the firstborn of the cattle. ◩(1) There will be loud crying all over the land greater than you have ever known. But there will be no deaths and no crying among the Israelites, so that you will know that the Lord makes a difference between the Egyptians and his own people. Then your officials will come to *me* and bow down and beg us to leave Egypt. And then—then *we will go out of Egypt!*" And Moses left the palace.

2. The Israelites prepare to leave Egypt. (Exodus 11:2–12:36)

(Moses 25, Aaron 32, leaders 31)
God had given Moses and Aaron specific instructions about how his people were to prepare for this last plague and for leaving Egypt. Moses *(place 25, 32 on the board)* called all the leaders *(add 31)* together and explained the instructions to them so that they could take them to the people.

These instructions were very important. If the people had faith in God (if they believed what he said and trusted him to keep his promise) and followed his instructions exactly, their firstborn would be saved from death when God went through the land. And they would be ready to leave Egypt at a moment's notice. *(Remove 25, 32.)*

Sketch 30 — City Street

a. They ask neighbors for gold and silver. (Exodus 11:2, 3; 12:35, 36)

(People 35, 49)
The leaders said to the people *(add 35, 49)*, "God says that you should go to your Egyptian neighbors and ask for gold and silver." This might sound strange to us, but the Israelites had worked as slaves to the Egyptians for many long years without any pay. God made the Egyptians willing and they gave the Israelites many valuable things. These things helped pay for all their hard work and provided money they would need for their trip. It must have been exciting for them to think they were actually getting ready to leave Egypt! *(Remove all the figures.)*

Sketch 31 — City Street

b. They prepare their lambs. (Exodus 12:3-7)

(Man 36, children 12, 37, lamb 24[1])
Place 36, 12, 37 on the board.
The leaders also gave the people God's other instruction: "On the tenth day of the month, every father must choose a

Sketch 32 — City Street

one-year-old lamb *(add 24[1])* or goat for his family. If his family is too small to eat a whole animal, they may share it with a neighboring family. The lamb or goat must be a male and it must be perfect—without any injury or disease. Keep the lamb for four days. *(Leave all the figures on the board.)*

(Dead lamb 40, basin of blood 41, hyssop branch 39, blood spots 38[3])

"On the 14th day of the month, kill the lamb *(remove 24; add 40)* and save some of its blood in a basin *(add 41)*. Dip a bunch of hyssop *(add 39)* in the blood and put the blood on the top and sides of the door frame of your house *(add 38[3]*. (Hyssop is a common bushy plant that grows on rocky surfaces in that area.) Then take your whole family and go inside the house *(remove all the figures except 38[3]*, close the door and stay there until morning. The Lord will pass through the land that night and the firstborn of all the Egyptians will die. The only safe place will be inside a house that has the blood on the door."

Sketch 33 — City Street

▲ **Option #7**

Passover Meal: Provide samples of some of the foods the Israelites ate in their Passover meal— perhaps baked lamb chops and pita bread cut into bite-size pieces.

You may obtain more information on the Seder Meal, its meaning and the way it is conducted at your local library, on the Internet or from Christian organizations reaching out to Jewish people with the message of Christ.

c. They prepare a meal and pack their belongings. (Exodus 12:8-11)

(Man 10, woman 7, girl 11, boy 17)
Place all the figures on the board.

Inside the house the whole family was to get ready to leave. They must roast the lamb and prepare a meal. They were to make enough bread to eat and to take with them on their trip. Since they didn't have much time, God told them to make it without yeast. When it was baked, it was a flat bread like a cracker. ▲#7

They also had to pack their belongings and get ready to travel. They were to be dressed in their traveling clothes, have their shoes on their feet and their walking sticks in their hands before they ate their meal together. This showed their faith in God. They believed what he said and they obeyed his instructions. ▲#8

The meal that they were to eat together that night was called Passover ▲#9 because God had said he would pass through the land at midnight and all the firstborn of the Egyptians would die. But when he saw the blood on the doors of the Israelite homes, he would "pass over" them and no one there would die because they had shown their faith in God by obeying his instructions.

The Bible tells us that when the Israelites heard all this, they bowed down and worshiped God. They had seen God's power and they believed that he was going to deliver them from slavery. Then they did just exactly what God had told them to do. Can you imagine how they felt or what they said to each other as they packed and ate their last meal in Egypt? *(Allow for response.)*

Sketch 34 — Plain Interior

L-6   59

▲ **Option #8**

Mural scene.

▲ **Option #9**

Print word PASSOVER on a word strip or large card to use as a visual reminder.

▲ **Option #10**

Mural scene.

Perhaps some wondered if it would really happen. Pharaoh had already refused nine times to let them go. Maybe some thought that putting blood over the doors was a bit strange or that God's instruction to ask the Egyptians for their gold and silver was even more so. But they put their faith in God and his promise that he would free them from Egypt, and they did what he said.

3. **God strikes every Egyptian firstborn. (Exodus 12:29-34)**

At midnight, the Lord struck down all the firstborn in Egypt, from the palace to the prison, and even the cattle. We don't know exactly how he did it; we just know that in one night they all died. Pharaoh and his officials and all the Egyptians got up in the night and found the oldest son in every home dead. There was great crying and wailing and mourning throughout the land, just as God had said there would be. But there was no death and no crying among God's people, because God had "passed over" their homes when he saw the blood on the doors. ▲#10

(Pharaoh 1, Moses 25, Aaron 32)

Pharaoh *(place 1 on the board)* couldn't wait until morning. In the middle of the night he sent for Moses and Aaron *(add 25, 32)*. "Get out of our land!" he commanded. "Get away from us, you and all your people. Go, serve the Lord as you have said. Take your flocks and herds. Just get out! And," he said, "please pray for me!" What a strange thing for him to say. Was he at last beginning to recognize that Moses' God was the one true God?

(Blood spots 38[3], men 36, 10, woman 7, boys 17, 37, Egyptian 4, crowd 35)

Place 38(3), 36, 10, 7, 17, 37 on the board.

The Egyptians *(add 4)* rushed to their Israelite neighbors saying, "Hurry, get out! Get away from here or we shall all be killed!"

There was no time to bake the rest of the bread they had mixed, so they took the dough with them, wrapped up in bundles on their backs. Soon all the families *(add 35)* were ready to travel and lined up for their journey out of Egypt. Now they realized how important it had been to obey God in faith, for they had to leave quickly. ▲#11

And the Lord did as he had promised! He freed his people from slavery on that night. They had been in Egypt for 430 years. Now this huge group of people—probably close to two million plus all their animals—were finally going to the land the Lord had promised would be theirs. They were finally free! God had kept his promise!

Sketch 35 — Palace

Sketch 36 — City Street

▲ **Option #11**

Mural scene.

■ Conclusion

Summary

(People 35, man 36, hyssop 39, dead lamb 40, basin 41, cross 69)

The Israelites needed faith in God in order to leave Egypt. What is faith? *(Allow for response throughout.)* That's right; faith is believing what God says, trusting him to do what he promises and obeying him no matter what.

What did the Israelites *(place 35 on the board)* do to show they had faith in God? Yes, they believed God when he said he would pass over any home that had blood on the door, and they did what he said—killed their lambs and put the blood on their doors *(add 36, 39, 40, 41)*. They stayed inside their homes that night and trusted God to do what he had promised to do—pass over them.

Did God keep his promise? Yes, he did. How? He went through the land at midnight and the firstborn in every Egyptian home died—but *no one* died in the Israelite homes where the blood was on the door. Why was that? That's right; because they had faith in God. They believed what he said, they trusted him to do what he promised and they did what he told them to do, even though it may have seemed like a strange thing to do. And that night their children were safe and they were freed from slavery in Egypt. God kept his promise!

Sketch 37   Plain Background

Application

(Cross 69; memory verse visual)

God made a way for the Israelite children to be saved from death that night. The lambs died instead and the blood was put on the door of every home so that the firstborn in that house would not die. They were thankful!

Today we can be thankful because God has made a way for us to be saved from the punishment for our sins. As we have heard before, the Bible says that the punishment for our sins is death. It also says that God's Son, Jesus—who never sinned at all—came to earth and died on the cross *(add 69)* to take that punishment for us. Now, if we have faith in God, we can have God's gift of salvation—we can be saved from the punishment for our sins.

Let's say our memory verse *(add memory verse visual)* together one more time. *(Do so.)* What does it mean to be "saved by faith"? *(Response)* Yes, it means to *believe what God said*—that the punishment for sin is death and that Jesus died to take that punishment for us—to *trust God* to do what he promises—give us the gift of salvation—and *do what he says* we should do—receive Jesus Christ as our Savior. When we do that, God gives us the gift of salvation—we are saved through faith. ▲#12

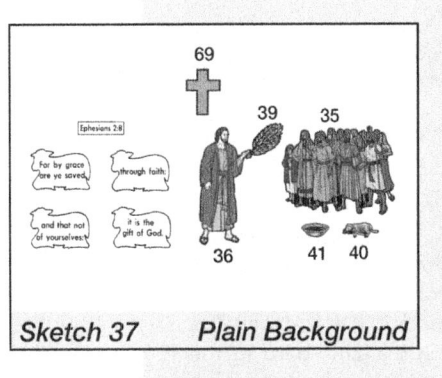

▲ Option #12

Object lesson: Gift wrap a box in which you have placed a red paper cross with the word SALVATION printed on it. Have a child open the box and show the gift God gives us when we receive Jesus as Savior.

Have you received God's gift of salvation? Have you believed that Jesus died to take the punishment for your sins and received him as your Savior, trusting God to give you salvation? If you have not, would you like to do that today?

Response Activity

*Distribute the **"God's Gift"** handouts and pencils. Have the children read the words aloud with you: "I have received God's gift of salvation." Wait quietly while they check the answer that applies to them. Encourage all who have answered Yes to print their name.* ▲#13

Then quietly read the last statement as the children listen: "Today, by faith, I receive God's gift of salvation by believing that Jesus died to take the punishment for my sins and receiving him as my Savior." Invite any who want to trust Christ as their Savior to come talk with you or a helper after class. Be prepared with literature to help them. When they have completed their "faith transaction," have them print their name and the date.

✎ TAKE HOME ITEMS

Distribute **memory verse tokens for Ephesians 2:8** *and* **Bible Study Helps for Lesson 6.**

▲ **Option #13**

Prepare for each child a small gift-wrapped box containing a paper cross on which is printed SALVATION. Attach the "God's Gift" card to the outside as a tag or tape it to the box. Follow the response instructions.

Israel Crosses the Red Sea
Theme: Deliverance

Lesson 7

❀ BEFORE YOU BEGIN...

It is nearly impossible for most of us to identify with the feeling of bondage the children of Israel experienced while slaves in Egypt or the exhilaration that was theirs when they saw Pharaoh's army destroyed in the Red Sea. This account of their deliverance by God's mighty hand is one of the most dramatic events recorded in Scripture.

Still, we all have needed to be delivered from a dangerous or hurtful situation at one time or another. And many of us understand the need to be delivered from some "besetting" sin that binds. God's enemy, Satan, is our enemy and our children's enemy. He constantly and cleverly tempts boys and girls to go their own way—to take what they want from the store, to lie or cheat at school, to sneak behind their parents' backs to play games and read magazines they know are wrong and harmful, to experiment with drugs to be part of the "in" crowd. Sadly, what begins as an adventure can soon become bondage. Through this lesson teach your children that the God who delivered Israel at the Red Sea is ready and able to deliver them from any sin that binds. *"The Lord knows how to deliver the godly out of temptations"* (2 Peter 2:9, NKJV).

☞ AIM:

That the children may

- Know that only God can forgive them when they sin and deliver them from sin's power in their lives.
- Respond by accepting God's forgiveness and asking him to deliver them from a sin that controls them.

📖 SCRIPTURE: Exodus 12:37-42; 13:17–15:21; Psalm 106:7-12.

♥ MEMORY VERSE: Daniel 3:17

Our God whom we serve is able to deliver us. (KJV)
The God we serve is able to save us. (NIV)

▲ **Option #1**

Definition word card:
Deliverance = Being set free or rescued

▲ **Option #2**

While looking at Daniel 3:17, take time to read (or have a child read) verse 18. Talk with the children about its implications—that these young men were willing to trust God even if he chose not to rescue them. Ask, do you remember what it means to trust or have faith in God? *(Response)* Yes, to believe what God says, trust him to do what he promises and obey him no matter what. Shadrach, Meshach and Abednego believed that God could rescue them from the danger if he chose to; they trusted him to take care of them if he did not rescue them; and they obeyed him, even though it meant being thrown into the fiery furnace. And we can read what happened: God rescued them *out of* the furnace! They were not burned and they didn't even smell of smoke! *(Allow children to amplify on the story as time permits.)*

📁 **MATERIALS TO GATHER**

Memory verse visual for Daniel 3:17
Backgrounds: Review Chart, Plain Background, General Outdoor, Palace, Red Sea Crossing, Land and Sea
Figures: R1-R7, 1, 3, 4, 7, 11, 17, 25, 34, 35, 37, 44, 45, 46, 47, 48, 49, 61, 62
Token holders & memory verse tokens for Daniel 3:17
Bible Study Helps for Lesson 7
Special:
- **For Memory Verse:** Newsprint & marker or chalkboard & chalk
- **For Introduction:** A piece of light-weight chain with a lock or a length of cord long enough to wrap around a child's wrists and tie him or her gently but securely; 3" x 5" card with ANGER printed on it
- **For Bible Content 1 & 2:** Wilderness map
- **For Summary:** Word strip GOD from Lesson 1
- **For Application:** Chain or rope from Introduction; red ribbon or yarn attached to the key for the lock or to scissors to cut the cord; word strips ANGER, SIN; list from Memory Verse
- **For Response Activity:** "Rope" handouts, pencils
- **For Options:** Materials for any options you choose to use
- **Note:** *Follow the instructions on page xii to prepare the word strips To prepare the "Rope" handouts, tie a piece of red yarn or ribbon to a short length of rope (6-10 inches) and staple or tape a 3" x 5" card to it.*

💼 **REVIEW CHART**

Display the Review Chart with R1-R5 in place and R7 in God's Supply Room ready to use when indicated. Place R6 on the Chart as you review last week's memory verse and theme with the children. Use the following questions to review Lesson 6.

1. What was special about the Passover lamb or goat? *(It was to be perfect; it could not be sick or injured.)*
2. What happened to the blood of the lamb? *(The father put it above and on both sides of the door.)*
3. What did God say would happen to those families who did not put the blood on their door? *(Their firstborn son and their animals' firstborn would die.)*
4. What is faith? *(Believing what God says is true, trusting him to do what he promises and doing what he tells us to do.)*
5. What gift do we receive from God when we put our faith in his Son, Jesus, as Savior? *(Salvation—being saved or delivered from the punishment for our sins)*

What will God give to the Israelites from his Supply Room today? What will they need as they begin their trip from Egypt to the promised land? *(Have a child take R7 from God's Supply Room and place it on the Chart.)* Yes, it's *Deliverance*. This big word means being set free or being rescued from something that is dangerous or wrong. ▲#1 In our Bible lesson we will discover how God delivered or rescued his people from their enemies, the Egyptians, and set them free.

♥ MEMORY VERSE

Use the verse visual and newsprint & marker to teach Daniel 3:17 when indicated.

Can you think of a time when you were in trouble and needed someone to deliver or rescue you? *(Allow for response throughout.)* The words of our memory verse were spoken by three men who were in serious trouble with their enemies. Their story is found in the Old Testament book of Daniel, chapter 3. ▲#2

Because Shadrach, Meshach, and Abednego refused to bow down and worship a statue of the king, the king threatened to throw them into a fiery furnace. Our memory verse was their answer to the king's threat. Find Daniel 3:17 in your Bible. Let's read it together. *(Do so; then display the verse visual).* ▲#3

> Our God whom we serve is able to deliver us.
> Daniel 3:17

Their words are true for you and me, too. Our God is able to deliver or rescue us from sinful actions, words, and attitudes and from our enemy Satan who tries to get us to go his way and not obey God's Word. Can you think of some things that boys and girls today need to be rescued from? *(List responses on newsprint or chalkboard. Suggest the following if necessary: consistently lying, cheating in school or at sports, acting out in anger, thinking bad thoughts, being selfish, watching violent TV programs, or playing violent video games.)* ▲#4

We might expect people who are not saved to do some of these things. Can God forgive them? What would they need to do to be forgiven? Do Christians sometimes have problems with these things?

God is the only one who can deliver us from these and other sins that sometimes control us. If we want him to deliver us, we must admit (confess) our sin and accept God's forgiveness. Then he will deliver us from its power over us by helping us to say no to it each day. Let's say our verse together aloud. *(Work on memorizing the verse.)* ▲#5

📖 BIBLE LESSON OUTLINE

Israel Crosses the Red Sea

■ Introduction

Danny's anger

▲ Option #3

Locate teaching pictures to visualize the fiery furnace scene.

Or, provide a large piece of newsprint or poster board with crayons or markers and have the children draw the scene, either individually or as a class.

▲ Option #4

Before class, print the suggested "thinking stimulators" on separate 9" x 12" cards.

In class, hand these to children to hold in front of the class as they are mentioned. Print children's responses on extra cards to be held in front of the class as well.

▲ Option #5

Memorizing the verse: Have the group say the verse several times together, emphasizing a different word each time—e.g., our, God serve, able, deliver, us. For variety, specify different groups to say it each time—e.g., all who are wearing a specific item of clothing (black shoes, blue shirt), those who are the oldest (or the youngest) in their family, etc.

▇ Bible Content

1. The Israelites leave Egypt.
2. God guides his people with a cloud.
3. Pharaoh pursues the Israelites.
4. God delivers his people.
   a. The Israelites cry out to God.
   b. God makes a path through the sea.
   c. God overthrows the Egyptians.
5. The Israelites praise God.

▇ Conclusion

Summary

Application
Acknowledging a sin that controls you

Response Activity
Asking God to deliver you from a sin that controls you

📖 BIBLE LESSON

▇ Introduction

Danny's anger

(Light-weight chain and lock or a length of cord, 3" x 5" card with ANGER printed on it)
Danny had trusted Jesus as his Savior, so he knew he was a Christian, but he had a big problem! Though he tried hard, he couldn't solve it by himself. Whenever he couldn't have his own way or something went wrong with his plans, he would get very angry and start yelling and saying things he would be sorry for later. his sinful anger seemed to take over and get him into trouble—and this happened over and over. Afterward Danny would feel terrible and wish he could take the angry words back—but, of course, he couldn't. Danny felt as though he were chained or tied up by his anger. *(Show the chain and lock or the rope. Then have an adult helper have his or her hands tied or chained. Leave the hands bound through the lesson.)*

We will let this chain (or rope) stand for Danny's sinful anger and reactions. *(Attach the 3" x 5" card to the chain or rope; have the helper struggle to be free.)* Just as it is impossible for [helper's name] to get free from this chain by himself, so it was impossible for Danny to get rid of his anger by himself. He needed someone more powerful to rescue him or deliver him from his "enemy"—his anger.

Today we will discover that God did this very thing for his people. He delivered them from their enemy, the Egyptians. The Israelites were powerless to defeat this great army by themselves. Let's learn how God rescued them. Find Exodus, chapter 14 in your Bible and place your bookmark there

---

▲ **Option #6**

Review of the Ten Plagues: Assign children different plagues to illustrate on 9" x 12" pieces of newsprint or poster board. Put the illustrations on a table in random order. Then have individuals choose them in the order they occurred and tell how they affected the Egyptians and Israelites.

◪ **Note (1)**

It is impossible to visualize 2,000,000 people on the Felt Board, so let your children know that figures 35 and 44 are merely representing the entire group of Israelites that traveled from Egypt to Canaan.

▲ **Option #7**

Show pictures of the Joseph story as a visual reminder for the children.

Bible Content

1. The Israelites leave Egypt. (Exodus 12:37–13:19)

In our last lesson we learned how the Lord struck Egypt with the tenth plague—the death of the firstborn son—and how Pharaoh sent for Moses and Aaron and told them to take all their people and their animals and get out of the land. ▲#6 Their Egyptian neighbors gave them gold and silver and clothing. In this way God provided the money and supplies his people needed for their journey. Now these same neighbors begged them to leave quickly before more people died.

(People 44, girl 11, boy 17, Moses 25, rod 34, cattle 45; Wilderness Map.)

Because they had obeyed God's instructions, the Israelites were all packed and ready to go. *(Place all the figures on the board.)* Before morning they were on their way, marching out of Goshen towards the desert *(indicate the route on the map)*. It must have been quite a sight, perhaps two million people plus all their animals—cattle, sheep, camels, and donkeys. ⌂(1) Probably most people walked, carrying some possessions on their backs. Others may have ridden on camels or donkeys. How do you think they felt? How would you have felt if you had been one of them? *(Have children give responses.)*

Moses also took Joseph's mummified body. Joseph had wanted to be buried in the land God promised to give them hundreds of years before. ▲#7 ⌂(2) *(Remove all the figures.)*

Sketch 38 — General Outdoor

(Tents 61, 62, Moses 25, rod 34, people 35, children 17, 37)

After that first day of walking, the Israelites made camp *(place 61, 62 on the board)* for the night at a place called Succoth. What a huge camp it must have been! Each family built their own fire and baked flat bread from the dough they had brought with them. Many of them probably still could not believe they were free from slavery!

That night the Lord gave Moses *(add 25, 34)* some special instructions for the people *(add 35, 17, 37)*. So that they would not forget how God delivered them from Egypt, they were to have a week-long celebration every year at this same time. During that special week they were to eat this same flat bread—bread made without yeast—and do no work. On the seventh day they were to have a special feast at which they would eat a lamb they had killed and roasted. God said that when their children or grandchildren asked why they did this, they were to tell them how they had put the blood of a lamb on the sides and top of their doors to protect the oldest son

Sketch 39 — General Outdoor

⌂ Note (2)

Joseph, the first Israelite to live in the land of Egypt, was sold by his jealous brothers when he was just 17, taken to Egypt and sold to a man named Potiphar, falsely imprisoned and finally—by God's will—made prime minister, second only to the Pharaoh. In a time of great famine Joseph was reconciled with his brothers and brought his father Jacob and whole family to Egypt to live. There they grew into the great nation of Israel. (See Genesis 35-50 and *God Calls Us, Footsteps of Faith, Old Testament Volume 1,* Lessons 13-15.)

L-7

◩ **Note (3)**

This all happened about 1500 years before the birth of Christ. To this day Jewish people all over the world celebrate Passover in April of every year, about the same time as our Easter celebration. The lambs that died in Egypt that night were a picture of how the Lord Jesus Christ would someday die for the sins of the whole world. John the Baptist called Jesus the Lamb of God (John 1:29). Thousands of Jews from around the world were in Jerusalem for the Passover Feast when Jesus died on the cross (1 Corinthians 5:7b).

Sketch 40 — General Outdoor

Sketch 41 — Palace

▲ **Option #8**

Mural scene.

in every family from death, and how God had delivered them out of Egypt. This special feast was called the Feast of Passover because God "passed over" the homes where the blood was on the door and those children were safe. ◩(3) *(Remove all the figures.)*

2. God guides his people with a cloud. (Exodus 13:20-22)

(People 44, cloud 46, fire 47; Wilderness Map)

God knew that the Israelites *(place 44 on the board)* could not find their way alone on this journey, so he guided them in some special ways. During the day, he used a huge pillar or column of white cloud *(add 46)* to show them the way. At night, the cloud changed to a pillar of fire *(remove 46; add 47)* that gave them light in the darkness and kept wild animals away. When the Lord wanted them to stop or stay in one place to rest, the cloud stood still. When he wanted them to continue the journey, the cloud moved ahead. ▲#8

The Lord also directed the route they took. The shortest way from Egypt to the land God had promised to them was along the coast of the Mediterranean Sea, straight across the desert and north to the land of Canaan *(indicate on the map)*. But the Philistines, a very war-like people, lived along that route. God did not want his people to become discouraged and turn back if they had to fight with them, so he led them by a longer but safer way. They followed the cloud for several days until they came to the edge of the Red (or Reed) Sea *(indicate on the map)*. There the pillar of cloud stopped, and the people set up camp.

3. Pharaoh pursues the Israelites. (Exodus 14:1-9)

(Pharaoh 1, servant 3, Egyptian 4)

While the Israelites were traveling, the Egyptians were mourning the death of their firstborn children. Soon, however, Pharaoh *(place 1 on the board)* began to realize what it would be like without their slaves. "Why did we let them go?" he said to his officials. *(add 3, 4)* "Who will make bricks and build our cities? Who will do the work they did? We must bring them back!"

Pharaoh's spies told him that the Israelites had camped by the Red Sea. "Good!" he said, "we can trap them there against the sea and they won't be able to escape!"

(Chariots and horses 48)

Pharaoh hurriedly called up his army with all their horses and chariots *(place 48 on the board)*, climbed into his own chariot and started out to chase down the Israelites. This was the greatest and most powerful army in the world at that time! They could travel much faster than the people who were walking; soon they could see the Israelites camped for the night along the shore of the Red Sea. *(Remove 48.)*

Sketch 42   General Outdoor

4. **God delivers his people.**
   (Exodus 14:10-31; Psalm 106:7-12; 148:8b)

   a. **The Israelites cry out to God.**

(Cloud 46, people 35, 49, Moses 25, rod 34, fire 47) Place 46 on the board.

As the Israelites *(add 35, 49)* were settling down for the night, they heard a noise. When they looked out into the distance, they could see the Egyptian soldiers rushing toward them! What could they do? They couldn't go forward because the sea was in front of them. They couldn't go back because the army was behind them. And the desert was around them! There was nowhere to run! ▲#9

Read Exodus 14:10 to see what they did. *(Wait for response.)* That's right; they were terrified and they cried out to the Lord. They knew they could not fight against Pharaoh's army, and they were sure they would all be killed or taken back to Egypt as slaves. They were helpless, so they cried out to God for help.

But then, because they were so scared, they did something else. Read verse 11 to see what that was. *(Wait for response.)* Yes, they began to blame Moses *(add 25, 34)*. "Why did you bring us out of Egypt?" they said. "It would have been better for us to go on serving the Egyptians than to die out here in the wilderness." ▲#10

Moses said to them, "Don't be afraid. Just stand still and you will see how the Lord will deliver you. You will never see this army again. The Lord will fight for you today and he will save you. The only thing you have to do is watch and see what God will do." They must have wondered what would happen next.

Then the Lord said to Moses, "Raise your staff high *(extend 34 upward)* and stretch it out over the sea to divide the waters so the Israelites can cross over on dry ground." Suddenly, the pillar of cloud *(remove 46)* that had been leading them moved around behind *(add 47)* them so that it was between them and the Egyptians. For the Israelites it was a pillar of fire to give them light, but for the Egyptians it was pitch black. They couldn't see where they were going or what they were doing. It must have been an amazing sight!

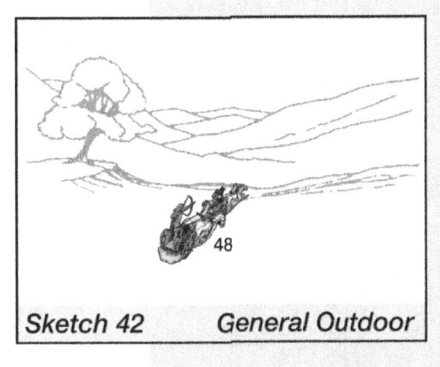

Sketch 43   General Outdoor

▲ **Option #9**

Mural scene.

▲ **Option #10**

Choose several children to read Exodus 14:11-13, imitating the way the Israelites might have sounded in their fear.

b. God makes a path through the sea.

(Moses 25, rod 34, people 44)
When Moses *(place 25, 34 on the board)* stretched out his staff over the sea, God sent a strong east wind that blew all through the night, dividing the sea and drying up the muddy bottom. As soon as it was dry, the Israelites *(add 44)* marched right into the midst of the sea on dry ground! There was a wall of water on their right side and another wall of water on their left side! Can you imagine their how amazed they were as they crossed over? God had done a miracle for them! *(Leave all the figures on the board.)* ▲#11

Sketch 44 — Red Sea Crossing

▲ Option #11
Mural scene.

▲ Option #12
Have children take the parts of Moses, the Israelites and the Egyptians and act out the story from Parts a, b, and c as the teacher reads aloud Exodus 14:10-14; 21-28. Encourage them to be creative and make props for the water.

c. God overthrows the Egyptians. ▲#12

(Horses and chariots 48)
It took quite a while for all the people and their animals to get across the sea. *(Remove 25, 34, 49; move 44 farther up the path.)* As soon as the Egyptians could see what was happening they rushed into the path with their horses and chariots in hot pursuit of the Israelites *(add 48)*. They didn't understand what had happened. They must have thought they could go anywhere the Israelites could.

Moses had told the Israelites, "The Lord will fight for you," and that's just what happened. Read verse 25 to see what he did. *(Wait for response.)* That's right; God took the wheels off their chariots! Can you imagine that? All the chariots suddenly without wheels and the horses trying to pull them? What a mess! Soon the Egyptians were saying, "Let's get out of here! The Lord is fighting for them against us!" And they tried to get back to the shore.

By this time the Israelites were safely on the other side *(remove 44)*. God said, "Moses, stretch out your hand over the sea, so that the waters can cover the Egyptians and their chariots and horses." Moses stretched out his hand, and as the sun was coming up all the water suddenly went back to its place. The Lord swept all the Egyptians into the sea and not one of them survived! *(Remove 48.)*

5. The Israelites praise God.
(Exodus 15:1-21)

(People 31, 35, 49, Miriam 7)
How do you suppose the Israelites *(place 31, 35, 49 on the board)* felt as they watched God at work for them? *(Response)* As they stood on the shore of the sea watching the waters cover the army, they knew the Egyptians would never hurt them again. They knew that their God, the holy and living God, had delivered them in this wonderful way. Then they sang a beautiful song of praise. *(Have the children*

Sketch 45 — Land and Sea

turn to Exodus 15 and read verses 1-6 and 10-12 aloud as a group or individually.) ▲#13

Miriam (add 7), Moses' older sister, led the women in singing, "I will sing to the Lord, for he is worthy to be praised. He has won a great victory over the mighty Egyptian army!" ▲#14

■ Conclusion

Summary

(People 44, chariots 48, word strip GOD)
Who delivered the Israelites (place 44 on the board) from their enemy? (Allow for response throughout.) Yes, God did. (Add GOD.) Who was their enemy? That's right; the Egyptian army. (Add 48.) How did God deliver them? Yes, he did a miracle for them so they could escape and be free. He put the enemy to death.

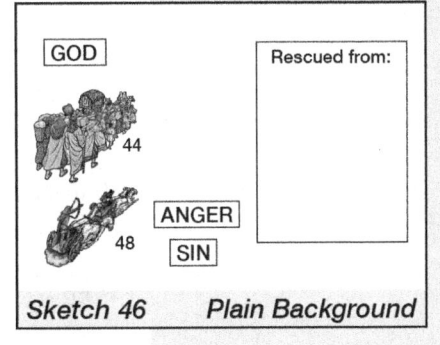

Application

(Scissors or key with red ribbon attached, chain or rope from Introduction; word strips ANGER, SIN; list from Memory Verse)

Do you remember what Joey's "enemy" was? (Have the helper wearing the chain or rope come to the front or hold up the chain or rope; allow for response throughout.) Yes, it was anger (place ANGER on the board) and his wrong responses to it. What did we call his anger? That's right; it was sin (add SIN). What did this enemy do in his life? It got him into trouble! He would get angry when things didn't go his way and respond by yelling mean and hurtful words. It was as if he were tied up and couldn't get free from his anger.

This rope (or chain) that stands for Joey's anger (indicate the person wearing the rope or hold the rope up) also stands for any sins from which we need to be delivered or set free. Can you think of some sin that keeps you "tied up" as Joey's did? Let's look at the list we made earlier. (Display the list; add any additional responses.)

Sometimes these things get control of us and we feel as though we can't stop doing them. It is as if we were tied up, like [adult's name] is tied right now. Every time we repeat the sin the "rope" gets tighter and heavier. (Have the adult acknowledge that the rope is tight. Be careful not to have it tight enough to hurt.) Satan's power is strong and he wants us to keep on sinning.

When we try to get free (have helper try to get out of the ropes or chain) what happens? (Ask the adult if he or she can get free.) That's right; we discover we can't do it by ourselves. We have no power or strength to stop sinning on our own.

Who can tell us what it will take to free [adult's name]? Yes, someone else must help or deliver him (her). Someone else must untie the rope

▲ **Option #13**

On newsprint, print Exodus 15:1-6 from one Bible version for all to read aloud together.

Sketch 46   Plain Background

▲ **Option #14**

Have the children sing a song that expresses God's victory over his enemies.

or unlock the chain. It's the same way with Joey and with us. We need someone stronger than ourselves and more powerful than Satan to rescue us. Who is that person? That's right; it is the Lord Jesus, God's Son. He is the only one who has the power and the right to forgive our sin and free us from Satan's power. He also can help us stop doing it again and again.

How can we get his forgiveness and help? That's right; we must ask him for it and trust him to do it. Just as [adult's name] must ask someone to deliver him/her and trust that it will be done. *(Have the adult call on someone to free him (her). Give the "rescuer" scissors or a key with red ribbon attached to do so.)*

Now [adult's name] has been delivered from the ropes. The red ribbon on the scissors (or the key) reminds us that Jesus shed his blood on the cross when he died and then rose again from the dead to win the victory over Satan's power to keep us "tied up" in sin. It also reminds us that only Jesus has power to deliver us from the sin in our lives.

Those of you who have asked Jesus to be your Savior are free from Satan's power and can come to Jesus any time for help to be delivered from a sin in your life. Pray and ask God for his help and power. He promises to give it and to free you from that sin. *(Have the children say Daniel 3:17 together.)*

Response Activity

Invite any who are not sure they know Christ as Savior to come after class to talk with you so they can be sure their sin is forgiven.

*Distribute **"Rope" handouts** and pencils. Explain that the rope reminds us of sin that can "tie us up" and control us while the red yarn reminds us that God's power can deliver us from that sin.*

Encourage the children to think of one "enemy" sin they need to be rescued from (looking at the chart if they need to) and print it on the card attached to the rope. Have them take the handout home and put it where they will see it every day. It will be a reminder to ask God for his help and power to stop doing that sin and to trust him to deliver them this week.

Close by giving the children time to silently ask God to deliver them this week from the specific sin they have printed on the card. Then pray aloud, asking God to help each child gain victory over their sin.

Be sure to give opportunity next week for the children to share what God did for them.

✍ TAKE HOME ITEMS

*Distribute **memory verse tokens for Daniel 3:17** and **Bible Study Helps for Lesson 7**.* ⌂(4)

⌂ Note (4)

Prepare now to help your children maintain the habit of daily Bible reading when this series of lessons is finished. Contact BCM International for information about Mailbox Bible Club. See the Materials list on page 180.

God Supplies Manna and Quail
Theme: Food

Lesson 8

❃ BEFORE YOU BEGIN...

We take so much for granted! It's so easy to go thoughtlessly about our day, eating, working, sleeping, enjoying our home and spending our money—and giving very little thought to the God who provides it all. It's so easy to look to our pay check (or our parents) rather than the One who cares most about us and has promised to supply our needs. In our materialistic age, it's so easy to confuse needs with wants—and to expect to have them all.

The Israelites were completely dependent on God, but they looked to Moses and Aaron when they didn't have food. God supplied their "needs" in manna and quail, but they murmured because they didn't have their "wants" (the bread and meat of Egypt). Our children need to learn that, ultimately, God is the One who supplies their needs and they should thank him for everything, even their daily food. That they can pray for a specific need and trust God to provide it. That he is not a heavenly vending machine who automatically gives whatever we ask for, but a loving Father who knows what is best and gives what will be for our good. *"My God shall supply all your need according to his riches in glory by Christ Jesus"* (Philippians 4:19, NKJV).

☞ AIM:

That the children may

- Know they can depend on God to supply material needs as well as spiritual.
- Respond by acknowledging God as the ultimate supplier of all their material needs and trusting him for a current specific need.

📖 SCRIPTURE: Exodus 15:22–16:36

♥ MEMORY VERSE: Matthew 6:11

Give us this day our daily bread. (KJV)
Give us today our daily bread. (NIV)

73

📁 MATERIALS TO GATHER

Memory verse visual for Matthew 6:11
Backgrounds: Review Chart, Plain Background General Outdoor, River, Plain with Tree, Wilderness,
Figures: R1-R8, 8, 11, 12, 23, 24(1), 25, 31, 35, 44, 45, 46, 49, 50(3), 51, 52, 53, 54, 62, 63, 89, 103
Token holders & memory verse tokens for Matthew 6:11
Bible Study Helps for Lesson 8
Special:
- **For Memory Verse:** Bread or rolls, enough for each child to have some.
- **For Bible Content 2:** Wilderness Map; a small stick
- **For Bible Content 4c:** Coriander or other small white seeds; crackers and honey
- **For Summary:** word strips FOOD, WATER, a small stick
- **For Application:** word strips FOOD, WATER, CLOTHES, HOME, TRUST
- **For Response Activity:** "My Needs & God's Answers" handouts, pencils
- **For Options:** Materials for any options you choose to use
- **Note:** Follow the instructions on page xii to prepare the word strips, and the "My Needs & God's Answers" handouts (pattern P-6 on page 171).

💼 REVIEW CHART

Display the Review Chart with R8 in God's Supply Room. Place R1-R7 in random order on a table or around the edges of the Chart. Allow individual children to choose a review symbol and place it on the Chart as they briefly tell how God gave that thing to the Israelites, then recite the corresponding memory verse. Use the following questions to review Lesson 7. ▲#1 ▲#2

1. What did God use to guide the Israelites as they left Egypt? *(A pillar—or column—of cloud by day and a pillar of fire by night)*
2. How did the cloud show the way? *(It moved ahead of them and stopped when they were to rest.)*
3. What was the purpose of the pillar of fire? *(To give light at night and keep wild animals away.)*
4. Why did Pharoah decide to chase the Israelites? *(He realized he was losing his construction workers.)*
5. How did God deliver the Israelites from the Egyptians? *(He made a dry path through the sea so they could cross over.)*
6. What happened to the Egyptian army? *(Everyone drowned in the sea.)*
7. What are some things you and I need to be delivered from? *(Bad habits, wrong attitudes, telling lies, etc.)*

▲ **Option #1**

Divide the class into small groups (two to four students each) or treat a small class as one group. Print on slips of paper or 3" x 5" cards phrases describing scenes from Lesson 7: for example, Egyptians giving gold to Israelites, the Israelites leaving Egypt at midnight, the pillar of cloud guiding the Israelites, the Israelites crossing the sea. Give one to each group and have them pantomime (act out without words) their scene as the others try to guess what it is.

▲ **Option #2**

Give each child paper and crayons or washable markers to illustrate a scene from Lesson 7 and then have them describe it to the class. This could be done as a pre-session activity and then used as review.

Can you think of some important things the Israelites will need as they travel through the desert? *(Allow for response throughout.)* Let's look in God's Supply Room to see what God will provide for them in this lesson. *(Have a child take R8 from God's Supply Room and place it on the Chart.)* What does it say? Yes, it is *Food*. Where would two million people get enough food and water to keep themselves alive as they travel through the desert? There were no supermarkets or convenience stores in those days.

We will learn today how God provided all the food and water they needed in places where it seemed impossible. And this will help us to understand that when we trust in him, God can supply whatever we need as well.

♥ MEMORY VERSE

Use bread or rolls and the verse visual to teach Matthew 6:11 when indicated.

Do you ever get hungry? *(Allow for response throughout.)* What kind of food really satisfies you? *(Response)* Is anyone hungry right now? How do you know that? Yes, God put within us a hunger signal so that we know when our bodies need food. We must eat food to grow and have healthy bodies. If we don't eat as we should, our bodies will get sick and eventually die.

I brought a little snack to class today. *(Show bread and cut off a small portion for each child.)* This bread will help satisfy our physical hunger. God knows we need food to stay alive. In fact, he made us that way. Jesus recognized our need for food when he included it in the prayer he taught his disciples. Here are his very words: "Give us this day our daily bread." *(Display the verse visual.)*

These words in Matthew 6:11 tell us that God is the source of all that we need to live each day. But you are probably thinking, God doesn't give me food; my parents do! It is true that your parents work hard so they can grow food or buy food at the market, but God is the one who sends the sunshine and rain and makes the food grow. (See Psalm 104:14; 145:15).

Jesus' words also let us know that we should depend on God to meet all our physical needs. We should not take the food we eat for granted or feel it is something we deserve. All that God provides for us are his gifts of love; they should remind us of him. That's why we pray before we eat. We thank him for the food he has provided and for those who have prepared it for us.

Many people do not have enough to eat because we live in a world that is not perfect. It is filled with sin. Droughts, floods, diseases and wars bring famine and suffering. We should be very grateful to God for what we have when we think of so many who have so little. *(Work on memorizing the verse).* ▲#3

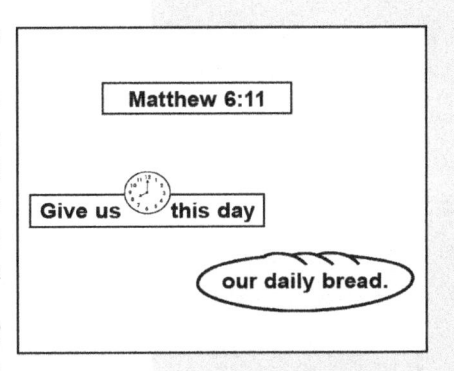

▲ Option #3

Memorizing the Verse: Place a roll of white shelf paper or wide adding machine tape on a table. Have the children, one at a time, use a crayon or a washable marker to print a word from the verse along the paper until the verse is complete, including the reference. Cut the words apart and scramble them on a table. Then have the children choose verse pieces from the scramble and place them in proper order on a table, tape them on a wall (use masking tape) or tack them to a bulletin board. Say the verse together as each piece is added.

📖 BIBLE LESSON OUTLINE

God Supplies Manna and Quail

▪ Introduction

Our need for food

▪ Bible Content

1. God leads his people.
2. God supplies water.
3. God gives rest.
4. God supplies food.
   a. The people complain.
   b. God provides meat.
   c. The people gather manna.

▪ Conclusion

Summary

Application
God will supply your needs

Response Activity
Trusting God to supply your needs

📖 BIBLE LESSON

▪ Introduction

Our need for food

When you are hungry, what do you do about it? *(Allow for response throughout.)* Yes, you look for something to eat—in your home or a store or a restaurant. For most of us it's not too hard to find something. Can you imagine what it would be like to be hungry or thirsty and not find anything to eat or drink anywhere around? Perhaps when you are traveling and far from a place to eat, or it is the day before grocery shopping when it seems there's nothing in the house to eat? It's hard for us to imagine because we have so much, but that is exactly how it was for the Israelites when they were journeying to their new land.

Back in Egypt they probably had their own gardens where they grew fresh vegetables to eat. In the middle of the desert there were no rivers or streams or fountains, no gardens or fields of vegetables, hardly any wild animals to eat—and certainly no grocery stores or fast food restaurants! Of course, they could have killed and eaten their cattle and sheep, but then they would not have had them to provide milk and butter or to sacrifice to God when they worshiped. They could not hope to live through the trip without water and food. Where would they find enough for them all?

Today we will see some of the miracles God did to provide exactly what his people needed. See if you can discover one way he did this. Find Exodus, chapter 16, in your Bible and place your bookmark there.

■ Bible Content

1. God leads his people. (Exodus 15:22)

(Cloud 46, people 44)
After they had crossed the Red Sea and were delivered from the Egyptians forever, the children of Israel *(place 46, 44 on the board)* continued their journey. Do you suppose they talked to each other about the great miracle God had done to save them from the Egyptians? How could you forget crossing the sea on a dry path with great walls of water standing on either side of you! Perhaps they wondered what their new land would be like. That land, called Canaan, was the place God had promised to Abraham and his descendants so many years before. Now it would soon be theirs!

As they marched along, they left the green trees and grass behind and began traveling through desert or wilderness country, always following the pillar of cloud as it moved ahead of them. There was no shade to protect them from the hot sun. The desert sand was hot under their feet and they probably became tired from walking hour after hour. *(Leave all the figures on the board.)*

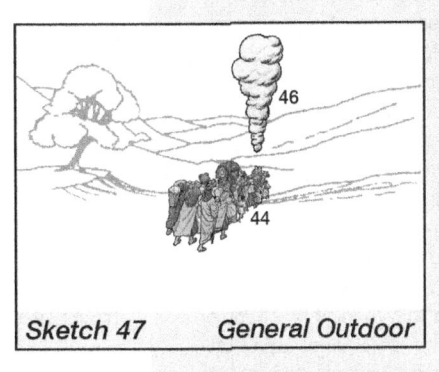

Sketch 47   General Outdoor

▲ Option #4

Locate pictures of Middle East desert areas in resource books or on the Internet to help your children understand the type of terrain the Israelites were facing.

2. God supplies water. (Exodus 15:23-25)

Water was a problem in the desert. They carried it in special bags made of animal skins that kept the water cool for a long time, but it was hard to find and they soon ran out. The desert was hot and dry and they became very thirsty. Sometimes in the desert there are small springs or wells of water where travelers can fill their bottles, but the Israelites found none of these along their way. The Bible says they traveled for three whole days without finding water. They must have been worried. ▲#4

(Moses 25, child 12, group 35, cows 45, sheep 24[1]; Wilderness Map; a small stick)
Place all the figures on the board.
At last they came to a place called Marah *(indicate on the map)* where there was water. How glad they must have been to see it! Eagerly they pressed forward to get a cool drink, but when they tasted the water, it was so bitter they couldn't drink it! There must have been minerals or chemicals in it from the surrounding soil that made it taste bad. That's why the place was called Marah, which means *bitter*. Have you ever tasted

Sketch 48   River

L-8

▲ **Option #5**

Mural scene.

▲ **Option #6**

A small experiment: Take to class a pan or container of water into which you have poured enough salt to make it undrinkable. Ask for a volunteer to taste the water to demonstrate. Then have another child throw the stick into the pan of water and have someone else do the "taste testing." The fact that there is no change in the water illustrates that the change agent was not the stick, but God's mighty power.

Sketch 49 — Plain with Tree

Sketch 50 — Wilderness

water like that? *(Allow for response throughout.)* Did you like it? How do you think the people felt then? Yes, they probably were disappointed and maybe even afraid. What would they do now?

Instead of looking to God who had provided everything else they needed, they turned on Moses and began to complain: "What are we going to drink? Where can we get good water?" They had already forgotten the miracles God had done for them.

But Moses knew what to do. The Bible says he cried out to God for help. He prayed because he knew he couldn't take care of all these people by himself. ▲#5

God answered by showing Moses a piece of wood *(show the tree limb or stick)*. Moses threw the piece of wood into the water and God made the water taste good, the way it was supposed to. The Israelites could drink as much as they wanted. They could fill all their water bottles and water their animals! God had done another miracle to show his people they could trust him for all they needed. ▲#6

God then made a promise to his people: "If you will listen to my voice and obey my commands, I will keep you from getting sick and none of the diseases which I brought upon the people in Egypt because of their sin will come upon you." That was certainly a wonderful promise. How would you like it if God said, "If you obey me, you will never get a cold or have to stay in the house because you don't feel well?"

3. **God gives rest.**
   (Exodus 15:26,27)

(Cloud 46, Moses 25, girl 11, woman 8, men 63, group 31, well 23, tent 62; Wilderness Map)

Then the pillar of cloud *(place 46 on the board)* began to move again and the Israelites *(add 25, 11, 8, 63, 31)* followed it to a place called Elim *(indicate on the map)*—a beautiful oasis where there were 70 tall palm trees for shade and 12 wells *(add 23)* of good water. They could have all the water they wanted! The pillar of cloud stood still, and the people were glad to pitch their tents *(add 62)* and enjoy the rest that God had provided for them. Once again God showed his people they could trust him to take care of their needs.

4. **God supplies food.**
   (Exodus 16:1-36)

   a. **The people complain.**

(Cloud 46, Moses 25, group 35, fire 47)

Soon the pillar of cloud *(place 46 on the board)* lifted and the Israelites *(add 25, 35)* followed it into a desert called the Wilderness of Sin *(indicate on the map)*. It was not necessarily a wicked place. That was just its name.

It had now been more than a month since they left Egypt. Their life was very different from what they had known before. They were running out of the bread they had baked or mixed up the night they left, and they didn't know where they would get any more. Soon they forgot how much they had suffered when they were slaves. All they could think of was the good food they had eaten in Egypt.

So they all began to complain against Moses and Aaron. "Why did you bring us out of Egypt?" they demanded. "At least there we had plenty of food. You've brought us into this desert to starve. We will all die of hunger." Of course, it wasn't true, but they were discouraged.

Moses and Aaron called the people together and said, "The Lord has heard your grumbling against him. When you complain against us, you are really grumbling against the Lord. He says he will provide food for everyone."

Suddenly the pillar of cloud began to glow *(remove 46; add 47)*. It was the glory of the Lord in the cloud. He wanted to show them that he had heard their complaining and that he was going to send them food. God knew that there were more than two million people and that they would be hungry every day. He knew it would take a lot of food to feed them, but they didn't have to worry. How would he do it? *(Remove all the figures.)*

▲ **Option #7**

Mural scene.

▲ **Option #8**

Mural scene.

b. God provides meat.

(Quail 50[3], 89, girl 51, man 52)
The Bible says that God began to provide in a special way that very evening. Read Exodus 16:13-15 to see what he did. *(Wait for response.)* That's right; God sent them quail—birds something like pheasants. *(Place 50[3] on the board.)* Great flocks *(add 89)* flew through the camp low enough for the people *(add 51, 52)* to catch them. They roasted them for supper. How good they must have tasted! God had provided meat for all of them! *(Remove all the figures.)* ▲#7

Sketch 51 — Wilderness

c. The people gather manna.

(Coriander seed or small white seeds, tray, crackers, and honey; people 53, 54)
When the Israelites awoke the next morning, they saw that the ground was covered with dew. Read verse 14 to see what they saw when the dew disappeared. *(Wait for response.)* Yes, they saw small, white round things that looked like thin flakes of frost covering the ground. *(Spread the coriander seed out on a plate.)* No one had ever seen anything like it before. It was God's special provision. ▲#8

Read verse 15 to find their reaction. *(Wait for response.)* That's right; they asked what we probably would have asked: "What is it?"

Sketch 52 — Wilderness

▲ **Option #9**

Definition word card:
Manna = "What is it?"

▲ **Option #10**

Prepare 4 word cards (9" x 12" construction paper or poster board). Print FOOD on one, WATER on the second, STICK THROWN IN WATER on the third, and QUAIL on the fourth.

In class, have the children match the "needs" cards with "God's provision" cards and hold them up or tape them to the board.

Sketch 53   Plain Background

Moses said, "It is the bread God is giving you to eat. You can bake or boil it or eat it just as you find it. Each morning you *(add 53, 54)* must gather enough for you and your family to eat that day, but no more. On the sixth day of the week, gather twice as much because there will be none on the ground on the seventh day. That is a day to rest and worship God."

Maybe the people thought it looked like very strange bread. They must have wondered what it would taste like. Read verse 31 to see what it was like. *(Wait for response.)* Yes, it tasted sweet, like crackers made with honey and it looked like a small white seed. *(Show the coriander seed. Distribute the crackers and honey for children to taste.)* The people did not know what to call it so it was named manna. (The word *manna* in Hebrew means "What is it?") ▲#9

The manna was nourishing and kept the Israelites strong and healthy while they traveled in the desert. It appeared every morning and melted away when the sun grew hot. When some of the people saved some for the next day, it got worms in it and smelled bad—except on the seventh day. They gathered twice as much on the sixth day so they could rest and worship on the seventh. When they obeyed the instructions for the Sabbath, they always had enough food for their families. God provided all the food they needed because he loved and cared for them.

Then Moses said, "God says we should keep some of this manna so that our children and grandchildren can see the bread he gave us to eat in the desert." So Aaron put some manna in a pot that they kept and carried with them so that people in the future would know what the Lord had done for them.

■ **Conclusion**

Summary

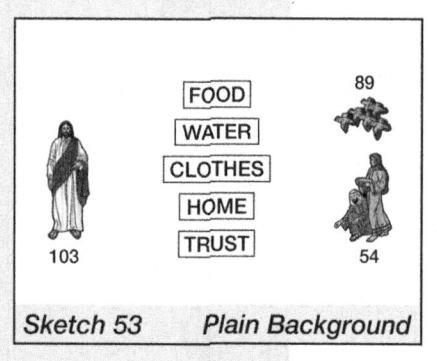

(Word strips FOOD, WATER; a small stick; people 54, quail 89)

Isn't it wonderful how God supplied for the needs of his people? What two things did the Israelites need to stay alive in the desert? *(Allow for response throughout.)* ▲#10 Yes, they absolutely had to have food and water *(place FOOD, WATER on the board)* to stay alive. How did God provide what they needed? *(*That's right; he provided good water after Moses threw the stick *(display the stick)* into the bitter water, and he sent quail *(add 89)* every evening and manna *(add 54)* every morning.

Application

(Word strips CLOTHES, HOME, TRUST; Jesus 103)

Let's think about some of the needs you and I have today. All of us need food, water, clothes, and a home *(indicate FOOD, WATER; add*

CLOTHES, HOME). What other kinds of needs do we have? *(Allow for response throughout; if necessary, suggest love, understanding, success at doing something, etc.)* ▲#11

Who supplies these needs for us? Yes, parents and teachers provide some of these needs, like food and clothing, a place to live and education. But God gave us our parents and teachers and he gives them strength to be able to work so that our needs are met. We should be grateful and thank God for providing in these ways.

But what happens when there is no human person to give us what we need? Maybe you feel as though no one loves you or cares about you or that you can never do anything right. Maybe you need shoes or clothing and there is no money for it. What can you do?

The Bible tells us that when we have trusted the Lord Jesus as our Savior *(add 103)* and belong to God's family, we can pray to God through Jesus' name, asking for what we need. He may not always give us what we ask for in just the way we think we should have it—the Israelites cried for bread and God sent manna—but we can trust *(add TRUST)* God to do what is best for us and always provide just what we need in just the right way. He loves us and promises to meet our needs.

Response Activity

Explain to the children that we cannot ask God to meet our needs until we have become part of his family by accepting Christ as Savior. Encourage any who have not trusted him to do so today.

Distribute **"My Needs & God's Answers" handouts** *and pencils. Have the children print one thing they need God to provide and add the date. Encourage them to pray each day for that need, then print how God provided it and the date he provided for it. They can add future needs and answers to prayer to the handout and keep it as a record of God's providing for them.*

If they need to accept Christ as Savior, have them print that on the handout as well.

✍ TAKE HOME ITEMS

Distribute **memory verse tokens for Matthew 6:11** *and* **Bible Study Helps for Lesson 8.**

▲ **Option #11**

Print suggestions on newsprint or chalkboard.

God Helps Israel at Rephidim
Theme: *Help*

Lesson 9

❃ *BEFORE YOU BEGIN...*

We often say, "I need your help" or hear, "How can I help you?" We all need help at some time or other. Most of us are willing to give help when asked, but sometimes when we are in need, we feel as though there is no one to ask. Or everyone is too busy. Or no one really cares. Or our problem is too small—or too big. Perhaps children feel this as much as anyone when they are "brushed off" or ignored or told, "Don't bother me!"

But God is *always* available; he *always* cares; no problem is too big or too small for him! He is "a very present help in trouble" for all his children, whether they are teacher or students. What a profound truth! What an important truth for boys and girls to understand at the earliest possible age.

God was always there for the Israelites, willing to help when they asked him, even when they became angry and complaining. Encourage your children to go to God first when they need help, rather than rely upon their own strength as the Israelites did. Teach them that whatever problem or difficulty they face is important to God and that he has all the resources necessary to provide the exact help they need. *"For He Himself has said, 'I will never leave you nor forsake you.' So we may boldly say: 'The Lord is my helper'" (Hebrews 13:5, 6, NKJV).*

☞ AIM:

That the children may

- Know that God is always with his children and will help them in difficult situations.
- Respond by asking God to help with a specific need they have.

📖 SCRIPTURE: Exodus 17; Deuteronomy 25:17-19

♥ MEMORY VERSE: Psalm 46:1

God is our refuge and strength, a very present help in trouble. (KJV)
God is our refuge and strength, an ever-present help in trouble. (NIV)

📁 MATERIALS TO GATHER

Memory verse visual for Psalm 46:1
Backgrounds: Review Chart, Plain Background, General Outdoor, Wilderness,
Figures: R1-R9, 12, 24(4), 25, 31, 34, 35, 44, 46, 55, 56, 57, 58, 59, 60, 62, 63, 72
Token holders & memory verse tokens for Psalm 46:1
Bible Study Helps for Lesson 9
Special:
- *For Review Chart & Bible content 1:* Wilderness Map
- *For Introduction:* "HELP WANTED" sign; newsprint & marker or chalkboard & chalk
- *For Bible Content 1:* Wilderness Map
- *For Application:* List from Introduction, marker or chalk
- *For Response Activity:* "Rock" handouts, pencils
- *For Options:* Materials for any options you choose to use
- *Note: To prepare the "HELP WANTED" sign,* print HELP WANTED! on cardboard or poster board (approximately 12"x18"). Use masking tape to attach a flat stick or a dowel to the back of the sign, leaving enough below the sign to use as a handle for carrying.
  Follow the instructions on page xii to prepare the "Rock" handouts (pattern P-15 on page 176.)

💼 REVIEW CHART

Display the Review Chart with R1-R8 in place and R9 in God's Supply Room. Use the following questions to review Lessons 7 & 8, locating places on the Wilderness Map.

1. How did God guide the Israelites on their trip? *(By a pillar of cloud by day and a pillar of fire by night.)*
2. What was the first stop on the Israelites' journey to Canaan? *(By the Red Sea; locate it on the map.)*
3. How did God deliver the Israelites from the Egyptians at the Red Sea? *(He made a dry path across the sea.)*
4. Where did they find bitter water? *(At Marah; locate it on the map.)*
5. What miracle did God do at Marah? *(He made the water good to drink when Moses threw a stick into it.)*
6. Name the place where they found 70 palm trees and 12 wells of water. *(Elim; locate it on the map.)*
7. What did the people complain about when they got to the Wilderness of Sin? *(They had no food to eat; find the place on the map.)*
8. How did God provide meat for the Israelites? *(He sent flocks of quail.)*

9. How did God give them bread? *(He put manna on the ground every morning except on the Sabbath.)*

As the Israelites continued to travel through the wilderness, the journey became more difficult. It would have been impossible for them to find what they needed or to know the way to go on their own. God knew what they needed and was ready to provide it. Let's look at the next piece in God's Supply Room to see what he is going to provide in today's story. *(Have a child remove R9 from God's Supply Room and place it on the Chart.)* Let's all read it together. *(Do so.)* Yes, God provides for his people all the *Help* they need. Our memory verse is his promise that he will do just that.

♥ MEMORY VERSE

Display the visual to teach Psalm 46:1 and read it aloud with the class.

| God is our refuge and strength, | a very present help in trouble. Psalm 46:1 |

What does the first part of the verse tell us about God? *(Allow for response throughout.)* Yes, it says that God is our *refuge* (a place of safety). We can go to him when we are afraid or in trouble. He is our *strength*. He is strong enough and powerful enough to protect us when we are in danger. And he will give us strength to do the right thing when Satan tries to get us to go his way instead of God's. Let's say that part of the verse together.

What does the last part of the verse tell us about God as our helper? That's right; God is our *very present help*. He is present—or right here with us—and he helps us and provides what we need when we need it. What does it tell us about *when* he helps us? Yes, he helps us immediately when we are in trouble. Does it mean that he will always take the trouble away? No, not always. But he will give us strength and courage to go through difficult times, when without his help we would be weak and fail.

Have you ever been in trouble and needed someone to help you? *(Encourage children to share kinds of trouble they have experienced; e.g., difficult school assignment, trouble at home, teasing on the playground, danger when alone.)* Let's repeat the last part of the verse together. *(Do so.)* Just think! God is right there with us to help us when we are in trouble. What a great relief to have God with us to help us in difficult situations, no matter how difficult it is. *(Work on memorizing the verse.)* ▲#1

📖 BIBLE LESSON OUTLINE

God Helps Israel at Rephidim

■ **Introduction**

Help wanted!

▲ Option #1

Memorizing the verse: To prepare, print the verse and reference by parts on several sheets of colored paper, each sheet a different color. Cut the sheets into puzzle pieces and hide the pieces around the room before the children arrive.

In class, divide the children into as many groups as you have colored sheets and assign a color to each group. At a signal, have them look for pieces of their color (being careful not to disturb the others), and put them together to complete the puzzle. Then see which group can say the verse correctly without looking at the words.

■ Bible Content

1. God provides water from a rock.
2. God helps his people fight an enemy.
   a. The Amalekites attack.
   b. Israel wins the battle.

■ Conclusion

Summary

Application
Identifying when you need God's help

Response Activity
Asking God for his help

📖 BIBLE LESSON

■ Introduction

Help wanted!

(HELP WANTED sign; newsprint & marker or chalkboard & chalk)

Have a child walk back and forth in front of the class carrying the HELP WANTED! sign.

Where do you often see a sign like this? *(Allow for response throughout.)* Yes, we often see it in a window (or name another place a child would be familiar with). What does a sign like this tell you? That's right; someone needs help.   ▲#2

Have you ever needed help, but thought it was hopeless—that you would never get it? *(If necessary, suggest something like a difficult homework assignment or a school project, a chore at home, a family break-up, or needing to tell the truth in a difficult situation. List the children's responses on newsprint or chalkboard. Save the list to use in the Application.)*   ▲#3

What did you do in that difficult situation? Did you try to do it all yourself and discover you needed help? From someone who could do the job or someone who understood what was happening and could help you get the job done—someone who was stronger and bigger than you?

The Israelites *really* needed God's help. They probably could have carried this HELP WANTED! sign *(hold up sign)* every day as they traveled through the desert. Moses had been telling them that God would help them. Today we will learn how God gave help to his people. Find Exodus, chapter 17, in your Bible and place your bookmark there.

▲ Option #2

Have a teacher or a child come into the room laden down with books, bags, etc., so that they need help even to get through the door or to the front of the room. Discuss with the class what the person needed—*help!*

▲ Option #3

Role playing "needs" situations: As time permits, choose individuals or pairs of children during your pre-session time and give them a situation you have written down. Give them opportunity before class begins to think and plan how they will role play it.

In class, have them present their role play and have the rest of the class guess what the need is.

Or, provide newsprint and crayons. Have every child illustrate a "need" situation, then show it to the class and describe it.

▲ **Option #4**

Dramatize Exodus 17:1b-7. Choose one child to be

Sketch 54 General Outdoor

Sketch 55 General Outdoor

narrator, one to be Moses, several to be Israelites and one to be the voice of God. Use the actual words in the text as your script. The children need not memorize them, but should be encouraged to read with emotion.

▲ **Option #5**

Mural scene.

▲ **Option #6**

Gather additional information and/or pictures about the Bedouins (desert nomads) from reference books or the Internet to show that this life style still exists today.

■ **Bible Content**

1. **God provides water from a rock. (Exodus 17:1-7)**

   (Cloud 46, people 44, Moses 25)
   After God gave the Israelites quail and manna, the pillar of cloud *(place 46 on the board)* lifted again and began to move. The Israelites *(add 44, 25)* packed up their tents and traveled onward. They were becoming stronger from walking and living outdoors. Every morning they gathered the manna as God had instructed. Each night they made camp when the cloud stopped. When darkness came, the cloud became a pillar of fire. *(Leave the figures on the board.)*

   (Wilderness Map; tent 62, child 12, group 35, sheep 24[4], men 63)
   Eventually, the pillar of cloud stood still at a place called Rephidim *(indicate on the map; remove 44, 46)*, and God's people set up their camp *(add 62, 12, 35, 24[4], 63)*. They were hot and tired and thirsty and longing for a cool drink, but there was no water there—not a well or a spring or a stream! What would they do? At Marah there had been water, even if it was bitter. God had made it good to drink. But here there was no water at all! Maybe some of them began to panic and wonder if they would die there.

   Read Exodus 17:2 to see what the people did. *(Wait for response.)* Yes, they complained to Moses and demanded, "Give us water to drink!" They weren't very nice about it. They wanted water and they wanted it right now! ▲#4

   How did Moses answer? *(Response)* That's right; he said, "Why are you so mean to me? What can I do? Why don't you trust God like he told you to?"

   The Lord had taken care of them in many wonderful ways, but now the people were thirsty and angry and frightened. They completely forgot how God had helped them at Marah, making the water good to drink, and how he was giving them food every day.

   They just kept on complaining: "Is this why you brought us out of Egypt, to let us and our children and our cattle die of thirst?" Their grumbling and complaining turned to angry shouts and threats until Moses feared that they were going to kill him.

   What would Moses do now? Read verse four to find out. *(Wait for response.)* He did the very best thing. He prayed to the Lord, "What am I going to do with these people? They're ready to stone me to death!"

   God loved his people. He did not get angry because they complained, even though he had reason to do so. He didn't punish them! He knew they needed water and he was ready to be their helper.

(Rock 55, Moses 25, rod 34, leaders 31, 63, water 56)
Place 55 on the board.

The Lord said to Moses, "Take some of the leaders with you and carry your rod in your hand. Go ahead of the people to the rock at Horeb *(add 25, 34, 31, 63)*. I will be there." Read verse six to find what God told Moses to do when he got there. *(Wait for response.)* Yes, he was to strike (or hit) the rock with his rod and water would come out of it.

Moses trusted God and obeyed. As he struck the rock with his rod, a stream of clear, fresh water *(add 56)* gushed out and ran down toward the people. It was another miracle from God! There was plenty of water for all the people and all their children and all their animals! They could drink all they wanted. God was their *very present help* in trouble. Surely they would never doubt again. *(Remove all the figures.)* ▲#5

Sketch 56 — Wilderness

Note (1)

The Amalekites were related to Esau, Jacob's twin brother (Genesis 36:12). He had married women who were not believers in the true God and their descendants were part of the heathen nations in the land.

2. God helps his people fight an enemy.
(Exodus 17:8-16; Deuteronomy 25:17, 18)

a. The Amalekites attack.

(People 44, cloud 46)
Place 44, 46 on the board.

The Lord had provided all their needs. Now the Israelites had to learn that there were enemies they must fight. In the desert around Rephidim lived a wild and warlike people called the Amalekites, nomads or Bedouins who wandered through the wilderness looking for good pasture for their flocks and herds. ⌂(1) ▲#6

The Amalekites considered that whole area their own and they did not want to share it, especially with a huge group of people like the Israelites. So they gathered all their warriors and came down from the hills in a surprise raid, killing many who were sick or weak or straggling behind at a slower pace. The Israelites were totally surprised! They had never expected or prepared for such a thing. *(Remove all the figures.)*

Sketch 57 — Wilderness

b. Israel wins the battle.

(Moses 25, Joshua 72)

Like many tribes in the wilderness, the Amalekites would attack and run back into the hills, then attack again later. What were God's people to do? They needed help and protection like never before.

Moses *(place 25 on the board)* knew he could trust God to help him and to protect the people and even to win the

Sketch 58 — Wilderness

L-9

victory. He must have prayed for help. Then he said to Joshua *(add 72)*, one of the younger leaders, "Choose some of our best men and go fight against these Amalekites. Tomorrow I will stand on the top of that hill and hold the staff of God in my hands." That meant that he would be praying during the battle and trusting God in a special way to help the men who were fighting. *(Remove all the figures.)*

(Moses 57, Aaron 58, Hur 59, battle 60)
Joshua obeyed Moses and took the men out to fight. Moses and Aaron and another leader named Hur *(place 57, 58, 59 on the board)* went up the hill so they could look down and see the battle *(add 60)*. There Moses lifted his rod toward heaven to show that he was depending completely on God for help in winning the battle. He knew that the people had their part to do, but the outcome was up to God. ▲#7

Read verse 11 to see what happened when Moses' hands were raised. *(Allow for response.)* Yes, the Israelites were winning the battle. Look at verse 11 again to see what happened when Moses' arms became tired and he let them down to rest. *(Wait for response.)* That's right; the Amalekites began to win. God wanted Moses to trust in him all the time.

But it was hard for Moses to keep his hands and arms raised toward God all the time, so Aaron and Hur found a big rock for him to sit on. Then they stood on either side of him and held his arms up towards God all day long, until the sun went down. They were trusting God, too. They were helping Moses to show that he was trusting God for the victory. ▲#8

Victory in battle depended on their continually trusting God to be their helper. Read verse 13 to see what happened as a result. *(Wait for response.)* Yes, Joshua and the soldiers defeated the Amalekites! God helped them and gave them the victory!

At the end of the day the Lord said to Moses, "Write this down in a book so that it will not be forgotten." God's people learned a big lesson that day—that they were not strong enough to win over their enemies by themselves. They needed God's help and they could trust him to give it.

▪ Conclusion

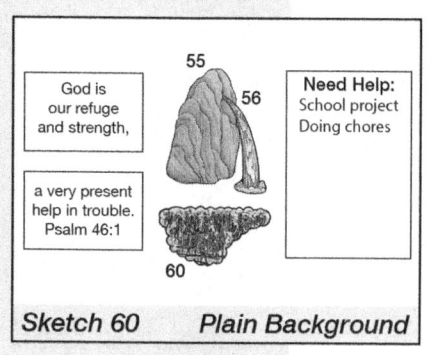

Summary

(Memory verse visual, rock 55, water 56, battle 60)
The Lord showed his people they could trust him for help when they needed it. *(Place the verse visual on the left side of the board and say the verse aloud together.)* He was their refuge and he gave them strength. Let's think about the kinds of help he gave them. *(Allow for response throughout.)* Yes, he gave them water from a rock *(add 55, 56)* and victory over the Amalekites *(add 60)*.

Sketch 59 — Wilderness

▲ **Option #7**
Mural scene.

▲ **Option #8**
Have several children demonstrate how Aaron and Hur helped Moses on the mountain.

Sketch 60 — Plain Background

What did Moses have to do for God to give help? Yes, he had to ask him for help and continue to trust in him. The Israelites were God's people. He loved them and would give them all they needed as they trusted him and obeyed.

Application

(List from Introduction, marker or chalk)
What does it mean to help someone? *(Allow for response throughout.)* That's right; to help someone is to make it easier for a person to do something or to give them what they need to do a job.

Let's look at our list of things we need help with. *(Display the list from the Introduction.)* Are there any other things that we could add to our list, something that you need help with right now? Maybe you need help in a difficult situation at home, at school or at church. Maybe you need God's help to be kind to someone you don't like. Do you find it hard to tell your friends about Jesus? Do you have a bad habit you want to get rid of? *(Add the children's responses to the list.)*

God wants to help you and me just as much as he wanted to help the Israelites. He wants to be our strength and refuge in tough times. If we belong to God's family through faith in Jesus Christ, we can go to him at any time for any help we need in any situation. It doesn't have to be big trouble. It can be anything we have printed on this list. God never gets tired of helping us because he loves us and cares about everything in our lives. What one thing do you need God's help with right now? It can be something from the list or something that you did not mention. Let's say our verse once more together as a reminder that God is willing to be our help right now in these situations. *(Do so.)*

Response Activity

*Distribute the **"Rock" handouts** and pencils. Have the children print on their handout the thing they need God's help with.* ▲#9

Remind the children that if they have never received Jesus as Savior, God wants to help them with that right now and they may talk with you after class.

Have the children pray silently, asking God for the help they need. Then lead in a closing prayer, asking God to help them depend on him for the help they need this week. Tell them to take their handouts home and put them where they will be reminded them to ask God for his help each day. Next week encourage the children to share how God helped them.

✍ TAKE HOME ITEMS

*Distribute **memory verse tokens for Psalm 46:1** and **Bible Study Helps for Lesson 9**.*

▲ **Option #9**

Collect enough small smooth rocks for everyone in your class. Use a permanent marker to print on each one "God's help" or "I need God's help." Give the rocks to the children and have them use thin permanent markers to print on them the thing they need God's help with. Help younger children if necessary. Have them take their rocks home as a reminder to ask God for help.

God Gives the Law
Theme: Rules

Lesson 10

❋ BEFORE YOU BEGIN...

Today's culture favors the idea that freedom is the inalienable right for people to do what is right in their own eyes. They set up their own rules and are accountable to only themselves. Having rejected or ignored the God of the Bible and the laws that reflect his holy character, they are ignorantly—or purposefully—doing what comes naturally.

The children of the 21st century are caught in a stranglehold of confusion and conflict, groping in the darkness of sin. Many have few adult models to look to for answers because often their parents and friends are themselves prisoners of anti-God philosophies and practices.

This lesson is a unique opportunity to bring the light of God's truth to your children. Be careful to present these truths clearly and unashamedly, making sure they understand what is at stake in living a life that pleases God in an unfriendly culture. *"My son, do not forget my law, but let your heart keep my commands; for length of days and long life and peace they will add to you" (Proverbs 3:1, NKJV).*

☞ AIM:

That the children may

- Know that God set the standard for right and wrong as revealed in the rules he has given in the Bible.
- Respond by choosing to obey God's rules in order to show others what God is like.

📖 SCRIPTURE: Exodus 19:1–20:26; 23:20–24:7; Deuteronomy 5:1-33

♥ MEMORY VERSE: Psalm 40:8

I delight to do thy will, O my God; yea, thy law is within my heart. (KJV)
I desire to do your will, O my God; your law is within my heart. (NIV)

📁 MATERIALS TO GATHER

Memory Verse Visual for Psalm 40:8
Backgrounds: Review Chart, Plain Background, General Outdoor
Figures: R1-R10, 10, 25, 35, 40, 46, 49, 52, 57, 61, 62, 63, 64, 105
Token holders and memory verse tokens for Psalm 40:8
Bible Study Helps for lesson 10
Special:
- *For Review Chart:* Figures 1, 9, 13, 18, 24, 25, 32, 40, 48, 54, 55, 56, 60, 89, 95, plague figures 106-112
- *For Introduction & Summary:* Newsprint & marker or chalkboard & chalk
- *For Bible Content 1:* Wilderness Map
- *For Bible Content 3:* "Ten Commandments" poster
- *For Application:* Selected verses printed on newsprint—choose from exercises listed
- *For Response Activity:* "My Choice" handouts, pencils
- *For Options:* Materials for any options you choose to use
- *Note: Follow the instructions on page xii to prepare the "Ten Commandments" poster (pattern P-16 on page 177) and the "My Choice" handouts (pattern P-7 on page 172).*

💼 REVIEW CHART

Display the Review Chart with R10 in God's Supply Room; have R1-R9 ready to use when indicated. Display Jochebed 9, Moses 13, Moses 18, sheep 24[1], Moses 25, Aaron 32, Pharaoh 1, snakes 95, plagues 106-112, slain lamb 40, Egyptian chariots 48, birds 89, manna 54, Amalekites 60, rock 55, water 56 on a table or the floor.

Review Lessons 1-9 by having the children take turns choosing one of God's provisions from R1-R9 and placing it on the Review Chart, then choosing one or more of the figures and placing them on the Chart, and finally telling how God provided what is written on the review symbol. For example: Wisdom: figures Jochebed 9 and baby Moses 18; God gave Jochebed wisdom to know how to protect Moses from Pharaoh. Then have the class recite the corresponding memory verse together.

God was now ready to give to his people something very important for their trip and for living together in the special land that he had promised them. Let's see what it is. (Have a child remove R10 from God's Supply Room and place it on the chart.) Yes, it is Rules.

What do you think of when you see this word? (Encourage response.) Often we think of rules as unpleasant—orders given to us that we don't like to obey. But did you know that the real purpose for rules is to make us happy and keep us safe? We have some rules in our class so that everyone here can have a good time. (Mention your basic rules and the reason for them.) ▲#1

▲ Option #1

Print classroom rules or home rules on newsprint or chalkboard. Print the children's thoughts or reasons next to each rule.

⌂ Note (1)

Paul's letter to the Galatian churches was written to tell Christians that they are neither justified by keeping the law of Moses, nor sanctified by keeping it. Therefore, the teacher must be careful not to give children the impression that they can *be* saved or *stay* saved by keeping the Ten Commandments. In fact, the teacher must be careful not to give the impression that Christians *can* keep the law by trying on their own.

This lesson seeks to lay a three-fold foundation: God knows what is right and wrong; he is the only one who can rightly determine what is right and wrong; he has a perfect right to say what is right and wrong.

Psalm 40:8
I delight to do thy will, O my God: yea, thy law is within my heart.

The Ten Commandments reflect God's perfect holiness, set the standard of what is right and wrong, clearly identify sin and show the need for the Savior and the salvation he provides.

For example, "Raise your hand when you want to answer" is so everyone can hear what you say instead of the confusing sound of all talking at the same time. You have some rules in your family. "Don't talk to strangers or go in a car with anyone you don't know" is to keep you safe. "Be in bed with the lights out at a certain time" is to help you get enough rest and feel good the next day. "Cross the street only when the light says to go" is to protect you from being hit by a car.

Rules let us know what is expected of us. They keep us safe and help us live with the people around us. Most rules are made by people who care about us and want us to live together happily and safely.

God loved and cared about his people. In Egypt they had lived by Egyptian rules, which had nothing to do with pleasing God or living his kind of life. Now they needed to know how God wanted them to live together—how they should treat each other, what they should do when they had disagreements or when one person broke a rule or hurt another person, what they should eat or not eat to stay healthy and how he wanted them to worship him instead of the idols of Egypt.

Today we will learn about some of the rules God gave his people because he loved them and wanted them to be happy living together. He also wanted them to show the nations around them by the way they lived what God is like.

♥ MEMORY VERSE

Display the visual for Psalm 40:8.

Our memory verse talks about God's law—his rules. Let's read it together. *(Do so.)*

When King David wrote these words, he was expressing how he felt about God's rules. Because he was a king, he knew how important it was to have laws to have a good kingdom with people doing what they were supposed to do. David knew that God's rules were just and good for him and for his people. He appreciated God's rules so much that he testified that he delighted in doing God's will as expressed in the laws God had given. ⌂(1)

These words are applied to Jesus in the New Testament (Hebrews 10:7) and show how he felt about God's law. We know that David did not always obey God's rules, even though he delighted in doing God's will. But Jesus did; he obeyed perfectly.

To have God's law in our heart means that we accept what God says is right and what he says is wrong, and that we do our part to live the way he tells us to. This includes choosing to obey God and trusting him for strength to do what is right no matter what. This verse challenges us to want to do God's will so much that we will live according to his rules. Keep in mind that it is one thing to *know* what is right; it is another thing to *do* what is right. Will you, like King David, delight to *do* (or live) according to God's rules? *(Work on memorizing the verse.)* ▲#2

📖 BIBLE LESSON OUTLINE

God Gives the Law

■ Introduction

Rules, rules, rules!

■ Bible Content

1. God's people arrive at Sinai.
2. God speaks to his people through Moses.
3. God gives his law to his people.
4. The people respond to God.

■ Conclusion

Summary

Application
   Practicing how to obey God's rules

Response Activity
   Choosing to obey God's rules

📖 BIBLE LESSON

■ Introduction

Rules, rules, rules!

(Newsprint & marker or chalkboard & chalk)
We've talked about some of the rules you should obey. Can you think of some others? *(List responses on newsprint or chalkboard; for example, doing dishes, cleaning your room, doing your homework before you watch TV, don't cheat, don't steal, don't carry a knife.)* Why are these rules necessary? *(Discuss)* Yes, they are for our good, even though we may not always like to obey them. *(Talk about why the rules you have listed are good or helpful.)* They are given to help us know how to be safe, how to live and work together well, and even to help us learn skills we will need later in life. ▲#3

What would happen if there were no rules in our world? *(Discuss)* There would be confusion in our homes and schools, even more accidents on our highways, and terrible fights and problems in our society. Good rules are very important.

Today we will learn about some very important rules or laws that God gave to his people. You may know some of them as the Ten Commandments. Let's find out what they were, how God gave them, and why. Find Exodus, chapter 19, in your Bible and place your bookmark there.

▲ Option #2

Memorizing the verse: Distribute the five pieces of the verse visual to five children. Each time a child adds a piece to the display (in the proper order), have the class repeat the verse aloud. When the verse is complete, have the class repeat the entire verse once more.

Distribute the visual pieces to another set of children. Have them, at a given signal, run to the front of the room and line up to display the verse in order. Have the other children check to see if they have done it correctly.

Continue with a different group until all have had an opportunity to participate. Time each group to see which can do it the quickest. Have the class repeat the verse each time it is displayed.

▲ Option #3

Collect and display pictures or samples of road signs for both cars and people. Discuss why it is important to obey these rules and the consequences of disobeying them or of not having such rules or signs.

Or, provide paper and markers or crayons. Have the children draw any "rule" sign they know and then let each "show and tell" their rule and why it is important.

■ **Bible Content**

**1. God's people arrive at Sinai.
(Exodus 19:1, 2)**

(Wilderness Map; cloud 46, Moses 25, people 35, 49, tents 61, 62)

Exactly three months from the day they left Egypt, the Israelites came to a very large plain (a flat, level area) in the Desert of Sinai *(indicate area near Mt. Sinai on the map).* There the pillar of cloud *(place 46 on the board)* stopped and all the people *(add 25, 35, 49)* pitched their tents *(add 61, 62).*

God's people would camp in this place, which was called Horeb, for a whole year. It was surrounded by rugged mountains. One of them—called Mount Sinai—was nearly a mile high! God had brought them there to give them his laws so they would know how he expected them to live together and worship him. God's Word had not yet been written down, so the only things most of them knew about God were the things Moses and Aaron had taught them.

**2. God speaks to his people through Moses.
(Exodus 19:3-15)**

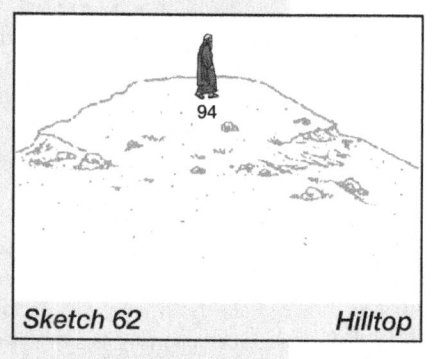

(Moses 25)

When the people had the camp all set up, Moses *(place 25 on the board)* climbed Mount Sinai to talk with God. Read Exodus 19, 5, 6 to find God's message for the people. *(Wait for response.)* ▲#4

God said, "If you obey me and live the way I tell you to, you will be my special treasure, above all the other people in the world. You will be a holy nation, my representatives to those other people." God is holy, which means he is separate from everything sinful or evil. He wanted his people to live holy lives, lives that were separate from sin, so that the nations around them would know what he is like.

Cloud 46, people 35, 49, tents 61, 62, Moses 25)
Place 46, 35, 49, 61, 62 on the board.

Moses came down the mountain *(add 25)* and told the Israelites what God had said. They quickly responded, "We will do whatever the Lord says," even though they didn't know what he would tell them to do.

Moses climbed back up the mountain *(remove 25)* to give God the people's answer. God said, "On a certain day I will meet with you on the mountain in a thick cloud so the people will hear me speaking with you and will always trust you as their leader. Tell them to prepare themselves." ▲#5

Sketch 61   General Outdoor

▲ **Option #4**

Have one child read aloud Exodus 19:5, 6. Ask the other children to tell in their own words what God's message meant.

Sketch 62   Hilltop

▲ **Option #5**

Mural scene.

Sketch 63   General Outdoor

They had three days to get ready. They had to wash their clothes and be sure everyone was perfectly clean. Then they placed a boundary (perhaps something like a fence) around the mountain. Any person or animal that went past the limits or touched the mountain would be stoned to death. God was trying to teach them to respect him for his mighty power and awesome holiness that separated him from everything sinful and evil. *(Leave the figures on the board.)*

3. God gives his law to his people.
(Exodus 19:16–20:21; Deuteronomy 5:1-33)

(Lightning cloud 105, Moses 25; Ten Commandments poster)

Early in the morning of the third day dark clouds covered the top of the mountain. *(Remove 46; add 105.)* Thunder rolled and lightning flashed as a very loud trumpet blast sounded. Then Moses *(add 25)* led all the people out of the camp to the mountain where God was going to give his law, his rules for them.

Read verse 18 to see what happened when God came down to Mount Sinai to meet Moses. *(Wait for response.)* That's right; thick smoke covered the mountain and billowed up like smoke from a furnace because the Lord had come down like fire. The whole mountain shook as though there were a violent earthquake, and the sound of the trumpet got louder and louder. Then the Lord spoke in a voice they could hear.

The people were terrified. They trembled and backed away and said to Moses, "You speak to us and tell us what God says, but don't let God speak to us directly or we will die!"

"Don't be afraid," Moses said to them. "God has come down so that you will realize how great and holy he is and will respect and fear him. Seeing his greatness and holiness will help you obey him and keep you from sinning." So the people stayed where they were as Moses *(remove 25)* went up the mountain and into the thick dark cloud where God met him.

There, for the first time, God gave Moses the special laws or rules he wanted the people to live by. Through these laws God was telling his people what is right and what is wrong. We call some of them the Ten Commandments. Let's find them in Exodus 20, beginning with verse two. *(Display the "Ten Commandments" poster. Assign individuals to read verses 3, 4, 7, 8-9, 12, 13, 14, 15, 16, 17 and have the class compare each reading to the command as it is written on the poster.)*

◸ (2) ▲#6

God also gave Moses the rest of the rules recorded in the book of Exodus. They were to teach the people three special things:
   a. What kind of person God is and how to please him.
   b. How to live with one another.
   c. How to worship God with sacrifices and prayer.

◸ **Note (2)**

Nine of the Ten Commandments are integrated into what comprises godly living for the New Testament Christian. The fourth one, dealing with the Sabbath, was a sign of the covenant relationship between Israel and Jehovah. It was kept on the seventh day and strictly enforced in the Old Testament. In contrast, there was more flexibility in the New Testament as to what day should be kept and what should be done on that day. From the 1st century AD, the Church has celebrated the resurrection of Jesus Christ in worship on the first day of the week. The principle of one day in seven for rest and worship stems from the creation model set by God and satisfies Christ's statement that the Sabbath was made for man.

▲ **Option #6**

Mural scene.
Have the children write the Ten Commandments into a space in the mural.

Sketch 64 — General Outdoor

(Allow the class to leaf through chapters 21-40 to see that many more laws were given. Remove figures 49, 105.)

4. **The people respond to God.**
   (Exodus 23:20-33; 24:3-7)

(Moses 25, men 63, man 10, altar 64, slain lamb 40)
When Moses *(add 25)* came down from the mountain, he told the people *(add 63, 10)* the laws that God had given him and some special promises God had made. God promised that he would send his angel ahead of them to bring them to the land he had prepared for them. He also promised that if they would listen to him and obey his laws, he would take care of them and protect them from their enemies.

Moses wrote everything God had told him in a book. Then he built an altar *(add 64)* and made an animal sacrifice *(add 40)* to God in front of all the people. He was worshiping God and showing the people how special God is. After that, he read to the people what he had written in the book. It was like a contract, a covenant or solemn promise, between God and the people. In it God told the people what he wanted them to do and promised to take care of them. The people promised to obey, saying, "We will do everything the Lord has said; we will obey."

Sketch 65   General Outdoor

■ Conclusion

Summary

(Newsprint & marker or chalkboard & chalk)
Who can tell me why God gave his people new laws or rules to live by after they left Egypt? *(List responses on newsprint or chalkboard, being sure to include the following if the children do not.)* Yes, he wanted them to know what is right and what is wrong, how to live together and solve their problems, how to stay healthy and how to worship him. He wanted them to live holy lives so they could be his special representatives to the nations who lived around them. The laws God gave them showed them how to do all these things. If they lived according to God's rules, they would be happy and God would be pleased. And the other nations would learn what God is like by watching them and seeing how different they were in the way they talked and how they behaved.

Application

(Selected verses printed on newsprint)
All of us who have received Jesus as our Savior are God's people, too. Instead of having a man like Moses to tell us what God wants us to do, we have God's Word, the Bible. God wants us to study it to find out how he wants us to live, and to choose to live by the rules he has

written there. Then our lives will be different from the people around us and we can be his special representatives (or examples) to them. Let's say Psalm 40:8 together. *(Do so.)*

Let's practice. *(Use one or more of the following scenarios—or some you choose to suit your children's needs—to help them understand how to apply God's Word to their own life situations.)*

1. If you are tempted to cheat on a test or a special project at school, what does God's Word say you should do? *(Display newsprint on which you have printed the words from Ephesians 4:25a and read them aloud together.)* How could you live by God's rules in this situation? *(Discuss, helping the children to apply the verse to the problem.)*

2. If someone says something mean about you and you feel like getting even, what does God want you to do? *(Display the words from 1 Thessalonians 5:15a or Ephesians 4:32 and read them aloud together.)* How can you obey God's rules when you feel like this?

3. If you feel like complaining because you don't have all the things your friends have, what does God want you to do? *(Display the words of 1 Thessalonians 5:18 and read them aloud together.)* What should you do to obey God's rule in this situation?

It's not always easy to follow God's rules and live the way God wants us to, but we don't have to do it alone. Because we belong to God's family we can always depend on him to help us. When we follow God's rules, we talk and behave differently from the people around us. That is one way they can learn what God is like. They may even ask us why we are different and we can then have an opportunity to tell them about God and his Son, Jesus.

Response Activity

Have the children bow their heads as you encourage them to choose to live by God's rules. Give them time to pray quietly, telling God they want to learn his rules and follow them.

*Distribute the **"My Choice" handouts** and pencils. Explain how to read one Scripture each day, print God's rule, make a check mark if they choose to obey and then ask God to help them obey that day. Next week ask them to tell how God helped them or what problems they had.*

Close by praying that God will help each one of them to choose to learn God's rules and trust him to help them live by them.

✍ TAKE HOME ITEMS

*Distribute **memory verse tokens for Psalm 40:8** and **Bible Study Helps for Lesson 10**.* ▲#7

▲ **Option #7**

Make copies of the "Ten Commandments" visual (pattern P-16 on page 177) to distribute to the children to take home as a reminder of the lesson.

The People Worship a Gold Calf
Theme: Correction

Lesson 11

❋ BEFORE YOU BEGIN...

We live in a society that is deeply grieved by the anti-social and frequently criminal behavior of many of our children, but we are often ambivalent about correcting and disciplining them. We range from too little discipline (permissiveness) to too much (abuse). Parents and other authority figures sometimes selfishly lash out at children in anger or woefully neglect them because they consider them a nuisance. It is not easy to teach the biblical truth that God, in love, chastens and corrects his children when they do wrong.

With utmost care, we need to teach our students that our Heavenly Father deals with his children perfectly, being neither too harsh nor too lenient, but always correcting appropriately and effectively—and always to help them learn to do right. Encourage them to accept correction without resentment. Assure them that they can rest confidently in their Heavenly Father's ability to always do what is right in disciplining them. *"My son, do not despise the chastening of the Lord, nor detest His correction; for whom the Lord loves He corrects, just as the father the son in whom He delights" (Proverbs 3:11-12, NKJV).*

☞ AIM:

That the children may

- Know that God loves his children and corrects them when they disobey.
- Respond by accepting God's correction through authority figures without resentment and as a reminder to obey him.

📖 SCRIPTURE: Exodus 24:12-18; 31:18; 32:1-35; 34:1-32; Deuteronomy 9:8-21; Acts 7:39-41

♥ MEMORY VERSE: Proverbs 3:11, 12

My son, despise not the chastening of the Lord...for whom the Lord loveth he correcteth. (KJV)

My son, do not despise the Lord's discipline...because the Lord disciplines those he loves. (NIV)

📁 MATERIALS TO GATHER

Memory verse visual for Proverbs 3:11, 12
Backgrounds: Review Chart, Plain Background, General Outdoor
Figures: R1-R11, 25, 31, 32, 34, 35, 40, 49, 57, 64, 70, 71, 72, 105
Token holders & memory verse tokens for Proverbs 3:11, 12
Bible Study Helps for lesson 11
Special:
- *For Review Chart & Memory Verse:* Newsprint & marker or chalkboard & chalk
- *For Summary:* Newsprint & marker or chalkboard & chalk; "God's Correction" chart
- *For Response Activity:* "God's Correction" handouts; crayons or washable markers
- *For Options:* Materials for any options you choose to use
- *Note: To make "God's Correction" chart, print three headings across the top of newsprint or chalkboard: "God said...," "Israelites disobeyed by...," "God corrected with..."; print "Why did God correct?" in the bottom center of the chart.*
  Follow the instructions on page xii to prepare the "God's Correction" handouts (pattern P-8 on page 172).

💼 REVIEW CHART

Display the Review Chart with R1-R10 in place and have R11 in God's Supply Room, ready to use where indicated. Use the following questions to review Lesson 10.

1. Why did God give his law to the Israelites? *(To show them how they were to live together and worship him)*
2. Where did Moses go to receive God's laws? *(Up Mount Sinai to meet with God)*
3. How did God show that he was on the mountain with Moses? *(Through smoke and fire, thunder and lightening)*
4. What did the people do when they heard God's voice? *(They became afraid and moved away from the mountain.)*
5. What promise did God make to his people? *(He would protect them, provide their needs and guide them to the land.)*
6. What did Moses do with the laws God spoke to him? *(He wrote them down in a book.)* ▲#1

Print on newsprint or chalkboard a math problem with an incorrect answer (for example, 12 + 10 = 20) or a misspelled word.

Look at this math problem (or spelling word) that I have put on the board. Is it right—or correct? No, it is not. What is wrong with it? *(Response)* Yes, the answer is wrong (or the word is misspelled). Who can correct it? *(Have a volunteer come and make the change.)* Now is it right? Yes, we have *corrected* the mistake. We have changed it from wrong to right. ▲#2

▲ Option #1

Use the following questions as a Bible drill for the group or as a written worksheet for individuals. (Questions may be used with a variety of Bible translations.)

1. Exodus 17:3: What did the Israelites do when they were unhappy with Moses? *(Murmured or complained)*
2. Exodus 17:4: What did Moses do? *(Cried to God or prayed)*
3. Exodus 17:6: What did God tell Moses to do? *(Hit or strike the rock)*
4. Exodus 19:5: What did God say his people would be if they obeyed him? *(His treasure or possession)*
5. Exodus 19:16: What did the people hear at Mount Sinai? *(A trumpet and thunder)*

Correction

11 Proverbs 3:11a, 12a

6. Exodus 19:19: How did God speak to Moses? *(With a voice)*

▲ Option #2

Definition word card:
Correct = to change from wrong to right.

▲ **Option #3**

Definition word card:
Chasten = Discipline or train

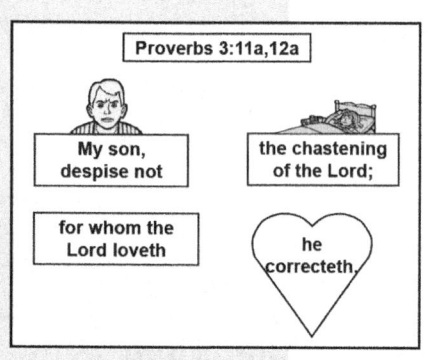

▲ **Option #4**

Memorizing the verse: Display the pieces of the verse visual in random order. Specify different groups of children to say the verse correctly and choose one of their members to put the pieces in correct order. Examples of "groups": all children wearing a certain color, all who have brown hair, all who are 10 years old, etc. Continue until all children have participated. Finally, remove the visual pieces from the board and have the class repeat the verse together.

What would happen if you made this mistake on a test in school? *(Response)* It would be marked wrong and you would get a lower grade. You might even have to write the incorrect problem (or word) correctly several times to help you remember the right answer. Would this "correction" be good for you? Why? *(Response)* Because it would help you remember the right answer and remind you not to make the same mistake again.

Did you know that God also corrects people when they are wrong? He often corrects those who break his rules. *(Have a child take R11 from God's Supply Room and place it on the Chart.)* The purpose of his correction is to help us do the right thing after we have sinned and to remind us not to disobey him again. He corrects us because he loves us.

♥ **MEMORY VERSE**

Use the verse visual and newsprint and marker or chalkboard and chalk to teach Proverbs 3:11, 12 when indicated.

Today's memory verse tells us that God corrects the people he loves. *(Display the verse visual and read it together with the class.)*

Whom does God love? *(Response)* In one sense he loves everyone and he showed that by sending the Lord Jesus to die for the sins of the whole world. But God loves believers in a special way. He is particularly concerned that people in his family, people who have believed in Jesus, should learn to obey him and do what is right.

What does our verse tell us that God does for the people he loves? *(Response)* That's right; he *chastens* them. To *chasten* (or chastise) means to discipline or train. ▲#3

When some people hear the word *chasten*, they think immediately of punishment. Punishment can be part of God's chastening or discipline, but it is always in this life and not to be confused with punishment in hell for those who do not receive Jesus Christ as their Savior.

God chastens and disciplines believers when they sin to correct them so that they will learn to do right (Hebrews 12:5-11). He may allow something bad to happen to teach us a lesson. Or he may use a parent or someone in authority to correct us. He does this to help us remember to obey so that we may have lives that are happy and pleasing to him.

How does God say that we should act when we are chastened? *(Response)* That's right; we should not despise it. If you despised God's chastening, you would not take it seriously. You might laugh about it or ignore it. Or you might dislike it so much that you would do anything you could to avoid it. Any of those attitudes would be foolish and would displease God.

While we may not like the punishment we receive when we disobey, we can thank our loving heavenly Father that he is doing it for our good so that we will choose to obey him. *(Work on memorizing the verse.)*
▲#4

📖 BIBLE LESSON OUTLINE

The People Worship a Gold Calf

■ Introduction

Matt resents Dad's discipline

■ Bible Content

1. God gives Moses the Ten Commandments.
2. Aaron makes a gold calf.
3. God is angry at the people's sin.
4. The people are punished for their sin.
5. God writes the Ten Commandments again.

■ Conclusion

Summary

Application
  Resenting God's correction is sin

Response Activity
  Confessing the sin of resentment and accepting God's correction

📖 BIBLE LESSN

■ Introduction

Matt resents Dad's discipline

How do you act when your parents discipline you? Do you get angry? Do you pout? Do you talk back to them? Perhaps you behave like Matt did when his dad grounded him for being a half hour late getting home from school.

Tom had invited him to stop and play a new video game he had received for his birthday. Matt had completely forgotten that he had promised his dad that he would come straight home from school and help to rake leaves. Dad had been upset because Matt had been late several days this past week.

Matt slammed his books on his desk. "It's not fair," he muttered to himself. "I was only a half hour late. What's the big deal?" his dad had said that he would have to come straight home from school the rest of the week and there was to be no TV, no video games and certainly no basketball games with his friends. And... he had to get his homework done before dinner.

All through dinner Matt sulked, refusing to join in the conversation with his family. When dinner was over, Matt headed for his room. Soon after that there was a knock at his door and his dad asked if he could

▲ **Option #5**

Have the children take turns printing the Ten Commandments in order on poster board or chalkboard in pre-session time as a review.

▲ **Option #6**

Have the children role play Exodus 32:1-7 — one taking the part of Aaron; the others, the Israelites — reading the dialogue from Scripture as they go. Or, have a narrator read the Scripture and the children act out the parts.

Sketch 66 General Outdoor

come in. "I guess so," Matt growled. "It's your house. You make the rules around here."

Dad was quiet before he spoke. "Yes, Matt, your mom and I do make the rules for our family. God has given us that responsibility as your parents. I can see that you are angry with me because you've been grounded."

"But...," Matt started to protest.

"Matt, our rule is that you come straight home from school unless you have asked permission to do otherwise. You have been disobeying that rule all week. I know you think that your punishment is unreasonable, but maybe it will help you remember that you are to obey us. Matt, we love you and want you to learn to be obedient. But more importantly, God loves you and wants you to obey him."

What does God say about our attitude when we are disciplined? *(Response)* That's right; we are not to resent it. Let's say our memory verse together. *(Do so.)* What do you think Matt should do? *(Let children respond. Point out that Matt's disobedience and attitude was wrong and should be confessed as sin. He needs to ask his parents for forgiveness and accept their punishment without getting angry.)*

Today we are going to see what God did when the Israelites disobeyed his rules. Find Exodus, chapter 32, in your Bible and place your bookmark there.

■ **Bible Content**

1. **God gives Moses the Ten Commandments.**
   (Exodus 24:12-18; 31:18; Deuteronomy 9:8-11)

(People 49, lightning cloud 105)

The people *(place 49 on the board)* had watched Moses disappear up the mountainside when he went into the cloud *(add 105)* to meet with God. He was gone for 40 days and 40 nights. He did not eat or drink at all, but God took care of him and gave him strength. God spoke to Moses during that time, giving him still more instructions for the people. Then God made two stone tablets and personally wrote the Ten Commandments on them. *(Have the children locate Exodus 31:18 and read it aloud.)* ▲#5

God wanted his people to have a permanent copy of his most important laws. He wanted them to remember how much he loved them and wanted them to do right. Remember, they had all agreed, "Whatever the Lord says, we will do!"

But as the days went by, the Israelites became more and more anxious about Moses. They could still see the light on the mountain, so they knew God was there, but where was Moses? Why didn't he come back? He had been gone more than a month, but it must have seemed much longer to them. He hadn't taken any food with him. Maybe he was dead. Maybe he had gotten lost or abandoned them. What were they going to do? They were tired of waiting for something to happen *(Remove all the figures.)*

2. Aaron makes a gold calf.
(Exodus 32:1-6; Acts 7:39-41)

(Aaron 32, people 35)
Read Exodus 32:1 to see what the people did. *(Place 32 on the board.)* Some of them *(add 35)* came to Aaron, who was in charge while Moses was away, and said, "We don't know what happened to Moses. He brought us out of Egypt and now he is gone away and we have nobody to be our leader. Why don't you make a god to lead us?" They probably meant that they wanted a statue of the true God, but they were wrong to ask for such a thing. They were acting like the Egyptians who worshiped idols and tried to get their gods to help them do whatever they wanted. ▲#6

Do you remember the first two rules God had given to his people only a month before? *(Response; have the children read Exodus 20:1-3 aloud.)* That's right; they were not to make any image (or statue) as a god or worship any other god. Aaron should have reminded them of this, but he didn't. He was probably concerned about Moses, too. Maybe he thought he had to do something to satisfy the people. Read verse two to see what he did. *(Response)* Yes, he listened to the people and let them influence him. He told them to bring him all the gold earrings the Egyptians had given them. *(Leave all the figures on the board.)*

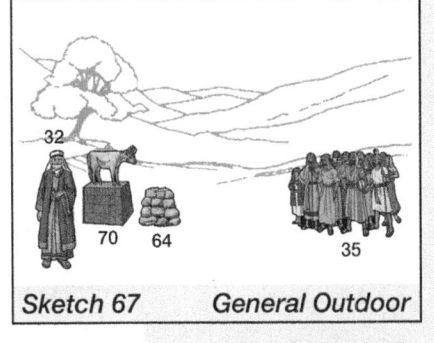

(Gold calf 70, altar 64, people 71, lamb 40)
Then Aaron melted all that gold and shaped it into a golden calf *(add 70)*. Cows and other animals were common objects of worship in Egypt. When the people saw it, they said, "Here is the god that brought us out of Egypt." Aaron placed the golden calf on a high platform where everyone could see it. Then he built an altar *(add 64)* in front of the calf and said, "Tomorrow is a feast day to the Lord. We will worship and celebrate."

Early the next morning the people *(add 71)* brought animals and other offerings to sacrifice on the altar *(add 40)*. Then they ate and drank and sang and danced around the altar of the golden calf as they had seen the Egyptians do in front of their gods. ▲#7

They had forgotten all about God's commandments. They had chosen to have a god they could see and touch, even though it could not meet their needs or hear their prayers or care about them. They had sinned against God and his law. *(Remove 40.)* ▲#8

▲ **Option #7**

Mural scene.

Sketch 67   General Outdoor

▲ **Option #8**

Show pictures of idols people worship today; for example, totem poles or Buddha. Then brainstorm with the class about other things people make a "god" or put in place of God in their lives. Print each one on a 4" x 6" card. Divide the children into groups of

Sketch 68   General Outdoor

3 or 4 and give each group one of the cards. Have them decide how their item can become a "god" to people, then illustrate it in a drawing, act it out in a skit or just tell the class about it.

3. **God is angry at the people's sin.**
   (Exodus 32:7-14; Deuteronomy 9:12-14)

   Up on the mountain Moses did not know what the people were doing down below. But God knew, because he sees and knows everything. "Moses," he said, "go down now because the people have sinned. They have already broken the rules I gave them and made themselves an idol in the shape of a gold calf. They have bowed down to it and sacrificed to it and said, 'This is the god that brought you out of Egypt.'" God was so angry with his people that he told Moses he wanted to destroy them and begin a new nation of people with Moses and his family.

   "But Lord," Moses said to God, "why would you destroy these people you have brought from Egypt? The Egyptians and other nations will say you are not great enough or strong enough to keep your promise—that you just brought them out here to kill them. Remember your promise to Abraham and Isaac and Jacob to make this nation great."

   God likes for us to remind him of the promises that he has made. God knew all along what he would do, but he wanted Moses to have a part in teaching this important lesson to the Israelites. He promised Moses that he would not destroy the nation. *(Leave all the figures on the board.)*

4. **The people are punished for their sin.**
   (Exodus 32:15-35; Deuteronomy 9:15-21)

   (Moses 25, Joshua 72)
   Moses started down the mountainside carrying the stone tablets God had given him. Part way down he met Joshua, his assistant, and they continued down together. Nearer the valley they could hear the people shouting. Joshua said, "It sounds like war." But Moses said, "It sounds more like singing to me." Have you ever heard all the noise and confusion when a lot of people are drunk and having a party? That's what it was like in the camp that day.

   When they got near the camp, Moses *(add 25, 72)* saw the gold calf and the people dancing around it, and he was furious! How could they do a thing like this? No wonder God was angry!

   In his frustration and anger, Moses threw the stone tablets God had made to the ground and broke them. He rushed through the crowd to the gold calf, pulled it down *(remove 70)* and smashed it into little pieces. Then he ground the pieces into fine powder, sprinkled the powder on the stream where the people got their water and made them drink it. The water probably tasted terrible and made them sick at their stomachs. That was one consequence of their sin—a strange punishment to remind them they needed to obey God. *(Remove 71, 72, 35.)* ▲#9

Sketch 69   General Outdoor

▲ **Option #9**

Mural scene.

104   L-11

(People 31)

Moses then turned to Aaron *(move 32 to the right of 25)*, "Why did you do this? Why did you allow the people to commit this great sin against God?"

Aaron answered, "Don't be angry with me. You know what these people are like; they sin so easily. When they asked me to make them a god they could see, I just told them to bring their gold. I threw it into the fire and out came this calf."

Aaron didn't admit to Moses that he had made the calf, but Moses knew. He also knew that God, who is holy and good, cannot tolerate sin, and that the people who had worshiped the calf must be punished because they had sinned against God. The people had to learn how terrible it was to break God's law and make their own god. They had to learn that God must punish sin. (1)

So Moses stood before the people and called out, "Who is on the Lord's side? Come and stand with me!" All the Levites came and stood with him *(add 31)*. Then Moses said to them, "Take your swords and go though the camp, killing people because of this terrible sin." Three thousand men died that day. After this, Moses said to the rest of the people, "You have committed a great sin, but I will pray for you." Then he prayed and asked God to forgive Aaron and the people. God did forgive them and he did not destroy them, but he had to chasten and correct them. He sent a terrible disease and many people got very sick.

The people who were left had lost loved ones and family members. Many of the people who could have helped them later were dead. It was a hard way for them to learn that God means what he says and that people suffer when they disobey God's rules. God wanted his people to understand that his laws were for their good and that it was very important for them to obey them. *(Leave 25 on the board; remove all the other figures.)*

Sketch 70   General Outdoor

Note (1)

The holiness of God is best understood by the punishment he has established for sin which is death. It is the only way we can grasp how offensive sin is to his holiness. God's punishment would be a vivid example that would be a lasting reminder to those who were left.

5. God writes the Ten Commandments again. (Exodus 34:1-32)

(People 35, 49, Moses 25)

After this the Lord said to Moses, "Carve two new stone tablets like I made before and bring them up the mountain tomorrow morning. I will write on them the words that were on the first tablets. Don't bring anyone with you and don't allow any people or animals to come near the mountain." *(Remove 25.)*

So Moses did as the Lord said, and once more he stayed on the mountain with God for 40 days and 40 nights without eating or drinking anything and God gave him strength. This time the people *(add 35, 49)* waited for Moses and did not

Sketch 71   General Outdoor

▲ **Option #10**

Mural scene.

Sketch 72   God's Correction chart

God said...	Israelites disobeyed by...	God corrected with...
No idols	Asking for a god	Death
No other gods	worshiping the calf	Bitter water
		Disease

Why did God correct?
Because God is holy
Because God wanted them to obey
so they wouldn't do it again

▲ **Option #11**

Make word strips for each phrase in Sketch 72 and place them on the felt board as you proceed through the Conclusion.

---

sin against God's law. They remembered the way God had punished some with death and the way he had chastened the rest with sickness. This correction helped them to obey the Lord.

When Moses *(add 25)* came down from the mountain, he was carrying the new stone tablets on which God had written the Ten Commandments. his face was shining with a wonderful light because he had been with God. Aaron and the people were afraid to come near him, but Moses called them together and gave them all the commands God had given him.   ▲#10

■ Conclusion

Summary

(Newsprint & marker or chalkboard & chalk ["God's Correction" chart])   ▲#11

How did the Israelites disobey God? *(Encourage response throughout; print responses under "Israelites disobeyed by...")* They asked Aaron to make an idol for them and then they worshiped it. What was God's rule about this? *(Print responses under "God said...")* That's right; they were not to have any other god or make any idols to worship.

Why did Aaron make the gold calf? Yes, the people were tired of waiting for Moses and wanted a god they could see to lead them.

How did God punish those who disobeyed him and did not believe his word? *(Print responses under "God corrected with...")* Yes, they were put to death. How did God correct the others? They all had to drink the bitter water that had the ground-up gold in it. Many others got sick with a terrible disease. They lost loved ones and family members. People who could have helped them were now gone. Sin is a terrible thing.

Why were they punished so severely? *(Print responses under "Why...")* Because God is holy and must punish sin. Because he wanted them to understand how important it is to obey. Because he knows that if sin is left unpunished, it will harm us and all those around us. Hopefully this terrible punishment would teach them a lesson and the next time they thought about disobeying God's law they would resist the temptation.

How do we know that God's people were corrected by God's punishment? Yes, they waited for Moses when he went up the mountain the second time and they did not disobey God's law while he was gone.

Application

Because God loves us, he wants us to obey him, too. He knows that learning to obey is for our own good, and so he gives us parents and teachers and others to help us learn this important lesson.

Disobeying what God tells us in his Word is sin. Because God is holy, he must punish sin today, too. Sometimes he has to use difficult circumstances or punishment by someone who is over us to correct us and help us remember not to do that wrong thing again. God corrects us because he loves us, and we should not resist or resent his chastening. How do you respond when your parents or teachers discipline you? Are you like Matt? Or do you accept discipline, recognizing that it is from the Lord to correct your wrong behavior and help you obey?

If you have been resenting your parents and teachers when they discipline you, then you need to confess your sin to the Lord. Ask him to use correction to remind you to obey him.

Response Activity

Distribute "God's Correction" handouts and crayons or washable markers. Have the children color the face that shows how they respond to the discipline they receive from their parents or teachers. Encourage those who resent this correction to pray silently, confessing their sin of resentment and asking God to help them see it as a reminder to obey.

Have the children print their name on the line below the "Accept" face if they are willing to accept God's correction that comes through their parents or teachers as from him and as a reminder to obey him.

Close in prayer, asking God to help the children accept correction without resenting it and in a way that helps them grow.

TAKE HOME ITEMS

Distribute **memory verse tokens for Proverbs 3:11, 12** and **Bible Study Helps for Lesson 11.**

Israel Builds the Tabernacle
Theme: Fellowship

Lesson 12

❋ BEFORE YOU BEGIN...

"I wish my daddy would come home. I miss him!" echoes through our society. Many children are lonely. It may be that Mom or Dad is missing from the home or working so that the children come home from school to an empty house. It may be that there are no other children to play with or that other children, for one reason or another, snub them. Or just that nobody pays much attention to them. They need fellowship.

The dictionary says fellowship is companionship, friendly association, or mutual sharing of experiences, activities, or interests; a union of friends or equals. Doesn't that sound like a place where you are accepted, cared about, encouraged, and enjoyed? Where you belong? And don't we have all that in "our fellowship…with the Father and with his Son, Jesus Christ"? Strive to make your class a place of fellowship for your children as they learn together what it means to be part of the family of God. And through this lesson teach them how to have fellowship with God—who will never leave them or fail them—and to begin a lifelong habit of daily quiet time with him. *"God is faithful, by whom you were called into the fellowship of His Son, Jesus Christ our Lord" (1 Corinthians 1:9, NKJV).*

☞ AIM:

That the children may

- Know that God loves believers and has made a way for them to fellowship with him.
- Respond by learning to fellowship with God through reading the Word, praising him, and praying.

📖 SCRIPTURE: Exodus 25–31; 33:7-11; 35:4–40:38

♥ MEMORY VERSE: 1 John 1:3

Our fellowship is with the Father, and with his Son, Jesus Christ. (KJV)
Our fellowship is with the Father and with his Son, Jesus Christ. (NIV)

MATERIALS TO GATHER

Memory verse visual for 1 John 1:3
Backgrounds: Review Chart, Plain Background, Wilderness,
Figures: R1-R12, 25, 34, 35, 46, 49, 61, 62, 73, 74, 75, 76, 77, 78, 79, 80, 81.
Token holders & memory verse tokens for 1 John 1:3
Bible Study Helps for Lesson 12
Special:
- **For Bible Content 2:** A small piece of wood painted gold, carved objects, an embroidered cloth
- **For Bible Content 5:** Chart of Tabernacle Design; pictures, replicas, charts or any other resources of the tabernacle; colored cloth, brass or silver objects to help the children imagine the materials used in the tabernacle
- **For Application:** Word strips: FELLOWSHIP WITH GOD, READ GOD'S WORD DAILY, TALK TO GOD IN PRAYER, SHARE, PRAISE, THANK, CONFESS, ASK; newsprint & marker or chalkboard & chalk
- **For Response Activity:** "My Fellowship with God" handouts, pencils
- **For Options:** Materials for any options you choose to use
- **Note:** Follow the instructions on page xii to prepare the Chart of Tabernacle Design (pattern P-2 on page 169) and "My Fellowship with God" handouts (pattern P-9 on page 173).

REVIEW CHART

Display the Review Chart with R1-R11 scattered around the edges and R12 in God's Supply Room. Have volunteers, one at a time, choose a symbol and place it on the Chart while giving the memory verse which accompanies it. Use the following "True or False" statements to review lesson 11. Ask the children to give correct answers for the false statements.

1. God called Moses to the mountain to give him the law. *(True)*
2. Moses spent 30 days and 30 nights on the mountain with God. *(False; Moses spent 40 days and 40 nights on the mountain.)*
3. Aaron forced the Israelites to make a gold calf. *(False; Aaron made the gold calf.)*
4. God wrote the Ten Commandments on a scroll for Moses. *(False; God wrote them on clay tablets.)*
5. The Israelites disobeyed one or more of the Ten Commandments God had given. *(True)*
6. God punished with death all those who worshiped the gold calf. *(True)*
7. God corrects and disciplines us when we sin because he loves us and wants us to remember to obey him. *(True)*

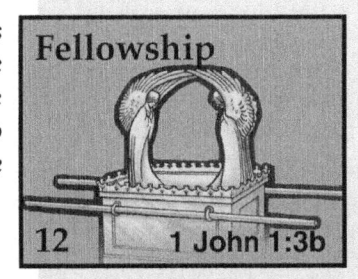

▲ **Option #1**

Definition word card:
Fellowship = Friendship

▲ **Option #2**

Memorizing the verse: Divide the class into two teams and play "ping pong" by having each team say a word from the verse when you point to them. For example, point to one team and have them say 1 John.

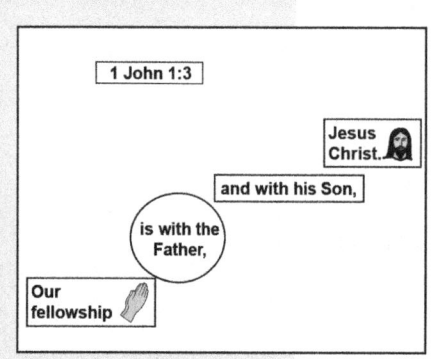

```
1 John 1:3

                        Jesus
                        Christ.
            and with his Son,
    is with the
    Father,
Our
fellowship
```

Point to the other team and have them say 1; then to the first team again and have them say 3. Then go back and forth as they say one word at a time until they have finished the verse.

Do this the first time with the visual displayed. Then remove visual pieces one at a time—having the group repeat the verse each time—until they can say the verse without help.

Variation: See how quickly the class can say the verse in ping pong fashion without mistakes.

Today we are going to discover something very wonderful that God gives to all who have trusted in his Son, the Lord Jesus Christ, as Savior. *(Remove R12 from God's Supply Room and place it on the Chart.)* It is called *Fellowship*. Has anyone heard this word before? Who knows what it means? *(Response)* ▲#1

Very simply, fellowship means having a friendship with someone. What does it mean to have a good friend? *(Response)* Yes, friends like to do things together. Friends care about each other and help each other. Sometimes they just enjoy being together and talking about things that interest both. Friends say thank you for help and take time to listen or just to be there in a difficult time. The time we enjoy together with a friend is called fellowship.

♥ **MEMORY VERSE**

Use the visual to teach 1 John 1:3 when indicated.

Our Bible verse talks about fellowship. *(Display the verse visual.)* Let's read it together. *(Do so.)* Who does this verse tell us we can have fellowship with? *(Response)* That's right; God himself and his Son, Jesus. Isn't it wonderful to think that the mighty God, the one who created everything that exists, wants to be our friend, to have fellowship with us? The book of 1 John, where this verse is found, was written to people who had already received the Lord Jesus as Savior and been born into the family of God. So we know that it is saying that God wants to have fellowship with his children.

Perhaps you're wondering how we can have fellowship, or a friendship, with God when we can't see him. We have already learned that the Holy Spirit comes to live in us when we receive Jesus as Savior and that he is always with us. He wants us to spend time with him by reading his Word, by thanking him and praising him, and by talking to him in prayer. God talks to us in his Word, telling us about himself and his promises and what he wants us to do. We talk back to him by thanking him for all he has done, praising him for how great he is and praying about many things, including ourselves and our own needs. Then we are enjoying fellowship, or friendship, with him and he with us.

However, our fellowship or friendship with God is different from fellowship with a friend here on earth. Sometimes our earthly friends disappoint us or move away, but God will *never* stop being our friend and wanting our fellowship. He will *never* leave us. He will always be there for us even when everyone else seems to not care about us. He is the best Friend of all! *(Work on memorizing the verse.)* ▲#2

BIBLE LESSON OUTLINE

Israel Builds the Tabernacle

Introduction

Andy's story

Bible Content

1. God gives Moses the pattern for the tabernacle.
2. The people build the tabernacle.
3. Moses sets up the tabernacle.
4. God fills the tabernacle.
5. God teaches through the tabernacle.

Conclusion

Summary

Application
Learning ways to have fellowship with God

Response Activity
Reading God's Word and praying to God

BIBLE LESSON

Introduction

Andy's story

Andy came to Sunday school every week. He claimed to have received Jesus as his Savior, but he was a very angry boy. He acted real tough with everyone and often got himself into trouble. But no matter how badly things went for him, he always gave his teacher a big hug before racing out the door. Mrs. Baldwin knew he was listening in class, because he gave right answers and asked good questions. But he never enjoyed the other children and often ran out of class angry.

One Sunday Andy arrived carrying a big bag of snacks—and he was the only one who came that morning. When he saw that he and his teacher were alone, he announced, "I will set up the class today!" So Mrs. Baldwin watched as Andy put the felt board in place and then arranged three chairs up close around the board.

"Why have you put three chairs by our board?" she asked.

"One for you, one for me and one for our snack!" answered Andy.

Andy offered the snack to Mrs. Baldwin and then said, "I will help tell the Bible story today. Could I put the people on the board? Oh yes, and I want to help read the words from the Bible." They had a wonderful time reading God's Word and learning the Bible lesson as Andy helped to tell the story and put "the people" on the board.

Then, to Mrs. Baldwin's amazement, Andy said, "Can we pray together now? I need to pray for my dad and mom and sister, and for me because I am very angry with them."

"Of course," said Mrs. Baldwin. Andy prayed aloud for the very first time, talking to God about his family and asking forgiveness for his anger and bad attitude. Then Andy thanked God for the great Sunday school class that day and for his teacher!

After Andy helped Mrs. Baldwin straighten up the room, he hugged her very tightly and ran happily on his way. Then she realized that the two of them had just had the best Sunday school class ever! They had enjoyed reading God's Word, learning the truths of the Bible lesson, and praying together. Instead of going away angry like he usually did, Andy went home like a new boy because of that time of quiet fellowship with his teacher and with God.

God knew that his people would need to have fellowship with himself as they traveled through the wilderness. They would need to know he was not just with them in the pillar of cloud and fire, but even closer—right there in the middle of their camp—so they could come to him anytime to praise him or talk to him about their problems or pray for forgiveness. Find Exodus, chapter 35, in your Bible and place your bookmark there. Today we will learn how God did all this for his people.

▪ Bible Content

1. **God gives Moses the pattern for the tabernacle. (Exodus 33:7-11; 25:1–27:21; 30:1-9, 17-21; 31:1-11, 18)**

Sketch 73 — Wilderness

(People 35, cloud 46 tent 61, tent of meeting 62)

When the Israelites *(place 35 on the board)* were traveling in the desert, how did they know that God was with them? How did they know where they were to go? *(Response)* That's right; they could always see the pillar of cloud *(add 46)* or the pillar of fire. When the cloud moved, they followed; when it stopped, they stopped.

When the people set up their tents *(add 61)*, Moses would pitch "the tent of meeting" *(add 62)* by itself outside the camp. People could go there to ask for God's special help. Whenever Moses went to the tent of meeting, the people would stand outside their tents, watching. While Moses was in the tent, the pillar of cloud *(move 46 to the entrance of the tent)* would come down to its entrance and stay there, and all the people would pray as they stood by their tent doors. The Bible says that God spoke with Moses face to face just as you would speak to one of your friends.

We don't know exactly how he did this. Perhaps he appeared in a human body. Moses understood everything that God said, and he knew that God loved his people.

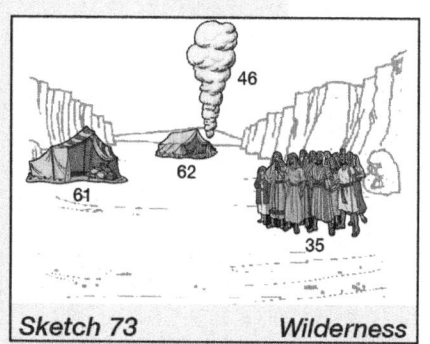

Then, while Moses was on the mountain receiving God's law, God said to him, "Have my people make a sanctuary (a consecrated or set-apart place) for me so that I may dwell with them." God wanted his people to know that he was with them all the time, that he had a permanent home among them. He wanted them to have a place where they could come to confess their sins and worship him and tell him their needs, a place where they could have real fellowship with him.

God told Moses exactly how to make this sanctuary, or special tent, that was later called the tabernacle. He told Moses what materials to use, what colors everything should be and how to put it all together. Moses brought all these instructions down from the mountain along with the stone tablets on which God had written the Ten Commandments. *(Remove 46)*

2. **The people build the tabernacle.**
   (Exodus 35:4–38:31; 39:32-43)

(Moses 25, people 35, 49, people bringing gifts 73; a piece of wood painted gold, carved objects, embroidered cloth)

When Moses *(add 25)* told the people *(add 35, 49)* that God wanted them to build a special tent for him, they were glad. This was something they could understand and obey. Read Exodus 35:5 to see what God said the people should do. *(Wait for response.)* That's right; God wanted them to bring an offering. Moses said, "Here is a list of what we need: gold, silver and bronze; blue, purple and scarlet yarn; fine linen cloth, animal skins, acacia wood, precious jewels, olive oil for the light and special spices for incense."

Sketch 74 — Wilderness

The people *(add 73)* gladly gave many of the beautiful things the Egyptians had given them when they left Egypt. They loved God and appreciated his caring for them; they were excited about making a special place for him to live among them. They brought so much that soon Moses had to tell them not to bring any more! ▲#3

God had given some of his people special abilities to make the things needed in the tabernacle. Some could do fine carving; some could work with gold or silver; some could do beautiful weaving; others knew how to work with precious jewels. Moses called these people together and asked them to train others to help them so that the work could go more quickly.

Some men made boards from the hard, strong wood of acacia trees, which grew in the wilderness. Others covered the boards with gold to make the frame for the tabernacle *(display wood)*. Some men did fine carvings on wood and stone *(display carvings)*; others made parts of the tabernacle from gold, silver and brass. Some women sat at their spinning wheels making yarn; others dyed the yarn and then wove it into beautiful curtains for the tabernacle and special clothing for the men who would serve God there. Still others did fine embroidery stitching on the curtains and the clothing *(display cloth)*.

▲ **Option #3**

Mural scene.

3. **Moses sets up the tabernacle.**
   (Exodus 40:1-33)

(Tabernacle 74, cloud 46)
It took several months, but at last the work was done. The people brought all the things they had made to Moses. How glad they must have been that God had used their talents and abilities to create his special home among them. Moses inspected everything they brought and saw that it was done just as the Lord had commanded and he blessed them.

Then the Lord spoke to Moses. Read chapter 40, verse 2, to see what he said. *(Allow time for response.)* That's right; he was to set the tabernacle up on the first day of the month. That was exactly one year from the day they left Egypt!

According to God's pattern, the tabernacle was always to be set up in the center of the camp and its entrance was to face towards the east *(place 74 on the board; have the children find the east side of the classroom)*. The people were to pitch their tents around it in a certain order, so that wherever they were, each tribe or family group could always see the tabernacle. ◳(1)

On this special day the people watched intently as Moses and the men carefully set up the framework for the tabernacle tent *(indicate each part as you speak)*, hung the curtains and covered the whole thing with the animal skins. Then Moses put each piece of furniture exactly where God's pattern said it should be and offered sacrifices to God. Finally, they set up the curtains that formed the courtyard, hung the curtain in the entrance-and all the work was finished! *(Leave 74 on the board.)*

Sketch 75   Plain Background

◳ **Note (1)**

The twelve tribes of Israel were descended from the twelve sons of Jacob (see Genesis 35:22b-26). By this time each family had grown into a large group which was called a tribe.

▲ **Option #4**

Mural scene.

4. **God fills the tabernacle.**
   (Exodus 40:34-38)

Read verse 34 to see what happened next. *(Allow time for response.)* Yes, the cloud *(add 46)* that had rested on Mount Sinai all the time they had been camped in that place began to move! As the people watched, it came down from the mountaintop and covered the tabernacle and the glory of God filled the tent; they could see a special glow from within. ▲#4

Can you imagine how exciting that must have been for them? God was going to live right there among them and they would be able to come to him and have fellowship with him, just as God had planned. *(Remove 46.)*

5. **God teaches through the tabernacle.**

(Brass altar 75, burning sacrifice 76, washstand 77, table of showbread 78, altar of incense 79, lampstand 80, ark 81; Chart of Tabernacle Design; pictures/replicas/charts/resources of the tabernacle; colored cloth, brass or silver objects)

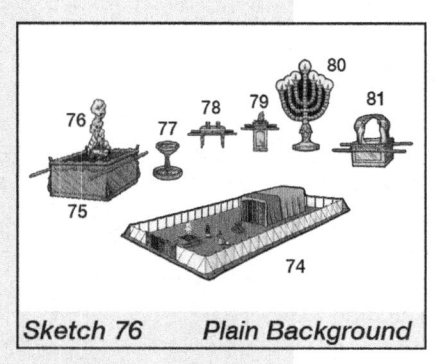

Sketch 76   Plain Background

God was very particular about how the tabernacle was built because he wanted his people to think about him, what he was like and what he had done for them when they came there. And because God knew that he was going to send Jesus into the world to die for sinners, he made everything in the tabernacle to teach something about Jesus. It was part of the way that he was preparing them for the coming of the Savior.

Let's pretend that we are walking through the tabernacle to see exactly how it was built and what some of the lessons were that God wanted to teach. ▲#5

▲ **Option #5**
Mural scene. (Include each piece in the tabernacle.)

When you approached the tabernacle, the first thing you saw was the **Courtyard** (sometimes called the **Outer Court**). It was a large area around the actual tabernacle tent and it was surrounded by a wall of heavy white linen curtains *(indicate it on 74)*. The people would come into the Courtyard to worship God, but they were not permitted to go inside the tabernacle tent. The white curtains and the fact that ordinary Israelites were not permitted inside the tent reminded them that God is holy—totally separate from everything sinful and bad. The single entrance reminds us that there is only one way to come to God. Jesus said that he is that only way to God.

There were two pieces of furniture in the Courtyard. The first was a large square brass altar *(add 75; indicate altar on 74)* where the priests offered sacrifices to God for the sins of the people. The people also brought animals here to be offered as sacrifices. The brass altar reminds us that a holy God must punish sin with death. When Jesus came, he was called the "lamb of God who takes away the sin of the world." *(Add 76; indicate sacrifice on 74)*.

The second piece of furniture was the laver or washstand—a big brass bowl *(add 71; indicate it on 74)*. It was made from brass mirrors the women had given. (In those days mirrors were made from highly polished brass instead of glass as they are today. The women's mirrors were melted down and made into the big bowl.) The priests who led the people in worship and the Levites who worked at the tabernacle washed their hands and feet at the washstand after they made the animal sacrifices and before they entered the tabernacle tent. The washstand reminds us that God forgives sin and cleanses our hearts. Jesus not only died for our sins; he forgives us and makes us fit to stand before God.

The **Tabernacle** tent itself was made from heavy linen curtains woven with blue, purple and scarlet threads and beautifully embroidered with pictures of cherubim, who are special angels. The curtains were fastened together with gold rings and hung over frames made from acacia wood covered with gold. One curtain hung over the entrance to the tent and a second one divided the tent into two rooms. The whole tent was covered with many animal skins sewn together to protect it from the weather.

The first room in the tabernacle was called the **Holy Place** *(indicate it on the Chart of Tabernacle Design)*. Only the priests who led the people in worship could go into this room. It contained three pieces of gold furniture.

The table of showbread *(add 78; indicate it on the chart)* displayed 12 loaves of bread which were replaced once a week. They reminded the priests of the 12 tribes of Israel and of God's promise to provide for his people's needs. Jesus would say, "I am the bread come down from heaven," meaning that he would satisfy the people.

The lampstand *(add 80; indicate it on the chart)* had seven branches with small cups that looked like flowers at the end of each one. These cups held olive oil which was kept burning day and night to provide light in the Holy Place. Jesus said, "I am the light of the world."

A special incense made from fragrant spices was burned on the altar of incense *(add 79; indicate it on the chart)* day and night to make a sweet-smelling perfume that rose up toward heaven. This special incense was used only in worshiping God and never burned anywhere else. This altar reminds us that our prayer should be going up to God continually, like the incense. The Bible tells us that Jesus is always praying to the Father for us.

The second room was smaller than the first and was called the **Most Holy Place** or the **Holy of Holies** *(indicate it on 74 and on the chart)*. It contained the most important piece of furniture—the ark of the covenant *(add 81)*. The ark was a gold box that had a gold lid called the mercy seat. Two gold statues of the angels called cherubim faced each other on the lid. Their wings stretched out to cover the special place in the middle where the High Priest sprinkled blood from a sacrifice made outside. A ball of light that represented God hovered over the mercy seat.

Inside the ark there were the two stone tablets on which God had written the Ten Commandments and a jar of the manna God used to feed his people in the wilderness. Only the High Priest, the leader of all the other priests, was permitted by God to enter the holy of holies and he could go there only once a year (on the Day of Atonement) with the blood of a sacrifice for the sins of the people. The ark reminds us that God wants us to come to him, but there must first be a sacrifice for sin. Jesus was our sacrifice and in a special way the cross was the mercy seat for our sins. *(Remove all the figures except 74.)*

■ Conclusion

Summary

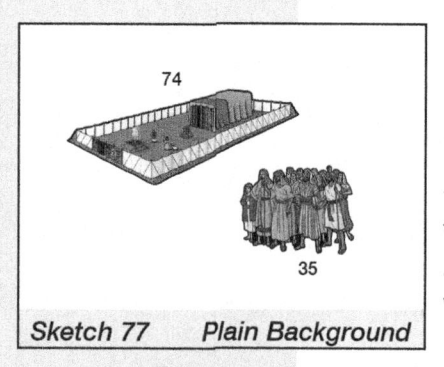

Sketch 77   Plain Background

(People 35)
Add 35 to the board.
What was God's plan to remind his people about what he was like and to encourage them to have fellowship with him? *(Allow for response throughout.)* That's right; it was the beautiful tabernacle. Why would God go to all that trouble? Yes, he loved them very much and wanted them to know about him. He also wanted to prepare them for the Savior he would later send into the world.

What are some of the things that the Israelites would have been reminded about God when they went to the tabernacle? Yes, he is holy; he was always with them; they could come to him anytime; he would forgive their sins: he wanted them to praise and worship him. ▲#6

Whenever they saw the tabernacle, they were reminded that their God was with them and that they could go to him whenever they needed to confess their sins and be forgiven, to praise him, to thank him, or to ask for his help. God had made a way for his people to come to him and enjoy fellowship with him as their God.

Application

(Word strips FELLOWSHIP WITH GOD, READ GOD'S WORD DAILY, TALK TO GOD IN PRAYER, SHARE, PRAISE, THANK, CONFESS, ASK; verse visual, a copy of Lesson 12 Bible Study Helps, newsprint & marker or chalkboard & chalk.) ▲#7

Today we can be thankful that God has made a way for us to have fellowship with him *(place FELLOWSHIP WITH GOD on the board).* Let's review our verse by reading it aloud together *(add the verse visual).* Belonging to God's family by receiving Jesus as our Savior gives us the right and the privilege to be friends with God and to have fellowship with him. *(Remove the verse visual.)*

Earlier in the lesson we talked about ways to have fellowship with God. Do you remember what they are? *(Response)* That's right; one way is by reading God's Word each day and studying it in Sunday school or Bible class or church. As we do this, we learn to "hear" what God tells us about himself and how he wants us to live. That's why we have our Bible Study Helps for you to read at home each week. *(Add READ GOD'S WORD DAILY.)*

Another way to have fellowship with God is to talk to him in prayer. *(Add TALK TO GOD IN PRAYER.)* We pray "in Jesus' Name" because he is the only way to God. Just as we do with our friends, we can share with God anything we're thinking or whatever is important to us, whether it is good or bad. *(Add SHARE.)* God is interested in us because he loves us.

We can also talk to God by praising him. *(Add PRAISE.)* What are some things we should praise God for? *(Print responses on newsprint or chalkboard; if necessary suggest the following: his greatness, his love, his holiness, or his power).*

Thanking God is also a way of talking to him. *(Add THANK.)* God loves to have us notice what he gives us or does for us and say thank you. What are some things we can thank God for right now? *(Print responses on newsprint or chalkboard).*

A very important part of having fellowship with God is confessing any sin we have done *(add CONFESS)* and knowing he will forgive

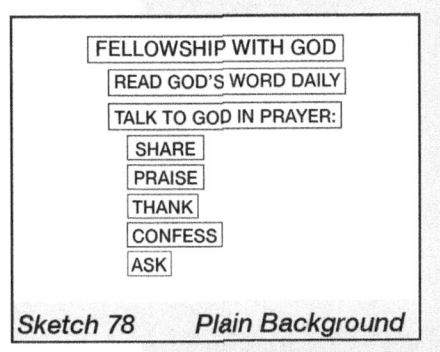

▲ **Option #6**

Print responses, as they are given by children or teacher, on newsprint or chalkboard.

```
FELLOWSHIP WITH GOD
READ GOD'S WORD DAILY
TALK TO GOD IN PRAYER:
   SHARE
   PRAISE
   THANK
   CONFESS
   ASK
```
Sketch 78   Plain Background

▲ **Option #7**

Before class, prepare this chart on newsprint or chalkboard, either in its entirety or in outline form you can add to as you teach. Allow space for recording responses.

us because Jesus died for us. Then we can freely ask God to supply our needs. *(Add ASK.)* What are some needs you have right now? *(Encourage response; if necessary suggest the following: someone to help with a school project, willing to be obedient in school, a job for a parent, or health for a friend.)*

Aren't you glad that God really wants to be our friend, to have fellowship with us? And that we can come to him anytime through Jesus? What kind of fellowship are you having with God today?

Response Activity

Encourage any who are not sure they belong to God's family to talk with you about receiving Jesus Christ as their Savior.

Give opportunity for your children who are believers to thank God for the privilege of having fellowship with him. Distribute the **"My Fellowship with God" handouts** *and pencils. Then explain how to fill in the blanks on the handouts and give the children time to work on completing them. Encourage the children to use their handout as a reminder of how they can have fellowship with God every day.*

TAKE HOME ITEMS

Distribute **memory verse tokens for 1 John 1:3** *and* **Bible Study Helps for Lesson 12**.

The Priests Offer Sacrifices
Theme: *Cleansing*

Lesson 13

❋ BEFORE YOU BEGIN...

The old saying, cleanliness is next to godliness, is not biblical, but it does express the fact that being clean is very important in many modern societies. Scientists spend much time and money developing formulas for removing dirt and grime from people and their belongings. But the most important and effective formula for cleansing was given to Christians by God in 1 John 1:9: *Confession = forgiveness and cleansing*.

It is vital for the Christian to know that when he received Christ as his Savior, he was cleansed from his sin by the blood of Christ and was born into the family of God. This sure knowledge gives assurance and security in the storms of life. It is equally as important for the believer to understand his responsibility to confess daily sins in order to maintain an open and growing relationship with God. Use this opportunity to help your children learn this important truth and begin forming the habit of recognizing and confessing daily sin in order to have a healthy and happy relationship with God. *"How can a young man cleanse his way? By taking heed according to Your word" (Psalm 119:9, NKJV).*

☞ AIM:

That the children may

- Understand that God has made a way for his children to be cleansed from the daily sins they commit.
- Respond by confessing their sins to receive God's forgiveness and cleansing.

📖 SCRIPTURE: Exodus 28; Leviticus 1; 16.

♥ MEMORY VERSE: 1 John 1:9

If we confess our sins, he is faithful and just to forgive us our sins, and to cleanse us from all unrighteousness. (KJV)

If we confess our sins, he is faithful and just and will forgive us our sins and purify us from all unrighteousness. (NIV)

📁 MATERIALS TO GATHER

Memory verse visual for 1 John 1:9
Backgrounds: Review Chart, Plain Background, General Outdoor
Figures: R1-R13, 10, 31, 40, 41, 49, 69, 74, 75, 76, 77, 78, 79, 80, 81, 85, 86, 87, 88, 103.
Token holders & Memory verse tokens for 1 John 1:9
Bible Study Helps for Lesson 13
Special:
- **For Review Chart:** Figures 74-81
- **For Memory Verse:** Teacher or child with dirty hands, basin with water, hand soap, towel; newsprint & marker or chalkboard & chalk
- **For Bible Content 1:** Word strips LEVITICUS, HOLY, SINNER
- **For Bible Content 3:** Blue-colored linen or fine cloth, a piece of embroidered cloth, small tinkling bells, a real pomegranate or a picture of one, gemstones
- **For Summary:** Word strip FORGIVENESS
- **For Application:** List from Memory Verse
- **For Options:** Materials for any options you choose to use
- **Note:** Follow the instructions on page xii to prepare the word strips.

💼 REVIEW CHART

Display the Review Chart with R1-R12 placed randomly around the edges and R13 in God's Supply Room. To review, have the children, one at a time, choose a symbol and give one incident they recall from that lesson about Moses or the Israelites. Ask another student to suggest a way God can supply that for us today.

Use the following questions, statements and visuals to review the tabernacle and its significance from Lesson 12. As each child answers correctly regarding the tabernacle, have him (or her) place the corresponding figure on the board.

1. Why did God want his people to have the tabernacle? *(So they would remember he was always with them and have a place to worship him)*
2. Where was the tabernacle set up? *(In the center of the camp)*
3. What does the word tabernacle mean? *(A tent or temporary living place)*
4. How did Moses know how the tabernacle should be built? *(God showed him the pattern.)*
5. Name three kinds of materials that were used to build the tabernacle. *(Gold, silver, brass, animal skins, linen cloth, blue, purple and scarlet thread, wood, precious jewels)*
6. Where did Moses get all the materials that he needed for the tabernacle? *(The people gave offerings of what they had.)*

7. Where did the priests sacrifice animals? *(On the brass altar)*
8. I am the basin where the priests washed after offering sacrifices. What was I called? *(The washstand or laver)*
9. I am the second room in the tabernacle where only the high priest could enter once a year. What am I? *(The Holy of Holies or the Most Holy Place)*
10. I am the *only* piece of furniture in the Holy of Holies. What am I? *(The Ark of the Covenant)*
11. I am the piece of furniture in the Holy Place where sweet spices burned day and night. What am I? *(The altar of incense)*
12. The priests always kept 12 loaves of bread setting on me. What am I? *(The table of showbread)*
13. Olive oil burned in my lamps day and night to provide light in the Holy Place. What am I? *(The lampstand)*

Ask a child or teacher to come to class with dirty hands; have a basin of water, hand soap and a towel prepared.

Now let's look in God's Supply Room to see what God is providing for us today. *(Have a child take R13 from God's Supply Room, read it, and place it on the Chart.)* Who knows what this word *Cleansing* means? *(Allow for response throughout.)* Yes, it means to make clean. You can see the word *clean* in the word *cleansing*. Let's do a little experiment to help us understand its meaning.

Have you noticed [individual's name] hands today? *(Have the child or the teacher show their dirty hands)*. What's wrong with them? That's right; they're dirty. How shall we get them clean? Perhaps we can just brush the dirt off *(attempt to do so)*. Oh, no, that doesn't work. Perhaps [individual] can shake the dirt off *(try)*. That doesn't seem to work either. How do we get dirty hands clean? We wash them with soap and water. Let's see what happens when we do that. *(Demonstrate by washing hands; show results.)* What happened? Yes, the hands are clean. They've been washed or cleansed by the soap and water.

♥ MEMORY VERSE

Use the visual and newsprint and marker or chalkboard & chalk to teach 1 John 1:9 when indicated.

Can soap and water make us clean from sin? *(Response)* No, of course not. God is the only one who can do that. When we believe that Jesus died for us on the cross and ask him to forgive our sin and be our Savior, God forgives us. Then, just as we can no longer see the dirt on our hands when we have washed it away, God says he no longer sees our sin. Instead, he sees us as clean from all our sin because we have trusted in what Jesus did for us.

But even after we have trusted Jesus as our Savior we sometimes do and say and think things that are wrong, that do not please God. When that happens, do we need to be saved again? No. Once you receive Jesus and are born into the family of God, you belong to

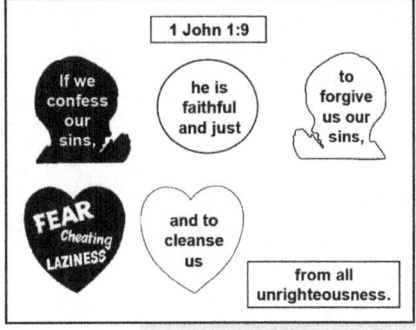

▲ **Option #1**

Definition word card:
Confess = to admit without making excuse.

▲ **Option #2**

Memorizinig the verse: Choose five children to hold up the verse visual pieces in front of the class as everyone reads the verse aloud. Then have one child hand his piece to another who is seated and go back to his own seat. Have the class or an individual repeat the verse, filling in the missing words. Continue until all five children have given away their verse pieces and returned to their seats.

Then have the children holding the visual pieces come to the front and display them in correct order. Have the class say the verse once again with the visuals in place; then remove the entire visual and say the verse one last time together.

---

him forever. But when we sin, when we do something that displeases our heavenly Father, we feel "dirty" on the inside and God is not happy with us. We feel very uncomfortable with God and may find it difficult to pray. It's something like when we disobey our parents or get into an argument with a friend. We don't feel comfortable with that person until we have said we were wrong and make things right between us.

Our memory verse was written to people who had already received Jesus as their Savior, but sometimes they did or said wrong things. Look in the book of 1 John near the end of the New Testament, chapter one and verse nine. *(Allow time to find the verse; then display the visual.)* Let's read it together. *(Do so.)*

What should we do when we sin? *(Response)* Yes, *confess* our sin. To *confess* means to "admit without making excuse." ▲#1

When we confess our sin to God, we tell him exactly what we have done and call it what he calls it—sin! *(Indicate examples in the dark heart and have the children give some of their own; e.g., lying about [something specific], stealing answers from someone else's paper, thinking bad thoughts about someone. List responses on newsprint or chalkboard.)*

Is it easy to admit that we have done wrong? No, it isn't. God already knows what we have done, but he wants us to admit it and take responsibility for our behavior.

Look at the verse again. What does it say about God? *(Response)* Yes, he is *faithful*—he will always do what he says; he keeps his promises. And he is *just* or fair in everything he does.

Next, when we confess to God something wrong we have done, what two things will he do for us? *(Response)* First, he will "*forgive* us our sin." Who knows what it means to forgive someone? *(Response)* That's right; it's to stop being angry with them, to give up trying to punish them or get even with them. And second, he will *cleanse* us or make us clean from the wrong or sinful action we have confessed to him. Then we can feel clean and comfortable with God again. Isn't that a wonderful thing to know? *(Work on memorizing the verse.)* ▲#2

📖 BIBLE LESSON OUTLINE

The Priests Offer Sacrifices

■ **Introduction**

Amanda is forgiven.

■ **Bible Content**

1. God's people need forgiveness and cleansing.
2. God said, "Bring an offering when you sin."
3. God chose the tribe of Levi to serve him.
   a. The priests wore special garments.
   b. The priests offered sacrifices.

c. The high priest went into the Holy of Holies once a year.

■ Conclusion

Summary

Application
Recognizing need to confess sin.

Response Activity
Confessing sin to receive forgiveness and cleansing

📖 BIBLE LESSON

■ Introduction

Amanda is forgiven.

Amanda needed help. Today was the weekly spelling test. She really needed to pass it, but she had not studied as she should have. "What am I going to do?" she asked herself. "I know! I'll just write the hardest words on my hands. Mrs. Smith will never notice if I look at my hands during the test, and I'll get those hard words right." Amanda got through the test without being caught and she received one of the highest marks in the class. It wasn't hard!

But Amanda had received Jesus as her Savior a few months before, and she knew that what she had done was wrong. But when Mrs. Smith praised her for studying so hard and all the kids were glad for her, she didn't let the cheating bother her. For the next two weeks, she used the same trick and it worked every time! But one day she was careless when she handed her paper to Mrs. Smith and she noticed the words on her hands. "Amanda," she said, "I want you to stay after class so we can have a little talk."

Amanda was scared. What would happen now? "I just won't admit it," she thought as she washed her hands. "She doesn't have any proof!" So Amanda refused to admit to Mrs. Smith that she was wrong or even that she had done it!   ▲#3

"Oh, Amanda," Mrs. Smith said, "I'm so sorry you're taking this attitude. I cannot trust you now. I'll have to watch you very carefully every time we have a test. Also, you will have to retake the tests you passed before." Of course, she did not get good grades this time.

Amanda felt terrible! She had disappointed Mrs. Smith and lost her trust. And she had sinned against God. As the weeks went by she began to feel dirty inside. Finally she could stand it no longer. "Oh, God," she prayed, "I'm so sorry I cheated. Please forgive me." The next day after school she went to Mrs. Smith and said, "I did it! I cheated and I'm really sorry. Please forgive me."

▲ **Option #3**

Have several children pantomime Joey's story to this point. Then ask the class to tell what Joey's sin was and what they think he should do to make it right.

"Yes, Amanda, I'll forgive you, " said Mrs. Smith. "And I'll be glad to help you study for future spelling tests any time you want to."

Amanda felt wonderful then—all clean on the inside! She had learned the hard way that it doesn't pay to do wrong. She had also learned that she could be forgiven and feel clean if she would confess what she had done.

Last week we learned how God came to live amid his people in the tabernacle. This week we'll learn about the special way he made for them to be forgiven and cleansed when they sinned so they could come into his presence and worship. When they were clean inside, they could go about their daily activities without feeling guilty, knowing that God would be with them and help them.

▲ **Option #4**

Use your GENESIS and EXODUS word strips to review briefly these books and have the children find them in their Bibles before you introduce Leviticus.

■ Bible Content

1. God's people need forgiveness and cleansing.

(Word strips LEVITICUS, HOLY, SINNER; people 49)
Open your Bibles to the third book of the Old Testament. It's right after the book of Exodus and is called Leviticus. *(If necessary, help the children find Leviticus 1:1. Place LEVITICUS on the board.)* ▲#4

This book is a collection of laws and instructions God gave Moses when he was on the mountain for a group of people called Levites. We are going to hear more about them in our lesson today.

God had a goal for his people *(add 49)*. Read Leviticus 19:2 to discover what it was. *(Have the children place their bookmark there and choose one child to read the verse aloud.)*

What did God say? *(Allow for response throughout.)* Yes, he told his people they were to be holy (separated from sin) because he is holy (sinless, separate from sin and evil). *(Add HOLY.)* Do you think it was possible for the Israelites to be holy? Why? Or Why not? It was not possible for them to be sinless or separate from sin like God is because they were sinners, just as you and I are. They acted and spoke and thought in sinful ways. *(Display SINNER.)* What, then, did God mean when he told them that they should be holy?

God meant that he wanted them to choose to separate themselves from sin, to live by his rules, to obey and honor him. That would make them different from the nations who lived around them. Then those other nations would see how different they were and would want to know more about the one true God.

Some of the Israelites rebelled against God and refused to obey him, like those who worshiped the gold calf. They didn't trust God and they were punished with death. But many of the people chose to believe in God's goodness and wanted to live God's way. They

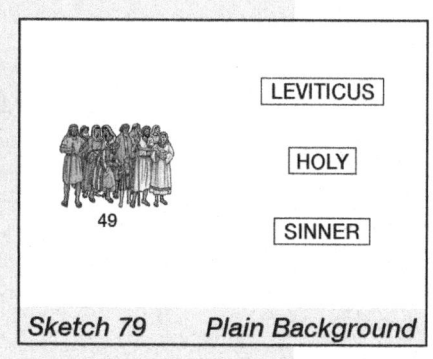

Sketch 79   Plain Background

separated themselves from sin and obeyed God's law most of the time. Still, because they were sinners, they sometimes did wrong things, so God made a way for them to be forgiven when they sinned. *(Remove 49 and all the word strips.)*

2. God said, "Bring an offering when you sin." (Leviticus 1)

(Tabernacle 74, man 10, lamb 86, goat 87)
God said to Moses, "When anyone sins, he must bring an offering to the entrance of the tabernacle *(place 74, 10 on the board)*. It must be a perfect male animal (no injury or sickness or defect) from the flock (sheep) or herd (goat or bull) *(add 86, 87)*. He must lay his hand on the head of the animal and confess that he has sinned before it is killed."

Of course, the animal couldn't really pay for the man's sin. Bringing the sacrifice showed that he believed God. It was a way for the man to confess that he had sinned and that he deserved to die. God forgave and cleansed him because of his faith in God. Then the man could go home rejoicing because God had made a way for him to be forgiven and cleansed from the sin he had committed.

Sketch 80   Plain Background

The sacrifice also was a wonderful picture of what God was going to do many years later when his Son, the Lord Jesus Christ, came into the world and died on the cross to take the punishment for all the sin of everyone who ever lived. *(Remove all the figures except 74.)*

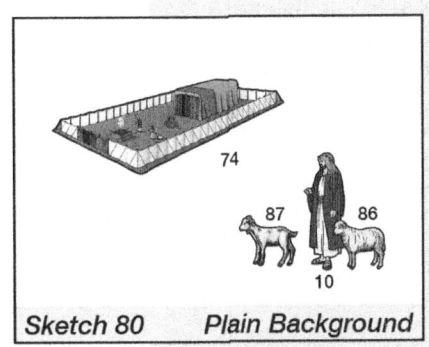

3. God chose the tribe of Levi to serve him (Exodus 28)

(High priest 85, brass altar 75, sacrifice 76, washstand 77, table of showbread 78, altar of incense 79, lampstand 80, Ark 81)
On the mountain God said to Moses, "I have chosen the tribe of Levi to serve me in the tabernacle. They are to help all the people make their sacrifices and worship me. Have all the other tribes provide their food and other needs so they can serve me there every day." This was a special honor! Moses and Aaron were from this tribe.

God also said to Moses, "Set apart your brother Aaron and his sons to be my priests and serve me in the tabernacle. Aaron

Sketch 81   Plain Background

will be the high priest *(add 85)* in charge of the entire tabernacle and the other priests." The priests were to represent the people before God.

God's special job for the other Levite men was to help the priests by taking care of the tabernacle. Some cut wood to keep the fire on the altar burning *(add 75, 76)*, or cleaned up after the animals were sacrificed and carried the ashes away from the altar, or washed all the silver bowls and platters used in worship. Others made sure there was

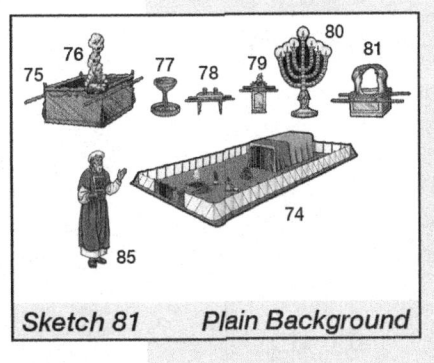

▲ **Option #5**

Mural scene.

▲ **Option #6**

Make replicas of the Ark and other pieces of tabernacle furniture from cardboard boxes. Spray with gold paint and attach rings at the proper places. Paint dowels or broom sticks for carrying poles. Have the children carry the replicas on their shoulders so they can experience what the Levites did.

▲ **Option #7**

Trace the outline of a child on a large piece of newsprint. Either before class or as you teach, sketch in each article of the priests' clothing. Involve the children by having them color the sketches or—if you have some who are capable—have them do the sketching as you teach.

▲ **Option #8**

Mural scene, High Priest.

always water in the washstand *(add 77)*, bread on the table of showbread *(add 78)*, incense on the altar of incense *(add 79)* or oil burning in the lampstand *(add 80)*.

The Levites also were responsible for moving the tabernacle when the people were traveling and setting it up in the new location. After the priests packed all the furniture from inside the tent according to God's instructions, the Levites packed everything else just the way God said they should. They moved the heavy boards, curtains and large pieces in wagons pulled by oxen, but they carried all the rest on their shoulders. ▲#5

The pieces of furniture were made with rings on the sides and special carrying poles which slid through the rings so the Levites could lift the furniture to their shoulders for carrying. The Ark of the Covenant *(add 81)*, which the High Priest cared for, also had rings and poles so the Levites could carry it. *(Indicate the rings and poles on 78, 79, 81.)* ▲#6 When the Levites died, their sons and grandsons continued this special service to the Lord. *(Remove all the figures except 85.)*

a. **The priests wore special garments.**

(Blue-colored linen or fine cloth, a pomegranate or a picture of one, small tinkling bells, embroidered cloth, gemstones)

God also told Moses to have special clothing made for Aaron and the other priests to show that they were set apart to serve him. Moses wrote God's instructions for these special garments in Exodus chapter 28. ▲#7

Aaron's garments were especially beautiful because he was the high priest and went into God's presence to represent the people. *(Indicate each article of clothing on 85 as you mention it.)* The garment he wore next to his skin was made of fine linen. Over this he wore a long blue robe *(show the blue cloth)* that reached almost to the floor. It had tassels around the hem that looked something like little pomegranate fruit *(show the pomegranate)*. Some were purple and some were red. Between the pomegranates hung small golden bells that jingled as he walked *(demonstrate the bells)*.

Over the blue robe Aaron wore a sleeveless linen garment called a tunic that was embroidered with gold, blue, purple and scarlet like the curtains of the tabernacle *(show the embroidered cloth)*. It had a belt of the same material. On each shoulder was a flat, gold-mounted onyx stone that had the names of six of the tribes of Israel written on it. ▲#8

On the front was a beautiful breast plate that was surrounded by braided chains of gold and had 12 precious stones (for example, ruby, emerald and sapphire) set in gold. *(Show the gemstones.)* The name of one of the 12 tribes was engraved on each stone. Every time Aaron went into the tabernacle, he was reminded that he was going to God for the people, for he wore their names on his shoulders and over his heart. He also wore a special linen hat called a turban. On its front was a gold plate that read "Holy to the Lord."

Skilled Israelite craftsmen made all the priests' clothing. The priests wore these special garments whenever they were serving the Lord in the tabernacle.

b. The priests offered sacrifices.

(High priest 85, man 10, lamb 86, slain lamb 40, basin 41)
The special work of the priests *(place 85 on the board)* was to offer the sacrifices. In addition to helping the people *(add 10)* when they brought animals *(add 86)* to be sacrificed for their own sins, they also made sacrifices for the sins of all the people. Every morning and evening they killed an animal *(remove 86; add 40, 41)*, caught its blood in a basin and poured it out at the foot of the altar. Then they burned the animal on the brass altar as an offering to God for the sins of all the whole nation. Seeing the innocent animal die in their place because of their sin was a daily reminder to the people that sin is a terrible thing in God's sight and must be punished by death. ▲#9

The priests also offered all the other sacrifices as God had instructed—some for special feast days and some for celebrations. Some required animals or doves or pigeons; others required grains. Whatever the sacrifice was, it must be perfect and undamaged—because it was for a *holy* God. How wonderful that God would make a way for his people to be cleansed and forgiven in their fellowship with him!

When Aaron and his sons died, their sons would become the priests and make the sacrifices. When they were gone, their sons would become priests, too. *(Remove all the figures except 85.)*

c. The High Priest went into the Holy of Holies once a year.
Leviticus 16) ▲#10

Sketch 82   General Outdoor

▲ Option#9
Mural scene.

▲ Option #10
You may omit this section when teaching younger children.

(Group 31, goats 87, 88)
God said that once every year the Israelites *(add 31)* were to keep a special feast day called the Day of Atonement. They were not to do any work. Instead, they were to spend the day thinking about and confessing their sins. This was a solemn day for all the people and especially for the high priest *(indicate 85)*. It was the one day out of the whole year when he could go into the Holy of Holies where the glory of God shone between the cherubim, and he always did it exactly according to God's instructions.

First, he washed his whole body with water and put on special plain white linen clothing. Then he brought before the Lord a young bull and two young male goats *(add 87, 88)*. He offered the young bull on the brass altar as a sacrifice for himself, for he, too, was a sinner and needed forgiveness. Then he took some of its blood in a

Sketch 83   General Outdoor

basin, some fire from the altar in a special pan called a censer and some sweet-smelling incense with him as he went into the Holy of Holies.

In the Holy of Holies the high priest put the incense on the fire in the censer, and its special fragrance filled the room like a cloud. He dipped his finger into the blood of the young bull and sprinkled it seven times before the mercy seat where the light of God's presence always stayed. Next, he left the Holy of Holies and offered one of the young goats *(remove 87)* on the brass altar as a sacrifice for the people's sin. Then he took some of its blood back into the Holy of Holies and sprinkled it seven times before the mercy seat.

All this time the people were watching and praying outside in the outer court. When they saw the high priest come out and sprinkle blood on the brass altar to show that it was cleansed too, they knew that God had accepted the sacrifice.

Finally, the high priest placed both his hands on the head of the living young goat and confessed all the sins of the Israelites before God. A trusted man was chosen to take this goat far away from the camp into the wilderness and set it free *(remove 88)*. This was a picture to the people that God was taking their sins far away so that they would never see them again. Of course, the goat did not take the sins away; God forgave them because he knew that Jesus would someday die for the sins of the world.

■ Conclusion

Summary

(Altar 75, lamb 86, goat 87; word strip FORGIVENESS)
How did God plan for his people to confess their sins and experience his forgiveness and cleansing? *(Allow for response throughout.)* The priests offered daily morning and evening sacrifices for the sins of all the people. Individuals who realized that they had sinned brought a perfect lamb or goat *(place 86, 87 on the board)* to be sacrificed on the altar *(add 75)* several times a year.

What did the person have to do before the priest took the animal away to be killed? That's right; he had to place his hand on the head of the lamb or goat and *confess* that he had sinned. What does it mean to *confess*? Yes, it means to agree with what God says about what we have done; to admit what we did and call it sin.

Why did the animal have to die? *(Response)* Because God said that the punishment for sin was death; the animal died to show that the worshiper deserved to die and to point to their coming Savior. Bringing the sacrifice was God's way for them to confess their sin and experience his forgiveness *(add FORGIVENESS)* and cleansing.

The problem was that it wasn't long after people left the tabernacle before they sinned again. How often did this sacrifice have to be made? *(Response)* Yes, it had to be done again and again, for they sinned and needed to confess over and over.

Application

(Jesus 103, cross 69, list from Memory Verse)

This special way God made for his people to be forgiven was a promise that one day his Son, Jesus, *(add 103)* would come as the Lamb of God (John 1:29) to pay for the sin of the world. It was also a picture of what he would do.

Like the lamb the people brought, Jesus did not deserve to die, for he had never sinned. He died on the cross *(add 69)* to pay for our sins once and for all and rose again so that we can someday live with God forever in heaven. By his death he also made a way for all of us who have trusted him as Savior to be forgiven and cleansed when we confess our daily sinful actions, thoughts, words and attitudes to him. He really is a wonderful Savior who loves us very much!

Let's look at the list we made earlier. *(Show list made during Memory Verse.)* If you have trusted Jesus as your Savior, think carefully about what is printed on it. Is there something here that you know you have done and need to confess so you can be forgiven and cleansed?

Response Activity

Have the children bow their heads in silent prayer. Encourage those who have trusted Christ as Savior to confess to God any wrong thing they have done and ask him to forgive them—then thank him for his forgiveness and cleansing. When you have said amen, remind them that this is something they should do as soon as they realize they have sinned, so that they can feel comfortable with God and please him.

Invite any who are not sure that they have received Jesus as Savior and been born into the family of God to come talk with you or a helper before leaving.

✍ TAKE HOME ITEMS

Distribute **memory verse tokens for 1 John 1:9** *and* **Bible Study Helps for Lesson 13**.

Israel Fails to Trust God
Theme: Thankfulness

Lesson 14

Part One: The People Complain About Manna

❋ BEFORE YOU BEGIN...

Listen to the voices around you: *Look out for number one! You deserve the best—you're worth it!* This attitude pervades the media, subtly infiltrates our thinking and results in greed, dissatisfaction, discontent—and complaining!

God's remedy is a shift in focus. *"Oh, give thanks to the Lord, for He is good!" "Giving thanks always for all things unto God." "Do all in the name of the Lord Jesus, giving thanks to God the Father through Him." (Psalm 106:1; Ephesians 5:20; Colossians 3:17).*

We must teach our children that being thankful is not an option, but rather something that pleases God, gives us joy, peace and contentment and makes other people want to be around us. That being unthankful and complaining leads to bitterness and jealousy—and can even drive people away. We must help them shift their focus to God, their loving Father and the giver of all things. *"Enter into his gates with thanksgiving and into his courts with praise, for the Lord is good and his mercy is everlasting." (Psalm 100:4-5, NKJV).*

☞ AIM:

That the children may

- Recognize that complaining is sin and does not please God.
- Respond by confessing their sin of complaining and choosing to be thankful.

📖 SCRIPTURE: Numbers 11:4–12:15

♥ MEMORY VERSE: Ephesians 5:20

Giving thanks always for all things unto God. (KJV)
Always giving thanks to God the Father for everything. (NIV)

📁 MATERIALS TO GATHER

Memory verse visual for Ephesians 5:20
Backgrounds: Review Chart, Plain Background, General Outdoor
Figures: R1-R14, 7, 24(4), 25, 32, 46, 49, 50(3), 51, 52, 61, 62, 89
Token holders & memory verse tokens for Ephesians 5:20
Bible Study Helps for Lesson 14, Part One
Special:
- *For Introduction:* A snack of some food the children probably would not enjoy
- *For Bible Content 1:* Word strips GENESIS, EXODUS, LEVITICUS, NUMBERS
- *For Bible Content 2:* Chart of Tabernacle Design
- *For Application:* Newsprint & marker or chalkboard & chalk
- *For Response Activity:* "My Thank You List" handouts, pencils
- *For Options:* Materials for any options you choose to use
- *Note: Follow the instructions on page xii to prepare the word strips and the "My Thank You List" handouts, (pattern P-10 on page 173).*

💼 REVIEW CHART

Display the Review Chart with R1-R12 in place and R14 ◰(1) in God's Supply Room. Review the Lesson 13 theme and memory verse as you place R-13 on the Chart. Have a child give the meaning of the verse. Use the following questions to review Lessons 11-13:

1. I was made from gold by Aaron and the Israelites worshiped me as a god. What am I? *(The gold calf)*
2. I became so angry at my people that I broke the tablets of stone. Who am I? *(Moses)*
3. I am the only person permitted by God to go before the Ark of the Covenant in the tabernacle. Who am I? *(Aaron or the high priest)*
4. I am the place where all the animal sacrifices were made. What am I? *(The bronze—or brass—altar)*
5. I was constructed according to the plans God gave Moses so the Israelites would have a place to worship him. What am I? *(The tabernacle)*
6. I am the animal an Israelite who had sinned brought to the priest. What am I? *(A lamb or a goat)*
7. I am the place where God gave Moses the laws written on the tables of stone. What am I? *(Mount Sinai)*
8. We are the special people God chose to serve in the tabernacle along with the priests. Who are we? *(The Levites)*
9. I am what the Israelites saw over the tabernacle to remind them of God's presence. What am I? *(The pillar—or column—of cloud or fire)*

Thankfulness

10/2

14   Ephesians 5:20

◰ Note (1)

The numbers on R14 review symbol refer to the 10 spies who gave a bad report and the 2 spies who gave a good report in the story found in Lesson 14, Part Two. Raise the children's curiosity this week by saying, "This symbol has a secret code that you may not be able to decode until next week."

▲ **Option #1**

For younger children:
Provide newsprint and crayons. Encourage them to draw a picture of a time when they complained and tell the class about it.

10. We are the two things God told Moses to put into the Ark of the Covenant. What are we? *(The tablets of stone and a pot of manna)*

When was the last time you whined about something you had to do or complained because you didn't have something? *(Allow the children to share their experiences.)* Have you ever said something like: "Why do I always have to do the dishes?" or "How come she got more presents than I did?" or "We always have food I don't like; I'm not going to eat it!" ▲#1

Do you like being around people who are always complaining or whining? *(Allow for response throughout.)* Why not? That's right; because they seem to be miserable and they make you feel miserable. They never seem to see the good things they have and so they are very unthankful people.

Do you think that a whining, complaining attitude pleases God? No, it doesn't, especially since he is the one who gives us everything we have. Have you ever given someone a gift or done something special for a person who didn't even say thank you? How did you feel? Probably very sad and maybe a little angry, too. That's how God feels when his children complain and are not thankful to him.

What kind of attitude does God want us to have? Let's look in God's Supply Room to find out. *(Have a child remove R14 from God's Supply Room, read it aloud, and place it on the Chart.)* Yes, it is *Thankfulness* or being thankful. What does it mean to be thankful? That's right; it means to be grateful or glad for something, to appreciate it, to say thank you.

♥ **MEMORY VERSE**

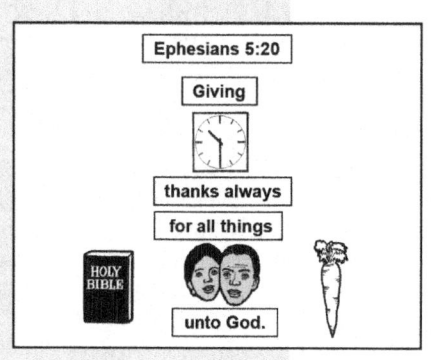

Use the visual to teach Ephesians 5:20 when indicated.
Let's look at today's verse to see what God says about this. *(Display the reference and the first two visual pieces; allow for response throughout.)* When are we to give thanks? Yes, we are to give thanks always! And what are we to give thanks for? *(Display the remaining visual pieces.)* That's right; for all things—for the things we have and the things that happen to us. And to whom are we to give our thanks? Yes, we are to give thanks to God.

Sometimes it's difficult to be thankful when we see others getting more than we have or another person making the team when we don't. But God wants us to understand that he loves us. He has a special plan for each of us and that plan is good. He knows exactly what we need because he loves us more than anyone else loves us. God's plan does not always include everything we want, but it does include what he knows is best for us. The Bible tells us that God wants us to trust him and be thankful for what he has done. God will help us to do that. *(Work on memorizing the verse.)* ▲#2

📖 BIBLE LESSON OUTLINE

The People Complain About Manna

■ Introduction
Being unthankful

■ Bible Content
1. Moses counts the people.
2. The people complain about the manna.
3. Miriam and Aaron complain against Moses.

■ Conclusion

Summary

Application
Recognizing that complaining is sin against God

Response Activity
Confessing sin of complaining and choosing to be thankful

📖 BIBLE LESSON

■ Introduction

Being unthankful

(A snack that children will not enjoy)
Are any of you hungry? I thought you might be so I brought along a snack. I hope you like it because I brought it especially for you. *(Distribute the snack and encourage the children to enjoy it. When some refuse to eat it or say they don't like it, respond accordingly. You might even prime some children ahead of time to say they dislike it and complain about it.)*

Why are you complaining about the snack? It's good for you and I brought it especially for you. *(Response)* You don't like it? You want me to give you something good to eat? Aren't you even thankful that I was thinking of you?

This is just a little example of what the children of Israel did when they did not like the food God gave them while they were traveling. Let's find out what happened to them and how they learned to be thankful.

▲ Option #2

Memorizing the verse: Have the children, one at a time, remove one piece of the verse and place it on the table as another child says the verse without the missing piece(s). Continue until all pieces have been removed and scattered on the table. Them have children who have not had a turn, one at a time, take a piece from the table and return it to its proper place on the board as the class repeats the verse. Finally, remove all the pieces and say the verse together again.

To help with choosing children for turns, ask for those who are wearing a certain color, or had homework for school or like peanut butter, etc., to volunteer for a turn.

Bible Content

1. Moses counts the people.

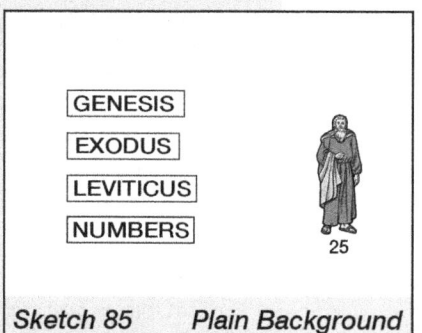

(Word strips GENESIS, EXODUS, LEVITICUS, NUMBERS; Moses 25)

What books of the Old Testament have we talked about? *(Allow for response throughout.)* That's right; Genesis, Exodus and Leviticus. *(Place GENESIS, EXODUS, LEVITICUS on the board.)* Who is the author of these books of the Bible? Yes it's Moses *(add 25).* He wrote exactly what God wanted him to say.

Today we are going to look at another book that Moses wrote, the fourth book of the Old Testament, the book of Numbers *(add NUMBERS).* Find Numbers, chapter 11, in your Bible and place your bookmark there.

This book is called Numbers because it tells how Moses and the other leaders counted all the people so they would know how many there were in each tribe. They counted them when they left Egypt (chapter 1) and they counted them again just before they entered the land God promised them (chapter 26). They were doing what we do today when we take a census to count how many people are living in our country. ▲#3

God told Moses to write down the names of all the men who were 20 years old or older because they would serve in the army and fight against their enemies. The total number of these men was 600,000. The only ones not counted as soldiers were the Levites whom God had chosen to serve him in the tabernacle.

Numbers is also called the book of murmuring or complaining. Let's see if we can find out why it got that name and how God worked to teach his people an important lesson—that a complaining and unthankful attitude is sin and doesn't please him. ▲#4

2. The people complain about the manna. (Numbers 11:4-34)

(Tents 61, 62, people 35, sheep 24[4], Moses 25; Chart of Tabernacle Design)

The Israelites had been camped at Mount Sinai for a whole year while God gave them their laws and they built the tabernacle. One morning they came out of their tents and saw that the cloud had lifted from the tabernacle. Do you remember what that meant? Yes, it was time to move on. So they packed their tents and all their belongings. And the priests and the Levites—according to God's special directions—took the tabernacle down and got it ready to move. Then they all moved out in the order God had given them, each tribe carrying its own banner or flag. What a sight that must have been!

Sketch 85   Plain Background

▲ **Option #3**

After introducing Numbers, review the first four books of the Old Testament, using the word strips and the method from the Option #2.

▲ **Option #4**

Word definition card:
Numbers = Book of murmuring or complaining.

Sketch 86   General Outdoor

They followed the pillar of cloud for three days, stopping to rest at night. Finally the cloud stopped where they were to set up their next camp. *(Place 61, 62, 35, 24[4] on the board; review the camp setup using the Chart of Tabernacle Design.)*

God continued to provide manna each day. *(Review with children what the manna was, using coriander seeds and honey to help them recall what it looked and tasted like. See Lesson 8.)* Every morning they gathered just enough for their family for that day. What did they do on the sixth day, the day before the Sabbath? *(Response)* That's right; they gathered enough for two days because God did not send any on the seventh day, which was the Sabbath—a day of rest.

The people were never hungry because God gave them all the manna they needed. Read Numbers 11:8 to see how they ate it. *(Wait for response.)* That's right; they ground it up and cooked it in a pot or else made it into loaves.

***   ▲#5

After a while, some of the people began to long for the food they had in Egypt. They started to complain. Their neighbors heard them and began to complain as well. Soon the whole camp was complaining. Moses *(add 25)* heard it and went out to see what the problem was. Read verse 10 to see what he found. *(Response)*

The people were standing at their tent doors wailing, "If only we had some meat to eat! Or some fish! Or some onions and garlic and cucumbers and melons like we had in Egypt! We're sick of this manna!" Instead of remembering how God had provided all they needed, they blamed him for not giving them what they wanted.

Moses heard their complaints and so did God. Look at verse ten again to see how they felt about it. *(Response)* Yes, God was very angry and Moses was displeased or troubled. He must have felt sad and discouraged, for he said to God: "Why have you brought all this trouble on me? Where can I get enough meat for all these people? I can't keep on taking care of them all by myself. It's too much for any man! If this is the way it's going to be, just let me die right now!"

God understood and said to Moses, "Choose 70 men who are leaders. I will give them special abilities and a real concern for the people so they will be able to help you watch over them." Moses was very thankful and he chose the men right away.

Then the Lord told Moses to say to the people: "Get ready, because tomorrow you will eat meat. The Lord heard you complain. He will give you meat and you will eat it, not just for one day or two or ten or twenty, but every day for a month until you are sick of it!"

"But Lord," said Moses, "where can we get enough meat for all those people to eat every day for a month? It wouldn't be enough if we killed all our flocks and herds and caught all the fish in the sea!"

But God said, "Do you really think I can't do what I promise? Just watch and see what I will do." So Moses went out and told the people what God had said. *(Remove all the figures.)*

▲ **Option #5**

Have the children pantomime the action as you read aloud the part of the story that is set apart by asterisks (***). Or, make copies of this section and have the children read and act out the parts.

Sketch 87 General Outdoor

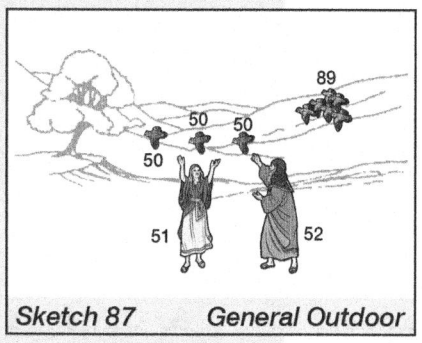

▲ Option #6
Mural Scene.

(Quail 50[3], 89, girl 51, man 52)
God sent a strong wind from the sea. It blew for two days and a night. Soon large flocks of quail *(place 50[3], 89 on the board)* appeared in the sky. They were flying so low that the people could easily catch and kill them *(add 51, 52)*. ▲#6

How exciting! The people caught birds until every family had bushels of them piled around their tents. They cooked quail and ate quail and then spread the leftover meat in the hot sun to dry so it would not spoil and they could eat it as they traveled. God had kept his word!

***

But the people's complaining and unthankful attitude was sin. They didn't appreciate what God had done for them, so he had to discipline them. As they ate the meat they had wanted so much, God sent a terrible sickness and many died because they had complained against God. God wanted his people to trust him, to believe what he said and to be thankful for what he gave them instead of complaining about what they did not have. He also wanted them to know that he disciplines his people when they sin.

3. Miriam and Aaron complain against Moses. (Numbers 12:1-15)

Sketch 88 Plain Background

(Aaron 32, Miriam 7, Moses 25, tabernacle 74, cloud 46)
You would think that the people would have learned that lesson, but Aaron and Miriam *(place 32, 7 on the board)* began to talk against Moses—their own brother! They said things like "Why should Moses be the leader? Hasn't God spoken through us as well? Why is he so special?" Sometimes brothers and sisters are jealous of one another, but Aaron and Miriam should have known better.

In Numbers 12:3 we read that Moses *(add 25)* was a very humble man. He didn't say anything to defend himself when his brother and sister talked against him. But God heard everything they said and he was angry. Suddenly he commanded all three of them to come to the tabernacle *(add 74)*. Then he came down in the pillar of cloud *(add 46)*, and said to Miriam and Aaron, "Why were you not afraid to speak against my servant Moses? He is faithful in everything he does and I tell him very clearly what I am going to do." Then the pillar of cloud moved away from them.

When Moses and Aaron looked at Miriam, they could hardly believe what they saw. Her skin had turned as white as snow! She had leprosy, a dreaded skin disease that makes people lose feeling in their hands and feet. Sometimes they hurt themselves and don't even know it. Sometimes parts of their body—like ears and nose and finger tips—fall off. According to God's rules she would have to live by herself outside the camp away from everyone else for the rest of her life, unless somehow, she was cured. This was terrible!

When Aaron saw this, he turned to Moses and said, "We have sinned and done a foolish thing. Please forgive us and please don't leave Miriam like this." He knew that he was guilty, too. God had chosen Miriam to teach everyone a serious and important lesson. So Moses prayed and asked God to heal Miriam.

"Yes," said God, "I will heal her, but because of her sin she must live outside the camp for seven days." And that's what happened. Miriam was shut out of the camp alone for a week. She must have thought a lot about what she had done. Probably Aaron and the people did, too. Maybe this time they would learn the lesson that God hates complaining. We can also learn from this that God is good and forgives believers when we confess our sins and begin living for him again. *(Remove all the figures.)* (2)

■ Conclusion

Summary

(People 35, quail 50[3], Miriam 7, Aaron 32)
What a sad lesson! God had to discipline his people. They were not thankful, and continually complained.

Why did God's people complain? *(Place 35 on the board; encourage response throughout.)* That's right; they were tired of eating manna every day. They wanted meat and some of the foods from Egypt. What happened when God sent the quail *(add 50[3])*? Yes, God sent a terrible sickness and many of them died. They did not trust God. They didn't believe that he would always do what was best for them. God wanted them to remember to trust him and thank him in the future.

Did they have anything to be thankful for? What? *(Discuss each item as it is mentioned. If necessary, suggest something like: God's protecting them as they traveled, providing food and water to keep them alive and healthy, or leading them in the right direction, etc.)* ▲#7

Were Miriam and Aaron *(add 7, 32)* trusting God when they complained because Moses was the leader instead of them? No, they weren't. Did they have anything to be thankful for? What? *(Response)* God had made Moses a great leader and given him wisdom and strength. He had allowed Aaron to help Moses by being High Priest and by encouraging the people to obey God. God was keeping his promises by leading them and giving them all they needed.

What did God do about their sin? *(Response)* He called them to the tabernacle and told them how wrong they were. Then he made Miriam sick with leprosy and she had to stay outside the camp for seven days.

◮ Note (2)

It appears that God chose to use Miriam as an object lesson to Moses, Aaron and all the people. Aaron was probably spared (though guilty) because he was the high priest and any deformity or affliction would have disqualified him.

Sketch 89   Plain Background

▲ Option #7

List responses on newsprint or chalkboard.

L-14-1

Application

Thankful	Unthankful
1.	1.
2.	2.

Sketch 90 — Chalkboard

(Newsprint & marker or chalkboard & chalk)
Print two column headings on newsprint or chalkboard: THANKFUL and UNTHANKFUL.

Do you ever whine or complain? Let's make a list of some of the things you complain about or find it hard to be thankful for. *(Print children's responses under UNTHANKFUL. If necessary, suggest food, clothing, mother's help, dad's hard work, sunshine, or good health.)* It's easy to not be thankful for things we have all the time and take for granted. It's easy to forget that God has given us all these things and wants us to trust him to take care of us in the future, too.

It's also easy to complain about things you do not have. What are some of those things? *(Add responses to this list; if necessary, suggest things such as a place on a team, a special honor, a popular toy or a pair of shoes.)*

Did you know that when you complain about things like this, you are sinning against God? You are really telling him that he is not taking care of you properly! What does our memory verse tell us we should do? *(Response)* Yes, we should always give thanks. Let's say our verse together. *(Do so.)*

God loves us and promises to supply all our needs. He wants us to be thankful for all he has given to us and trust him to provide all we need. Let's think about the THANKFUL part of our list. What are you thankful for today? *(Help them think about all they should be thankful for, and add their responses to the list.)* Let's stop and pray right now, thanking God for all he has done for us.

Response Activity

Distribute **"My Thank You List" handouts** and pencils. Have the children print on their handouts something they know they have complained about or have not been thankful for. Give them time to silently ask God to forgive them and help them be thankful instead during the coming week. Then have the children list three things for which they are thankful. Allow all who want to express thanks to pray aloud.

Encourage the children to use their handout as a reminder to give thanks daily or to ask God to help them be thankful. Give them opportunity next week to tell how God helped them. Close in a prayer of thanksgiving for all who are in the class.

✍ TAKE HOME ITEMS

Distribute **memory verse tokens for Ephesians 5:20** and **Bible Study Helps for Lesson 14, Part One.**.

Israel Fails to Trust God
Theme: *Thankfulness*

Part Two: The People Turn Back

Lesson 14

❃ BEFORE YOU BEGIN…

Your children will probably agree that no one likes a complainer! Yet how often we complain and grumble about what we do not have or when we find ourselves in a difficult situation. The Israelites did just that at Kadesh-Barnea. Their fearful complaining caused them to lose sight of God's goodness and faithful care, to refuse to trust God to keep his promises—and to suffer grave consequences.

It's much easier to complain when things don't go our way than to trust God to work out his good plan for us. We seldom stop to think that complaining and an unthankful attitude lead directly to anger and rebellion. That our thoughtless complaining can lead to severe consequences. Help your children to understand this and to recognize that their complaining is sin that they need to confess. Encourage them to ask God to help them focus on his goodness instead of on what they're unhappy about. And make it your goal to set a good example! *"I will bless the Lord at all times; His praise shall continually be in my mouth" (Psalm 34:1, NKJV).*

☞ AIM:

That the children may

- Know that refusing to trust God is sin.
- Respond by thanking God that He is trustworthy and trusting him for a specific need or situation.

📖 SCRIPTURE: Numbers 13–14; 20:1-13; Deuteronomy 1:19-46.

♥ MEMORY VERSE: Ephesians 5:20

Giving thanks always for all things unto God. (KJV)
Always giving thanks to God the Father for everything. (NIV)

📁 MATERIALS TO GATHER

Memory verse visual for Ephesians 5:20
Backgrounds: Review Chart, Plain Background Plain with Tree, Wilderness,
Figures: R1-R14, 21, 22, 25, 31, 32, 34, 35, 36, 55, 56, 61, 62, 63, 72, 90, 93
Token holders and memory verse tokens for Ephesians 5:20
Bible Study Helps for Lesson 14, Part Two
Special:
- **For Introduction:** Newsprint & marker or chalkboard & chalk
- **For Bible Content 1:** Wilderness Map
- **For Summary:** Word strips FEAR, GIANTS, CITIES, 40 YEARS, COMPLAINTS, ANGER, NOT ENTER LAND, SIN
- **For Application:** List made during Introduction
- **For Response Activity:** "I Will Trust God" handouts, pencils
- **For Options:** Materials for any options you choose to use
- **Note:** Follow the instructions on page xii to prepare the word strips and the "I Will Trust God" handouts, (pattern P-11 on page 174.

💼 REVIEW CHART

Display the Review Chart with R1-R14 scattered across the bottom of the Chart. Review the lesson themes with the children. Have the children say each verse, give its meaning, and place the corresponding review symbol on the Chart as you progress.

Ask for volunteers to pretend to be one of the Bible characters listed below as the children use the following questions (or ones they make up themselves) to interview them.

Moses:
1. How did you feel when the people began complaining? *(Sad and angry; not wanting to lead them anymore)*
2. Why did God send the quail to the Israelites? *(Because they had complained that they had no meat to eat.)*
3. What did God do when you needed help dealing with the people? *(He had me bring 70 leaders to the tabernacle where he gave them the spirit they needed to help lead the people.)*
4. How did God show you that he loved you and had chosen you to lead his people when Miriam and Aaron rebelled? *(He spoke to us from the pillar of cloud, calling me his faithful servant and saying that he tells me his will clearly.)*

▲ Option #1

Verse Relay:
Before class: Print the verse and reference on a sheet of paper in a way that you can cut the words and reference into separate pieces like a puzzle. Make a copy for each team you will have in your class (probably two or four, depending on the size of your group). Cut each sheet into pieces and put each set of pieces into an envelope, one for each team.

Thankfulness
10 / 2
14   Ephesians 5:20

In class: Divide the group into equal teams. Designate one child who can say the verse on each team to be "verse checker." Have the teams line up one person behind the other at one end of the room with their verse checker holding their envelope and facing them at the opposite end of the room.

continued on page 141

Israelites:
1. Why did you want to go back to Egypt? *(We were tired of the manna and missed the meat and other food we had there.)*
2. Why was God angry with you? *(Because we complained about the manna he supplied)*
3. What did God do about your complaints? *(He gave us so much meat that we got sick of it; he also sent an illness that caused some of us to die.)*

Aaron and/or Miriam:
1. Why did you complain and rebel against your brother? *(Because we were jealous.)*
2. Why were you jealous? *(Because God chose Moses and spoke through him and everyone thought he was special. After all, God had spoken through us, too!)*
3. How did God punish you? *(Miriam got leprosy and had to stay outside the camp for a week.)*
4. What lesson did you learn? *(God hates the sin of complaining and wants us to confess it.)*

♥ MEMORY VERSE

Use the visual to review Ephesians 5:20 and its meaning. ▲#1

continued from page 140

Explain the rules: At the signal, the first person on each team runs to their "checker," takes the envelope, empties it on the floor or a chair and puts the pieces in correct order. If the verse checker says it's right, the child runs back and tags the next person in line while the verse checker is gathering up the puzzle pieces and putting them back into the envelope. The next child in line then repeats the process. The team whose members all complete the puzzle correctly and then recite the verse together is the winner.

📖 BIBLE LESSON OUTLINE

The People Turn Back

■ **Introduction**

Have you been afraid to trust God?

■ **Bible Content**
1. Moses sends spies into Canaan.
2. The spies give their report.
3. The people refuse to trust God.
4. God judges the people.
5. Moses strikes the rock.

■ **Conclusion**

Summary

Application
Thanking God shows your trust in him

Response Activity
Thanking God to show your trust in him

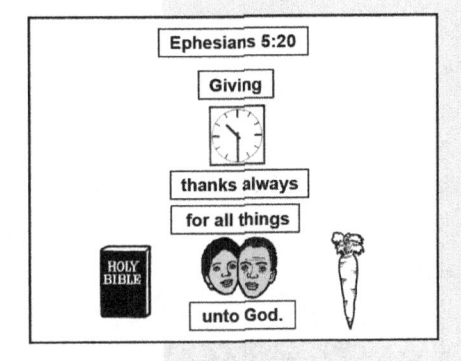

📖 BIBLE LESSON

■ Introduction

Have you been afraid to trust God?

(Newsprint & marker or chalkboard & chalk)
Have you ever been afraid to trust God to help you do something that was hard for you to do? What was it? *(Encourage children to share some of their experiences; list briefly on newsprint or chalkboard. If necessary, suggest something like: Saying no when friends wanted you to do wrong; standing up for someone others were making fun of; trusting God to provide something you needed when you had no money for it; witnessing about Jesus to someone on the playground.)* Why were you afraid? *(Discuss reasons with the children.)* Perhaps because of what other people might do or say? Or because you weren't sure that God would help you or provide for you? ▲#2

Sometimes it's easy to say that we trust God, but hard to really do it when we are faced with a hard situation. God's people—even Moses—had that problem, too. Listen to find out what happened when they failed to trust God in the wilderness. Find Numbers, chapter 13, in your Bible and place your bookmark there.

▲ **Option #2**

Put the children in pairs and have them act out a situation where they were afraid to trust God to help them. Have the rest of the class discuss what they could have done to show they were trusting God.

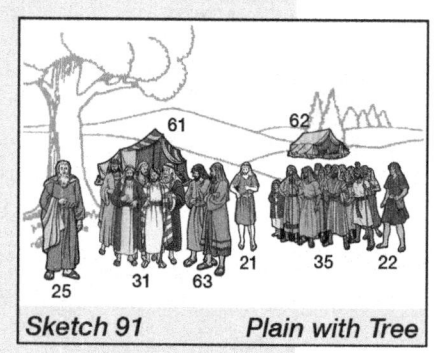

■ Bible Content

**1. Moses sends spies into Canaan.
   (Numbers 13:1-25; Deuteronomy 1:19-24)**

(Tents 61, 62, Moses 25, people 31, 35, spies; 21, 22, 63; Wilderness Map)
Place 61, 62, 25, 31, 35 on the board.
When Miriam was well and able to return to the camp, God led the Israelites on to a place called Kadesh in the wilderness of Zin *(indicate on the map)*. This place was not far from the land of Canaan which was going to be their new home. Do you think they were excited because they were finally so close to the land God had been promising for so many years?

Moses said to the people, "Look! There is the land the Lord your God has given you. Let's go up and take possession of it as he told us to. Don't be afraid and don't be discouraged."

But the people were afraid. They didn't know what the land was like or what kind of people lived there. Once again they forgot to trust God for courage and strength to do what he told them to do. Instead, they said to Moses, "Let's send some men to spy out the land. Then they can tell us what route to take and what the land is like and how big the towns are."

God told Moses to choose 12 men *(add 21, 22, 63)*, one from each of the tribes, to go into Canaan. God was patient with his people. He wanted them to recognize that he could give them this new country.

Sketch 91   Plain with Tree

Moses obeyed the Lord and sent the men on their way. *(Remove 21, 22, 63.)*

The spies spent 40 days (almost six weeks) looking over the territory that God had chosen. They saw that it was very good for growing fruits and vegetables and they carried some fruit back to prove it—figs and pomegranates and a bunch of grapes so big and heavy that it took two of them to carry it hanging from a pole across their shoulders! ▲#3

They also discovered that many of the people were very big and strong and lived in cities protected by thick walls. *(Leave all the figures on the board; move 25 and 31 to the right.)*

2. The spies give their report.
(Numbers 13:26-33; Deuteronomy 1:25)

(Men with grapes 90, Caleb 36)
When the spies *(add 90)* came back to the camp, Moses and the people gathered to hear their report. Read Numbers 13:27 to see what they said. *(Wait for response.)* They told how good the land was for growing things and for grazing their animals and showed all the fruit they had brought back with them. Maybe some of the people even got to taste it! How thrilling it must have been to hear about the good land God was giving them!

Then what did they say? Read verse 28. *(Wait for response.)* That's right; the spies said, "But...the people who live in the land are big and strong and so tall that they looked like giants to us. We felt as small as grasshoppers beside them. And the cities they live in are just as big and strong! They have high thick walls all around them." That didn't sound so good, and the people began to murmur to themselves.

Then Caleb *(add 36)*, one of the spies, stood and waited for them to be quiet. "We should go up and take this land for our own," he said, "for we can surely do it! We are God's chosen people!"

But ten of the spies said, "We can't attack those people! They are bigger and stronger than we are. We will never win a battle against them!" Because of what they said the people were scared and upset. They didn't believe God and they weren't grateful for what he had done for them.

Then Moses spoke to them: "Don't be afraid! The Lord your God is going ahead of you and he will fight for you, just like he did in Egypt. He will take care of you, just like he did in the desert. He has brought you safely all this way and he will give you the land just as he promised!"
◪(1) *(Remove 90.)*

3. The people refuse to trust God.
(Numbers 14:1-10a; Deuteronomy 1:26-32)

(Aaron 32, Joshua 72)
But during the night the people began to cry and grumble and complain: "We should have died in Egypt or in the desert. Why go into

---

▲ **Option #3**

Mural scene.

◪ **Note (1)**

God's command to the Israelites that they should destroy the Canaanites may seem extreme to us, but careful examination of Leviticus 18, where God lists their abominable practices, points out the utter degradation of their

Sketch 92   Plain with Tree

morality. Archaeological discoveries have confirmed this. While they had at one time a quite advanced civilization, it had by this time become decadent and ripe for destruction. In the name of their many gods, they practiced child sacrifice by burning, child prostitution, cultic worship and all sorts of depraved sexual perversions. Their extreme corruption and the danger they represented to the Israelites' worship of the one true God mandated their destruction.

Sketch 93 Plain with Tree

this land to be killed by the sword and have our wives and children taken captive? We should choose a new leader and go back to Egypt."

When Moses *(indicate 25)* and Aaron *(add 32)* heard that, they fell on their faces in front of all the people. *(Place 25, 32 in a prostrate position, then move them to the left side of the board.)* Caleb *(indicate 36)* and Joshua *(add 72)*, another spy who was also Moses' assistant, bravely faced the people and said, "The land we explored is a very good land! If we trust the Lord and he is pleased with us, he will give it to us. Don't rebel against him and don't be afraid of the people. The Lord is with us! With his help we will swallow them up."

What could the people have done to show that they did trust God? *(Response)* They could have said, "Moses is right! God has always helped us and taken care of us. Remember the Red Sea? And the manna? And the water? And how he gave us victory over the Amalekites? Forgive us, Lord, for doubting and complaining. Thank you for all you have done. We will trust you and go to the new land."

But they did not. They wouldn't listen to Joshua and Caleb. Instead, they threatened to stone them to death! *(Leave all the figures on the board.)*

4. God judges the people.
(Numbers 14:10b-45; Deuteronomy 1:32-46)

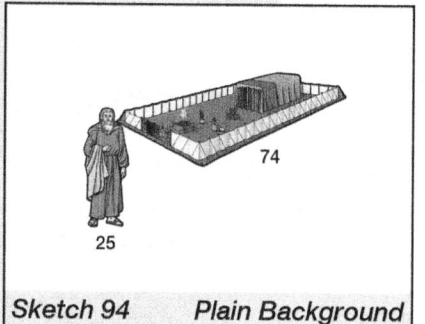

(Tabernacle 74, Moses 25)

God saw the people and heard everything they said. Suddenly he appeared outside the tabernacle *(place 74 on the board)* in a bright light that all the people could see. "How long," he asked Moses, *(add 25)* "will these people reject me and refuse to believe me despite all the miracles I have done for them? I will destroy them and make your family into a new nation greater and stronger than they."

"But Lord," pleaded Moses, "if you do that the Egyptians will hear about it and say you were not strong enough to take your people into the land. Please forgive them."

Sketch 94 Plain Background

"All right," answered God. "I will forgive them, but you must tell them this; 'Because you complained against me and refused to believe me, you will wander in this wilderness for 40 years—one year for each day the spies were in the land! Everyone who is 20 years old or older will die in this wilderness. But Caleb and Joshua and your children—the ones you said would be taken captive there—will live in the land I promised to give you.'" Then God sent a terrible sickness on the ten spies who gave the bad report and they all died.

When Moses told all this to the people, they began to mourn and cry. The next morning they got up early and said to Moses, "We have sinned. We will do what God said now and go into the land." They didn't ask God to forgive them. They weren't sorry they had sinned. They were sorry only because they were being punished.

"Don't go," said Moses, "because the Lord is not with you and will not help you. Your enemies will defeat you."

But the people went up to the land anyway, and were soon driven back by enemy soldiers. They still had not learned to believe God and trust him. And so they began 40 years of wandering in the wilderness.

5. **Moses strikes the rock.**
   (Numbers 20:1-13)

(Rock 55, people 35, Moses 25, rod 34, Aaron 32, water 56, people drinking 93)
Place 55 on the board.

There were many rocks, snakes and scorpions in this wilderness, but little water (Deuteronomy 8:15). One day the Israelites *(add 35, 25, 34, 32)* came again to Kadesh. There had been water when they were there before, but now they could find none for themselves or their animals.

Immediately the people began to complain and blame Moses and Aaron. "Why have you brought us into this terrible place to die? There is no grain or fruit or even water to drink! We wish we were dead!" It was so easy to forget that they were in the wilderness because they had refused to believe God and obey him, not because God had planned from the beginning for them to be there!

Moses and Aaron went to the tabernacle and fell on their faces before the Lord. God said to Moses: "Take your rod and gather the people together. Speak to the rock that is in front of them, and water will pour out of it, enough for all the people and animals to drink."

So Moses and Aaron called the people together and stood in front of the rock before them. Moses had always obeyed God, but this time something happened. Perhaps he was angry and frustrated with the people. Maybe he was just tired of all the problems. Whatever the reason, he spoke to the people instead of the rock: "Listen, you rebels; must we bring water out of the rock for you?" Then he raised his rod and hit the rock twice! At once the water *(add 56)* came gushing out in a great stream, so both people *(add 93)* and animals could have all they wanted. ▲#4

God provided the water for the people, but he was not pleased with Moses. Why was God unhappy with him? *(Response)* Yes, instead of speaking to the rock, he lost his temper and hit the rock twice with his rod. He disobeyed God; he didn't trust God.

What could Moses have done that day to show that he trusted God despite the things the people said and the way they behaved? *(Response)* He could have stopped to talk to God and say, "I thank you that you always keep your promises and you have always helped me, even when these people were so frustrating! I thank you that you will provide all the water we need for all these people and all their animals. Help me to trust you and obey you." And then he could have spoken to the rock as God had commanded. Remember our memory verse? Let's say it

Sketch 95 — Wilderness

▲ **Option #4**

Mural scene.

together. *(Do so.)* You see, stopping to thank God in the middle of a hard situation reminds us that God is in charge and will keep his promises.

But Moses didn't do that. And just as God had to punish the Israelites when they would not trust him, he now had to punish Moses and Aaron. The Lord said to them, "Because you have done this and have not trusted me, you cannot lead the people into the good land. you will both die here in the desert."

Moses was one of the greatest men who ever lived. God talked with him face to face as to a friend. The Bible tell us of just this one time when he did not obey God. Still, it was necessary for Moses and the people to understand that not trusting God was sin and that God must discipline him. It must have made Moses very sad to think he would never enter the land God had promised, but he knew he had sinned and he accepted God's discipline. As he faithfully continued to lead the Israelites day by day, he was continually reminded that his one act of disobedience had changed his life forever.

■ Conclusion

Summary

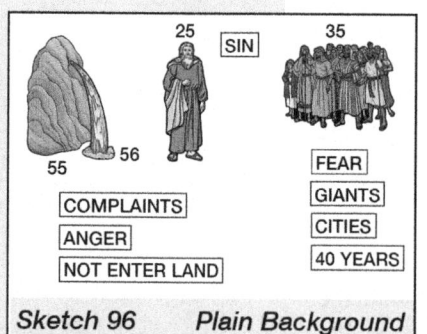

(People 35, Moses 25, rock 55, water 56; word strips FEAR, GIANTS, CITIES, 40 YEARS, COMPLAINTS, ANGER, NOT ENTER LAND, SIN)

Today we have learned about some people who failed to trust God. Who were they? *(Allow for response throughout.)* Yes, the Israelites and Moses. *(Place 35, 25, 34 on the board.)*

What did the Israelites fail to trust God for? That's right; they didn't trust him to help them take the new land from their enemies, even though he had promised he would. Why? Correct, they were afraid *(add FEAR)*. They believed the ten spies' report about giants and walled cities *(add GIANTS, CITIES)* instead of God's promises.

What happened because they would not trust God? God said they could not go into the land, but would have to wander for 40 years *(add 40 YEARS)* in the wilderness until all who had refused to trust God were dead. God continued to take care of them, but they missed out on the wonderful land and all the promises. How sad!

How did Moses fail to trust God? When the people complained *(add COMPLAINTS)* because they didn't have water to drink and blamed him and Aaron for bringing them into the desert, he lost his temper *(add ANGER)*. Instead of speaking to the rock *(add 55)* as God had told him to, he struck it twice with his staff.

What happened because Moses did not trust God? God gave the people water *(add 56)*, but said Moses and Aaron could not go into the new land *(add NOT ENTER LAND)*. That, too, was very sad.

The people and Moses all sinned *(add SIN)* by failing to trust God and they all experienced God's discipline as a result. What could they

Sketch 96   Plain Background

have done to help them trust God instead? *(Response)* Yes, they could have stopped to remember all God had done for them and the promises he had given them and said, "Thank you, we will trust you."

Application

Is it difficult for you to trust God and believe he will help you in a hard situation? Think about the things we discussed at the beginning of the lesson. *(Show the list from the Introduction.)* In these situations what do we do that shows we do *not* trust God? *(Discuss)* What could we do to show that we *do* trust God? *(Discuss. Suggest they take time to thank God because he is with them and will help them. Help them see that this will give them strength to do what is right.)*

When we don't trust God and do what he wants us to do, we too are sinning. What happens as a result? We miss out on seeing his power at work to help us and receiving the good things he wants to give us. Sometimes he disciplines us to correct us and help us remember to trust him in the future.

Is there something on this list or something in your life right now that you need to trust God for? Have you been afraid or complaining instead of thanking God that he is with you and trusting him to help you do the right thing? Let's say our memory verse together again. *(Do so.)* Will you thank God right now that he is with you and will help you in your hard situation?

If you have never believed that the Lord Jesus died for you and received him as your Savior, you can't expect God to help you when you need it and you can't know that you will go to heaven someday. The best way to show that you do trust God is to thank him for sending Jesus to die for you and receive him as your Savior.

Response Activity

Invite any who have never received Christ as Savior to come talk with you or a helper before they leave.

*Distribute the **"I Will Trust God" handouts** and pencils. Have the children print on their card one thing they will trust God to help them give thanks for. Encourage them to ask God to help them be thankful instead of complaining this week. Allow time for them to pray in class, either aloud or silently. Close the class by praying for them.*

✍ TAKE HOME ITEMS

*Distribute **memory verse tokens for Ephesians 5:20** and **Bible Study Helps for Lesson 14, Part Two**.*

Moses Makes a Brass Snake
Theme: Salvation

Lesson 15

❋ BEFORE YOU BEGIN...

The brass snake lifted up on a pole in the wilderness was a symbol of God's way of escape from death for his people. All they had to do when bitten was look at it and they would live. Those who looked, lived; those who refused, died. It was a matter of faith. What a graphic picture of how God would later send Jesus Christ into the world to be "lifted up" on a cross to take the punishment for our sin (John 3:14, 15). It is still a matter of faith.

This lesson gives you a golden opportunity to reinforce aspects of salvation that are clearly illustrated in the snake episode so that believing children can better understand the foundation points of salvation: 1) They deserve to die because of their sin; 2) Jesus took their place and bore the punishment they deserve; and 3) Accepting Jesus' death personally saves them once and for all.

As you prepare, ask the Holy Spirit to work mightily so that *every* child might clearly understand these wonderful truths, have assurance of their own salvation and a desire to follow Christ as their Master. *"These things I have written to you who believe in the name of the Son of God, that you may know that you have eternal life" (1 John 5:13, NKJV).*

☞ AIM:

That the children may

- Understand more fully the gift of salvation in Christ.
- Respond by thanking Jesus for dying for them and pledging their loving obedience to him the rest of their lives.

📖 SCRIPTURE: Numbers 20:1, 23-29; 21:4-9

♥ MEMORY VERSE: John 3:17

For God sent not his Son into the world to condemn the world; but that the world through him might be saved. (KJV)

For God did not send his Son into the world to condemn the world, but to save the world through him. (NIV)

📁 MATERIALS TO GATHER

Memory verse visual for John 3:17
Backgrounds: Review Chart, Plain Background, Wilderness
Figures: R1-R15, 10, 25, 31, 49, 61, 62, 63, 69, 95(3), 96, 102,103
Token holders & memory verse tokens for John 3:17
Bible Study Helps for lesson 15
Special:
- *For Bible Content 1:* Wilderness Map
- *For Summary:* Word strip SIN
- *For Response Activity:* "My Promise to Jesus" handouts, pencils
- *For Options:* Materials for any options you choose to use
- *Note:* Follow the instructions on page xii to prepare the word strip and the "My Promise to Jesus" handouts (pattern P-12 on page 174).

💼 REVIEW CHART

Display the Review Chart with R1-R14 in place and R15 in God's Supply Room. Use the following questions to review Lesson 14, Part 2.

1. When the spies returned from Canaan, what good things did they tell the people about the land? *(It was very good for growing fruit and vegetables.)*
2. What scary things did they say about the people and the cities? *(The people were so big that they felt like grasshoppers beside them, and the cities were large, surrounded by thick walls.)*
3. Why were the people afraid to go into the land? *(They were afraid they would be killed and their families taken captive.)*
4. What did Joshua and Caleb tell them to do? *(Go in and take the land for God would help them.)*
5. What did the people do? *(Refused to listen and talked about stoning Caleb and Joshua.)*
6. How did God discipline his people for their rebellion? *(Would not allow them to enter the promised land; instead, they had to wander in the wilderness for 40 more years.)*
7. How did Moses disobey God? *(He became angry and struck the rock instead of speaking to it.)*
8. What consequence did Moses suffer as a result? *(He was not allowed to enter the promised land.)*
9. Why did God discipline his people for complaining and being unthankful? *(Because it was sin—it showed they did not trust him and were not satisfied with what he provided for them.)*
10. What does God's word say about being thankful? *(We are to always give thanks to God.)*

In God's Supply Room we will find something very important that God wants to give to his people and to us. Let's see what it is. *(Have*

▲ **Option #1**

Definition word card: Save = to rescue.

a child take R15 from God's Supply Room and place it on the Chart.) It's *Salvation!*

We learned about this word in an earlier lesson. It means being rescued from danger. Today we will see how God rescued the Israelites from a dangerous situation. ▲#1

We will also learn how God wants to rescue or save us from sin and its punishment. Our memory verse will help us understand how he does that for us.

♥ **MEMORY VERSE**

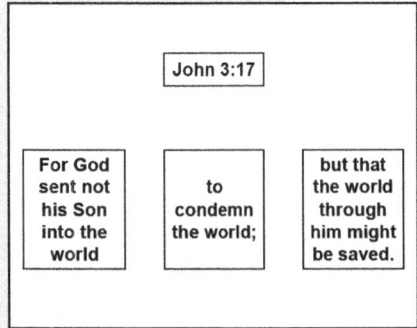

Display the visual to teach John 3:17.

As we read verse together, look for some things it tells us about God. *(Have the children read the verse aloud together; allow for response throughout.)*

John 3:17

| For God sent not his Son into the world | to condemn the world; | but that the world through him might be saved. |

What do we learn about God? Yes, God sent his Son into the world. Who can tell us what his Son was called? That's right; he was called Jesus Christ.

What else do we learn about God from this verse? He did *not* send his Son to condemn the world. Have you ever heard the word *condemn* before? *(Encourage children to tell where they have heard the word and what it means.)* This word is often used when a person is found guilty in court of breaking the law. To condemn someone is to strongly disapprove of them, to declare them guilty of doing something wrong, to give them a penalty or a punishment for that crime. The Bible tells us that everyone in the world has already been condemned or found guilty of sinning (Romans 3:23) and that the punishment for sin is death (Romans 6:23)—to be separated from God forever. ▲#2

▲ **Option #2**

Have the children locate Romans 3:23 and 6:23 in their Bibles so they can read them for themselves. Or, print the verses on poster board and display for all to see.

What is the third thing our verse tells us about God? Yes, that he sent his Son, Jesus Christ, to save—or rescue—the world from this punishment for sin. How did Jesus do that? *(Encourage response as you review Jesus' death, burial, and resurrection to pay for sin.)* Jesus was condemned to physical death on the cross; he took the punishment the world deserved. Because he is God and had never sinned, he rose from the dead, and now lives in heaven as the Savior of the world.

Did you know that this verse also contains our names—three times? Look at it carefully and see if you can recognize them. *(Allow children to try and guess where they see their names.)* That question was a little tricky. I was talking about the word "world" which really means you and me. We all can put our names there. *(Repeat the verse for the class and say your name each time "world" is mentioned.)* Let's say our verse together as it is written. *(Do so.)* Now let's say it again and put our own names in the place of the word "world" each time it occurs.

The word "world" means people—all of us here, our families and friends, our neighbors, the people in our town, the people in all the world! Jesus died for all the people of the world! When we receive him as Savior by believing in who he is and what he did for us, God forgives—or saves us from—our sin. Then we are no longer condemned, but are saved from the punishment of death (or separation from God) and made ready to live with him someday in heaven. What wonderful news! News that we can believe for ourselves and news to tell our friends and neighbors so that they, too, can be saved from their sin! How wonderful that God has provided salvation for us! *(Work on memorizing the verse.)* ▲#3

📖 BIBLE LESSON OUTLINE

Moses Makes a Brass Snake

■ **Introduction**

What does it mean to trust?

■ **Bible Content**

1. Miriam and Aaron die.
2. The people complain again.
3. The Lord sends poisonous snakes.
4. The people repent.
5. Moses makes a brass snake.

■ **Conclusion**

Summary

Application
 Understanding our salvation

Response Activity
 Thanking God for our salvation

📖 BIBLE LESSON

■ **Introduction**

What does it mean to trust?

Have you ever had to trust someone for something? Maybe to keep a promise or not to tell a secret or to help you with some homework. What were you really doing when you trusted them? *(Encourage children to share their thoughts on this.)* You were putting your faith in that person, counting on them to do what they said they would do.

Let's try a little experiment in trusting. *(Trust Fall: Before beginning, caution the class that this is a special experiment they are to do only with you, the teacher, never with each other. Ask for a volunteer who trusts you completely—a child small enough for you to catch easily—to stand at arm's length in front of you, facing away. Explain that when you reach the count of three, he is to look straight ahead, keep his knees straight and fall backward into your arms. Assure him that you will catch him.*

▲ **Option #3**

Memorizing the verse: Print each word of the verse on a separate paper plate. Scatter the plates on a table or the floor in the front of the room. Have the children come, one at a time, each choosing the plate having the next word of the verse on it. Then have them hold the plates up in front of the class so all can see if the order is correct.

When the verse has been approved, each child should give his (or her) plate to a child who is seated. At a signal from the teacher, those with plates must run to the front of the room and line up in proper order. The rest of the class can then check to see if the order is correct. Continue this until all have had a turn.

Or, scatter the plates around room and divide the class into two groups. At a signal, have one group quickly gather the plates and put them in order across the floor. Repeat with the second group. Try timing both groups to see which can do it more quickly and accurately. If time permits, repeat the game so teams can try for a better time.

As time permits, do the experiment with several children. Then discuss what you have done. Or, blindfold a child, then lead him between chairs, around tables, etc., in your classroom.)

How did [child's name] show trust? *(Response)* He fell backwards (or followed the leader) without hesitating. Why is that a difficult thing to do? *(Response)* Because you cannot see the person behind you, but must trust that he or she will catch you (or lead you right). *(If any children hesitated, discuss their responses and why it was hard to trust. Assure those children that it was all right to hesitate.)*

This little experiment can help us to understand what it is like to trust God completely. We can't see God and yet he asks us to trust him to do what he promises, even when it seems impossible! The Israelites, we have seen, had to have that kind of trust in God all during their journey. In this lesson, we find them dealing with a very dangerous situation that they had caused by their sin. They needed to decide whether they would trust God to solve the problem and save them. Find Numbers, chapter 21, in your Bible and place your bookmark there.

■ Bible Content

1. Miriam and Aaron die. (Numbers 20:1, 23–29)

(Wilderness Map)
The Israelites had been wandering in the wilderness for a long time now. Many who had rebelled and refused to go into the new land had already died. Miriam died while they were at Kadesh. Then God led them from Kadesh to Mount Hor which was near the border of Edom *(indicate on the map)*. ▲#4

Aaron died at Mount Hor and his son Eleazer took his place as high priest. The people mourned for Aaron a whole month. Moses must have missed him very much. Now he had no one to talk to or to pray with about the problems that came up.

2. The people complain again. (Numbers 21:4-6)

(Tents 61, 62, people 49, 63, 10, 31, Moses 25, snakes 95[3])

Place 61, 62 on the board.

Because so many of the older ones had died, younger men had now become the leaders of each tribe *(add 49)*. They were strong and healthy from living outdoors for so many years. They had often had to fight off enemies, so their soldiers had become skilled in using bow and arrow, swords and other kinds of weapons. God had continued to protect them and lead them, even though their parents had refused

Sketch 97   Wilderness

to obey him and go into the land. He gave them manna to eat every day and provided water for them and their animals. The Bible also tells us that their clothes never wore out and their feet never swelled from all the walking! (Deuteronomy 8:4).

From Mount Hor God led them toward the Red Sea. The people *(add 63, 10, 31)* were tired of traveling and became impatient and discouraged. Once again they began to complain and grumble against God and Moses *(add 25)*, just as their parents and grandparents had done. They said, "Why did you bring us up out of Egypt just to die in this desert? There is no bread! There is no water! And we hate this miserable manna!" *(Leave all the figures on the board.)*

3. The Lord sends poisonous snakes. (Numbers 21:6)

Read Numbers 21:6 to find out what happened when the people complained. *(Wait for response.)* What did God do? Yes, he sent poisonous (or fiery) snakes *(add 95[3])* into the camp to bite the people. What an incredible thing! Snakes do not normally gather in a place where people are living. They leave very quickly unless they are cornered. But God, who created snakes and has all power, brought them right into the camp. Many kinds of snakes lived in that desert. The Bible doesn't tell us which kind they were—only that they were poisonous and many people died. ▲#5

What a horrible time it must have been! Everywhere the people looked or moved, there was a snake ready to bite them. Probably they tried to chase them out of their tents and kill them, but many were bitten anyway and many died. What does this punishment tell us about what God thought about their complaining? *(Response)* Yes, he was disappointed that they would not trust him and he had to punish their sin. It seemed as if the Israelites just never learned their lesson. *(Leave all the figures on the board.)*

4. The people repent. (Numbers 21:7)

Now read verse seven to see what the people did. *(Wait for response.)* Yes, they came to Moses and said, "We sinned when we spoke against God and against you. Pray to the Lord that he will take the snakes away." How was that different from all the other times they had sinned by complaining? *(Response)* That's right; they admitted their sin. They had not done that before.

What did Moses do? Yes, he prayed for the people. How was Moses' action different from what he did in last week's lesson about the water and the rock? *(Response)* Moses did not get angry and disobey God this time. He was trusting God and obeying him. *(Remove 31, 49, 63, 10.)*

▲ **Option #5**

Mural scene.

5. Moses makes a brass snake. (Numbers 21:8-9)

(Brass snake 102, people 96)

When Moses prayed, God answered. However, the answer must have seemed very strange, even to Moses. Read verse eight to see what it was. *(Have one child read it aloud.)* Yes, God told Moses to make a snake out of metal and put it up on a pole so that everyone could see it. Then, whenever a person was bitten he or she could look at the snake and be healed.

Even though it seemed a strange thing to do, Moses obeyed God. He had learned how important it is to do what God tells you to do. He made a snake out of brass and put it up on a pole *(add 102)*. Then he said to all the people: "This is what God says: When you are bitten by a snake, look at the snake on the pole and you will live." ▲#6

If you had been there, what would you have thought? *(Responses)* Maybe some of the people thought that was a foolish thing to do and tried to take care of themselves. Perhaps others were afraid to go where they could see the snake or thought it was too far to go. We don't really know. All the Bible tells us is that anyone who was bitten and looked at the brass snake lived! *(Add 96.)* A mother could not look on behalf of her sick child; a father could not look on behalf of his family. Perhaps they pointed at the snake and said, "Look! Just look and you can be healed!" But everyone had to look at the snake for himself. And everyone who looked was saved from death.

■ Conclusion

Summary

(Word strip SIN; snakes 95[3], brass snake 102)

Why did God send poisonous snakes to bite the people? *(Allow for response throughout.)* Yes, they had sinned *(add SIN)* by complaining against God and Moses. Could they get rid of the snakes by themselves? No, they needed to be saved or rescued from death.

When did God begin to save them? Yes, when they admitted that they had sinned and asked Moses to pray for them. What did God tell Moses to do to help them? That's right; he was to make a metal snake *(add 102)* and put it up on a pole where everyone could see it.

Do you think it was hard for the Israelites to trust God's answer? Why? It must have seemed like a very strange thing to do—to look up at a snake on a pole to be saved from death. But when they did it, God healed them and they lived, just as he had promised! But everyone had

---

Sketch 98 — Wilderness

▲ **Option #6**

Mural scene.

Sketch 99 — Plain Background

to look for themselves. Doing what God told them to do showed that they trusted him!

Application

(Verse visual, Jesus 103, cross 69)
Just as God provided salvation for the Israelites in the wilderness, he has provided salvation for us, too. Just as they deserved to die for their sin, we all are sinners and deserve to die for our sin. They could not get rid of the snakes themselves and we cannot get rid of our sin ourselves. But God did a wonderful thing for us and we learned about it in our memory verse. What is it? *(Display the verse visual and read the words aloud together.)* Yes, God sent Jesus to save or rescue us.

Jesus *(add 103)* said that just as Moses lifted the snake up on a pole so the people could look and be saved, he was going to be lifted up on the cross *(add 69)* and die to take the punishment for our sin so we all could believe in him and be saved. Jesus did not deserve to die, but he took the punishment of death for our sin in our place. Now, when we believe that Jesus died for us and receive him as our Savior, we are saved from the punishment for our sin. God forgives us, we are born into the family of God and we receive eternal life, the kind of life that will live forever in heaven with him someday. ▲#7

Remember the little experiment we did at the beginning of our lesson? The trust fall? (Or the blindfold exercise?) Just as you trusted the teacher absolutely, you must trust God and put your faith in him alone. And then thank the Lord Jesus for dying in your place. The best way to thank him is to say to him, "I love you and will live to please you." Will you do that today?

Response Activity

Invite unsaved children to receive God's gift of salvation now.
*Distribute the **"My Promise to Jesus" handouts)** and pencils. Read over the handout with your children, pointing out the link between being thankful and showing it by loving and pleasing the Lord. Encourage them to sign their name and put the current date at the place provided. If any do not feel ready to sign their handout in class, encourage them to take it home and to do it there. Close in prayer asking God to help them to live out their intentions faithfully.*

✍ TAKE HOME ITEMS

*Distribute **memory verse tokens for John 3:17** and **Bible Study Helps for Lesson 15**.*

▲ Option #7

Object lesson: Cut out a red paper heart and print SIN on it. Cut out a red paper cross large enough to cover the word SIN; print JESUS across it and 1 John 1:9 at the bottom. As you teach, illustrate God's forgiving our sin by covering it with Jesus' cross.

Moses Goes to Heaven
Theme: Hope

Lesson 16

✿ BEFORE YOU BEGIN...

Hope is looking forward to something you really expect to happen. Without hope, people do not survive well. God's Word calls the hope we have in Christ "an anchor of the soul...sure and steadfast" (Hebrews 6:19). An anchor keeps a ship from drifting and holds it steady in a storm. John writes, *"When He is revealed, we shall be like Him...and everyone who has this hope in Him purifies himself, just as He is pure"* (1 John 3:2,3, NKJV). The confident hope that we shall someday see Christ and be like him is a sturdy anchor to hold us steady in the storms of life and a strong motivation to keep ourselves pure and obedient to God.

You and your students need this hope. It is based in our relationship with God. As you teach, trust the Holy Spirit to speak to each one according to their need so that they may go away with the settled confidence that their sin is forgiven and they belong to God's family now and forever—and that he lives in them to help them every day and will finally take them home to heaven to live with God. *"Blessed is the man who trusts in the Lord, and whose hope is the Lord"* (Jeremiah 17:7, NKJV).

☞ AIM:

That the children may

- Know that believers have hope for today and for the future because God keeps his promises.

- Respond by thanking God for the hope they have because of his promises to care for them each day of their lives and to take them to heaven someday.

📖 SCRIPTURE: Numbers 26; Deuteronomy 1:1-5; 6:4-9; 31; 32; 34

♥ MEMORY VERSE: Titus 2:13

Looking for that blessed hope, and the glorious appearing of...our Saviour Jesus Christ. (KJV)

We wait for the blessed hope – the glorious appearing of our...Savior, Jesus Christ. (NIV)

MATERIALS TO GATHER

Memory verse visual for Titus 2:13
Backgrounds: Review Chart, Plain Background, General Outdoor, Plain with Tree, Wilderness
Figures: R1-R16, 25, 31, 35, 36, 37, 46, 49, 69, 72, 74, 85, 94, 97, 98, 99(2), 103, 104
Token holders & memory verse tokens for Titus 2:13
Bible Study Helps for Lesson 16
Special:
- **For Bible Content 2:** Word strips PENTATEUCH, GENESIS, EXODUS, LEVITICUS, NUMBERS, DEUTERONOMY; "Ten Commandments" poster from Lesson 10
- **For Bible Content 4 & Summary:** Wilderness Map
- **For Application:** Newsprint & marker or chalkboard & chalk
- **For Options:** Materials for any options you choose to use
- **Note:** Follow the instructions on page xii to prepare the word strips.

REVIEW CHART

Display the Review Chart and put R1-R15 in random order on a table. Have R16 in God's Supply Room ready to use. Allow the children to take turns choosing a symbol (in whatever order they choose) and placing it on the Chart as the whole class recites the accompanying memory verse.

To review previous lessons, print the following words on small cards: Moses, high priest, tabernacle, Pharaoh, plagues, snakes, brass serpent, tables of stone, gold calf, manna, quail, giants, spies, desert, rock/water, Joshua & Caleb, grapes, 40 years. Place the cards in a bag or box. Have the children take turns removing a card from the bag or box and tell what they remember about the person, object, or place(s) written there.

Did you ever look forward to something special you knew was going to happen? What was it? *(Allow for response throughout.)* Maybe it was a special trip or a holiday or even something you had worked hard for, like making the ball team. How did the waiting make you feel? The final symbol for our Chart tells us what we need when we have to wait a long time for something special. *(Have a child take R16 from God's Supply Room and place it on the Chart.)* Yes, it is Hope.

What is hope? It is looking forward to something you really expect to happen. The Bible word for hope means happily looking forward to what God is going to do. ▲#1

The Israelites had hope! They were looking forward to entering the new land God had promised to give them. They knew that whatever God promised he would do.

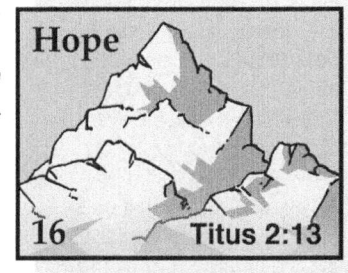

▲ **Option #1**

Definition word card: Hope = Looking forward to something you expect to happen.

▲ **Option #2**

Print Acts 1:11 on poster board for all to see and read together.

```
┌─────────────────────────────────────┐
│          Titus 2:13                 │
│                                     │
│  ┌──────────┐    ┌──────────┐      │
│  │ Looking  │    │ glorious │      │
│  │   for    │    │appearing │      │
│  │   that   │    │  of...our│      │
│  │ blessed  │    │ Saviour  │      │
│  │  hope,   │    │Jesus     │      │
│  │ and the  │    │Christ.   │      │
│  └──────────┘    └──────────┘      │
└─────────────────────────────────────┘
```

▲ **Option #3**

Memorizing the Verse: Have the children repeat the verse several times. Have different groups say it—those wearing a certain color; those who are oldest in their family, or youngest; those who have blue eyes, etc.

A variation: Starting at one side of class, have each child say one word of the verse in order, beginning with the reference. Do it first with the verse visual displayed. Then have a group of volunteers who wish to try it without the visual come to the front of the class and repeat it, one word at a time. The ones who miss their word must sit down. The object of the game is to remain standing throughout the entire verse. As time permits, allow other children to have a turn.

Our memory verse today tells us about the hope we have if we have received Jesus as our Savior.

♥ **MEMORY VERSE**

Use the visual and Jesus 103, cross 69 to teach Titus 2:13. Listen carefully to learn what the hope is as we read the verse together. *(Display the visual as you read.)* What is the hope? *(Allow for response throughout.)* Yes, it is the glorious or wonderful appearing of Jesus Christ *(add 103 beside the verse)*. We know that Jesus came to this earth many years ago. he lived a perfect life, died on a cross *(add 69 next to 103)* to take the punishment for our sins and came to life again so he could give us forgiveness and eternal life. A few weeks later his disciples saw him go up into a cloud and back to heaven to live with God the Father. They were sad, but the angels made a promise to them that is also for all of us who believe in Jesus. *(Have a child read Acts 1:11 aloud.)* ▲#2

What is the promise? Yes, that Jesus will come back to earth again the same way he went away. We know from other verses in the Bible (1 Thessalonians 4:13-18) that he will then take those who have trusted him as Savior back to heaven to be with him. He will change our bodies into the kind of bodies that can live forever in heaven! This is the blessed or wonderful hope of his glorious appearing. We do not know when it will happen—only God knows that. It may even happen before some of us die and go to be with Jesus. But we have his promise that it will happen! Because we know that God always keeps his promises, we can be sure he will come at just the right time!

Our memory verse describes this hope as blessed or happy! It will be a happy reunion when believers see Christ and are changed to be like him. Meanwhile, God wants us to live our lives to please him—to be like Christ in the way we think and act. He has given us his Word. to help us know how to do that. As we read it and obey it, we will get to know Jesus more and become more like him. The more we get to know him and become like him, the more we win look forward to seeing him and living with him forever.

Jesus' return will not be a happy event for everyone. If you know Jesus as your Savior but are living to please yourself, you will go to live with him forever in heaven, but you will feel ashamed when you meet him. Those who have not accepted Jesus as Savior will not get to see him or be with him; they will be separated from him forever.

When we have this wonderful hope, we should not get discouraged while waiting. Instead, we should live to please God so that others will want to know Jesus and be ready to meet him when he returns. *(Work on memorizing the verse.)* ▲#3

📖 BIBLE LESSON OUTLINE

Moses Goes to Heaven

▪ Introduction
Sandy's hope

▪ Bible Content
1. Moses renumbers the people.
2. Moses reviews the Law.
3. Moses appoints Joshua as the new leader.
4. Moses dies on Mount Nebo.

▪ Conclusion

Summary

Application
   Having hope in God's promises

Response Activity
   Thanking God for hope in Christ

📖 BIBLE LESSON

▪ Introduction

Sandy's hope

Sandy could hardly wait! Her dad had been away on a business trip for a long time but this weekend he would finally be coming home! Before he left, he said, "Sandy, I must go away for quite a while, but I know when I will be back. See, I have marked it in red on the calendar. I'm depending on you to work hard in school and help your mother while I'm away."

Sandy missed her dad very much, but she had real hope that he would be home again because he had promised. He sent her cards from the different countries he visited, always reminding her that he would be back.

Now that the day was almost here, Sandy was busy getting ready for his coming. She helped clean the house and even the garage! Sandy trusted her dad's word and expected to see him on Saturday, so she was looking out the window when he drove up. In great excitement she ran through the house and jumped into his waiting arms! "You came, you came. Just like you promised! I never gave up hope!"

The years in the wilderness had been difficult for the Israelites. Sometimes they must have wondered if they would ever see the land

▲ **Option #4**

Make three word strips or flashcards: 20 YEARS & OLDER, 600,000 MEN, 23,000 LEVITES.

▲ **Option #5**

To drill the first five books of the Bible, have the children remove the word strips from the board one at a time and each time repeat the books in order. Continue until all strips have been removed. Or, mix the word strips on the board and have the children put them in correct order.

Or, print the names of the books on paper plates. Hand them out to the children and have them run to the front of the room and stand in the correct order.

Sketch 100   Plain with Tree

Sketch 101   Plain Background

God had promised to give them. But they had hope because they had God's promises. In today's lesson we are going to see God doing some special things to show them that he will keep his word and take them into their new homeland.

■ **Bible Content**

1. **Moses renumbers the people. (Numbers 26)**

   (People 49, 31, Joshua 72, Caleb 36, Moses 25, high priest 85)
   The 40 years of wandering in the wilderness were almost over. All the Israelites *(place 49, 31 on the board)* who had been 20 years old or older when the people rebelled against God and refused to go into the new land God had promised had died and been buried, as God had said they would. The only ones remaining from their generation were Joshua *(add 72)* and Caleb *(add 36)*. *(If necessary and time permits, briefly review with the children the reasons for this and why Joshua and Caleb were still alive.)* The new leaders had probably been teenagers or children when God brought his people out of Egypt. It must have been very exciting to know that soon they would enter the land they had hoped to see for so long.
   God said to Moses *(add 25)*, "Count all the people so you will know how many men of this generation, 20 years old and older, will be able to serve in the army." (The last time they counted the people was before they refused to go into the land. All those men were dead now.) We can read about this in Numbers, chapter 26. ▲#4
   Moses and Eleazar *(add 85)*, the new high priest, did this while the people were camped on a plain near the Jordan River. They found there were more than 600,000 men who could be soldiers and 23,000 Levite men who took care of the tabernacle and led the people in worship.
   Counting the people also told them how many people were in each tribe so they would know how much land each tribe needed in the new land God was giving them.

2. **Moses reviews the Law (Deuteronomy 1:1-5; 6:4-9; 7-30)**

   (Moses 25; word strips PENTATEUCH, GENESIS, EXODUS, LEVITICUS, NUMBERS, DEUTERONOMY)
   Many of these Israelites had not been born or were not old enough to understand when God gave Moses *(place 25 on the board)* the Law at Mount Sinai and told him to write

it down so it would not be forgotten. We can be glad Moses obeyed, for today we can read God's law in our Bibles. Do you remember where we find it? *(Response)* Yes, in Exodus and Leviticus, the second and third books of the Old Testament. They are part of the Pentateuch *(add PENTATEUCH)*, a name for the first five books of the Old Testament. We have had lessons from the first four of these books. Let's say their names together. *(Add GENESIS, EXODUS, LEVITICUS, NUMBERS as the class repeats the words together)*

Today we will learn about the fifth book which is called Deuteronomy *(add DEUTERONOMY)*. Say that word with me. *(Help the children say the word correctly.)* Find Deuteronomy, chapter 1, in your Bible and place your bookmark there. Deuteronomy means "the Second Law." In this book Moses wrote a second time all the laws God had given his people to remind this generation of what God expected. ▲#5

(Moses 25, people 31, 35, 49; "Ten Commandments" poster) Place all the figures on the board.

One day Moses gathered all the people together on a great plain near their camp. He reviewed for them all that had happened since Israel left Egypt more than 40 years before. He probably talked a long time for there was a lot to tell! He reminded them of the times their fathers had sinned and how God had punished them, as well as how he had protected them and led them through the wilderness and kept their clothes from wearing out and given them food every day!

Moses also explained the law of God (Exodus 20) and begged the people to always obey it and never turn away from God. If they would obey God, he would bless them and make them successful in their new homeland. But if they turned away from him, God would turn away from them and allow their enemies to conquer them. *(Remove all the figures.)* ▲#6

Sketch 102   Plain with Tree

(Man 36, boy 37, stones 97)

Moses said, "Be sure to teach your children *(place 36, 37 on the board)* to fear God and obey his law." *(As time permits, have children look in Deuteronomy 6:7-9 for the ways they were to do this. For example, talk about it when sitting in your house, walking outside, going to bed or getting up. List responses on newsprint or print a list ahead of time and review it as the children read through the Bible passage.)*

He also told them to write parts of the law on large stones *(add 97)* and place them throughout the land so that all who passed by could read them and be reminded of the law of Israel's God. ▲#7

Moses wrote down all the words in Deuteronomy and the other four books of the Pentateuch, but they were God's words. Often we read,

Sketch 103   Plain with Tree

▲ **Option #6**

Display the Ten Commandments poster from Lesson 10.

Use the drawings the children made in Lesson 10 to review how we can obey the Ten Commandments.

Or, as time permits, have the children take turns acting out (in short skits or pantomimes) how they could obey a command. Have the others guess which command they are showing.

▲ **Option #7**

Wash a large stone and use a marker or paint to print one of the commands on it.

"And the Lord spoke to Moses saying..." Through the commands and promises written there God gave his people instructions about how to live and the hope that he would always be there to help them in any situation as long as they obeyed and honored him. *(Remove all the figures.)*

3. Moses appoints Joshua as the new leader. (Numbers 27:12-23; Deuteronomy 31; 34:9)

(Moses 25, Joshua 72, people 31, 35, 49)

Do you suppose that Moses *(place 25 on the board)* felt sad as he was preparing the people to enter the new land? Why would he feel that way? *(Response)* Yes, he knew he would not go into the land with them. Who can tell me why Moses could not go into the land? *(Response)* That's right; he disobeyed God by striking the rock instead of speaking to it as God had commanded.

Moses knew the people would need a new leader, so he prayed: "Please, Lord, appoint a man to lead these people so they won't be scattered and not know what to do."

The Lord said, "Lay your hands on Joshua before the priest and the people. Appoint him to be the new leader."

Moses obeyed. He called all the people *(add 72, 31, 35, 49)* together and said: "I am now 120 years old and can no longer lead you because the Lord said I cannot go into the land. The Lord himself will go ahead of you. He will destroy your enemies and you will take possession of the land. Joshua will be your leader. Don't be afraid, for the Lord God will never leave you." *(Have children look up Deuteronomy 31:6 and read it aloud.)* ▲#8

Then Moses laid his hands on Joshua's head to show that Joshua was being set apart to be the new leader. To Joshua he said, "Be strong and courageous. God has chosen you to lead these people into the land he promised to their forefathers long ago and to divide the land among them. He will go with you and never leave you. Do not be afraid or discouraged." *(Have the children read verses 7 and 8.)*

(Tabernacle 74, Moses 25, Joshua 72, cloud 46)
Place 74 on the board.

Then the Lord called Moses and Joshua *(add 25, 72)* to the tabernacle. There he came down in the pillar of cloud *(add 46)* to talk with them. He said to Moses, "You will soon die and Joshua will become the new leader. The people will disobey me after you are gone, just as they did while you were leading them. Write down this song and teach it to the

---

Sketch 104 — Plain with Tree

▲ **Option #8**

To bring Deuteronomy 31:1-8 to life, choose children to take the Parts of the people, Moses, Joshua and a narrator. Have the narrator read the dialogue directly from Scripture as the children pantomime their parts.

Sketch 105 — Plain Background

162   L-16

people. Singing it will remind them of my greatness—how I have taken care of them and provided for them—and of how important it is for them to obey me. Tell them that I will punish those who disobey." We can read Moses' song in Deuteronomy 32. *(As time permits, have the children turn to the chapter and read selected verses together.)* ▲#9

So Moses taught the people to sing the song. Then he said, "Remember all the words I have spoken to you today. Teach your children to live according to God's teaching. If you do this you will live long in the land God is giving you." Then he raised his hands and prayed for God to bless each of the twelve tribes.

4. Moses dies on Mount Nebo (Deuteronomy 32:48-52; 34:1-8)

(Moses 94, Wilderness Map)
Then God said to Moses *(place 94 on the board)*, "Go up Mount Nebo and I will show you the land I am giving to the people. You may not go there because you did not trust me and honor me before the people, but you may see it."

Mount Nebo was near the Israelites' camp, right across the Jordan River from the city of Jericho *(indicate on the map)*. When Moses got to the top, the Lord let him see all the land called Canaan—high mountains, beautiful blue sea and rich farming land. God said, "This is the land I promised to Abraham, Isaac, Jacob and all their descendants." How kind it was of God to allow Moses to see the wonderful land to which he had been leading the people for so many years. He had trusted God to take them to the Promised Land and here it was!

Sketch 106   *Hilltop*

Moses died there on the mountain alone with God. The Bible says that he was as strong as when he was younger and that his eyes were bright and clear. He didn't die because he was old (120 years), but because his job was finished. Then God buried him in a secret place.

God didn't want people to know where Moses was buried. He had been a great man and some people would probably have tried to worship him at his grave site, instead of remembering that he taught them to worship only the Lord God.

From the New Testament we learn that when a believer dies ("absent from the body"), he goes immediately to live with God in heaven (2 Corinthians 5:8). Moses probably didn't know all about that. What a wonderful surprise it must have been when he closed his eyes on earth and opened them again in heaven. All these years he had lived by faith and hope. Now he saw the Lord; his faith and hope were fulfilled. God always keeps his promises.

▲ **Option #9**

Have several children read aloud Deuteronomy 32:1-6, 9-14 and 39.

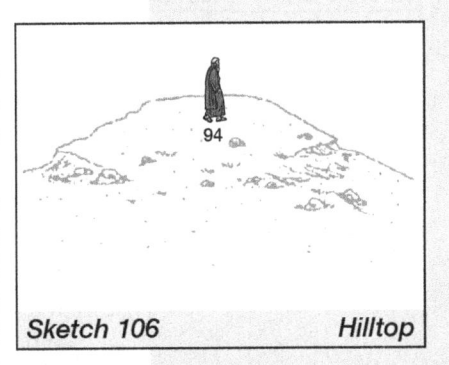

■ Conclusion

Summary

(Moses 25, people 49, Wilderness Map)

What did God promise Moses? *(Place 25 on the board; allow for response throughout.)* Yes, he would show Moses the land before he died. What did God promise his people? *(Add 49.)* That's right; he would give them a land of their own where they could settle down and live. God would keep his promise.

This is the last lesson about the Israelites' travels in the desert. Did God take his people to the Promised Land? Today we saw him bring them right up to the edge of their new land. They were just across the river from Jericho *(indicate on the map)*, a great walled city in Canaan. To see how God helped them conquer Jericho and the other cities in the land, you will have to read Joshua, the next book of the Old Testament.

Sketch 107   Plain Background

Application

(Newsprint & marker or chalkboard & chalk; cross 69, arrows 99[2], girl 98, boy 104, Jesus 103)

What can we learn about God from the Israelites? *(Print responses on newsprint or chalkboard. If necessary, suggest something like God guides us, provides our needs, or must punish sin.)*

We also learn that God means what he says, that we can trust him to take care of us and to keep his promises. This gives us hope. The Israelites lived long before Jesus *(add 69; add 99[1] to the left side of 69)* came, but God was preparing for the time when he would come to earth.

We *(add 98, 104)* live long after Jesus died on the cross *(add 99[1] to the right side of 69)*. What promise does God give us today? *(Response)* Yes, that when we have trusted in Jesus as our Savior from sin, we have the hope (or confidence) that we will live in heaven someday with God. What promise and hope does our memory verse give us? Let's say it together. *(Do so.)* Jesus *(add 103)* is coming back again to take us to be with him! *(Move the arrow on the right side of 69 and point it towards 103.)* The Israelites had to be prepared to enter the new land and we need to be prepared for Jesus' return. Only God knows when that will be. We should take the time now to be sure we are ready for him.

Are you ready? Have you asked Jesus to be your Savior? Have you thanked him for forgiving your sin and giving you the hope of going to heaven? Are you obeying God's Word and living the way it teaches so that you won't have to be ashamed when Jesus returns?

Response Activity

Invite any who have not trusted Jesus as Savior to receive him now so they will be ready to meet him when he returns.

Allow time in class for each one to pray a sentence prayer, saying "thank you" to God for the hope they have because he promises to take care of them all of their lives and take them to heaven someday.

✍ TAKE HOME ITEMS

*Distribute **memory verse tokens for Titus 2:13** and **Bible Study Helps for Lesson 16**.*

RESOURCE SECTION

Use the materials in this section to help your children
incorporate the Bible truths they are learning
into their daily lives in a practical way.

Reproduce the patterns as handouts
for the specific lessons where they are recommended.

*Permission granted to reproduce materials in this section
for use with **God Provides for Us** lessons.*

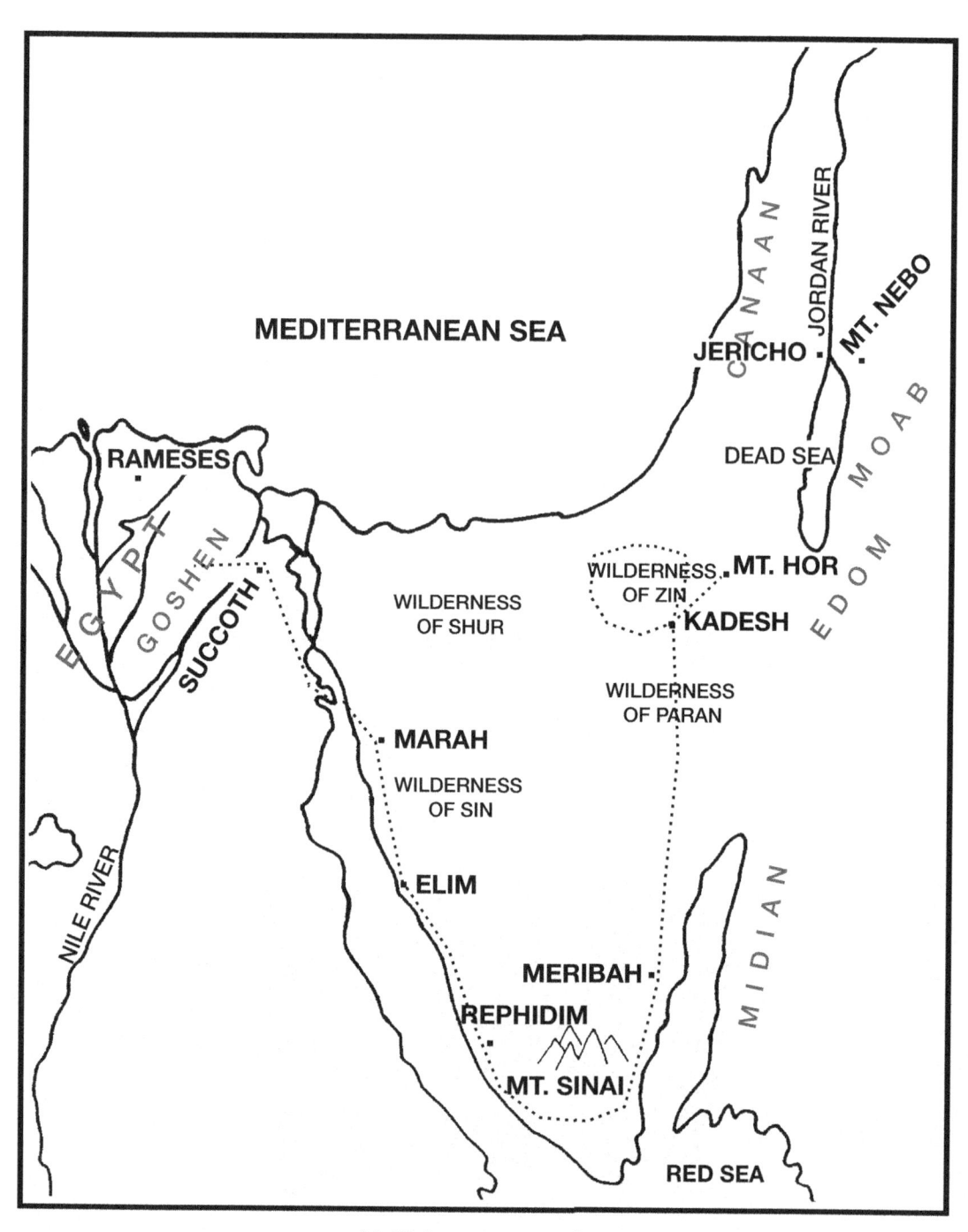

Wilderness Map

Chart of Tabernacle Design

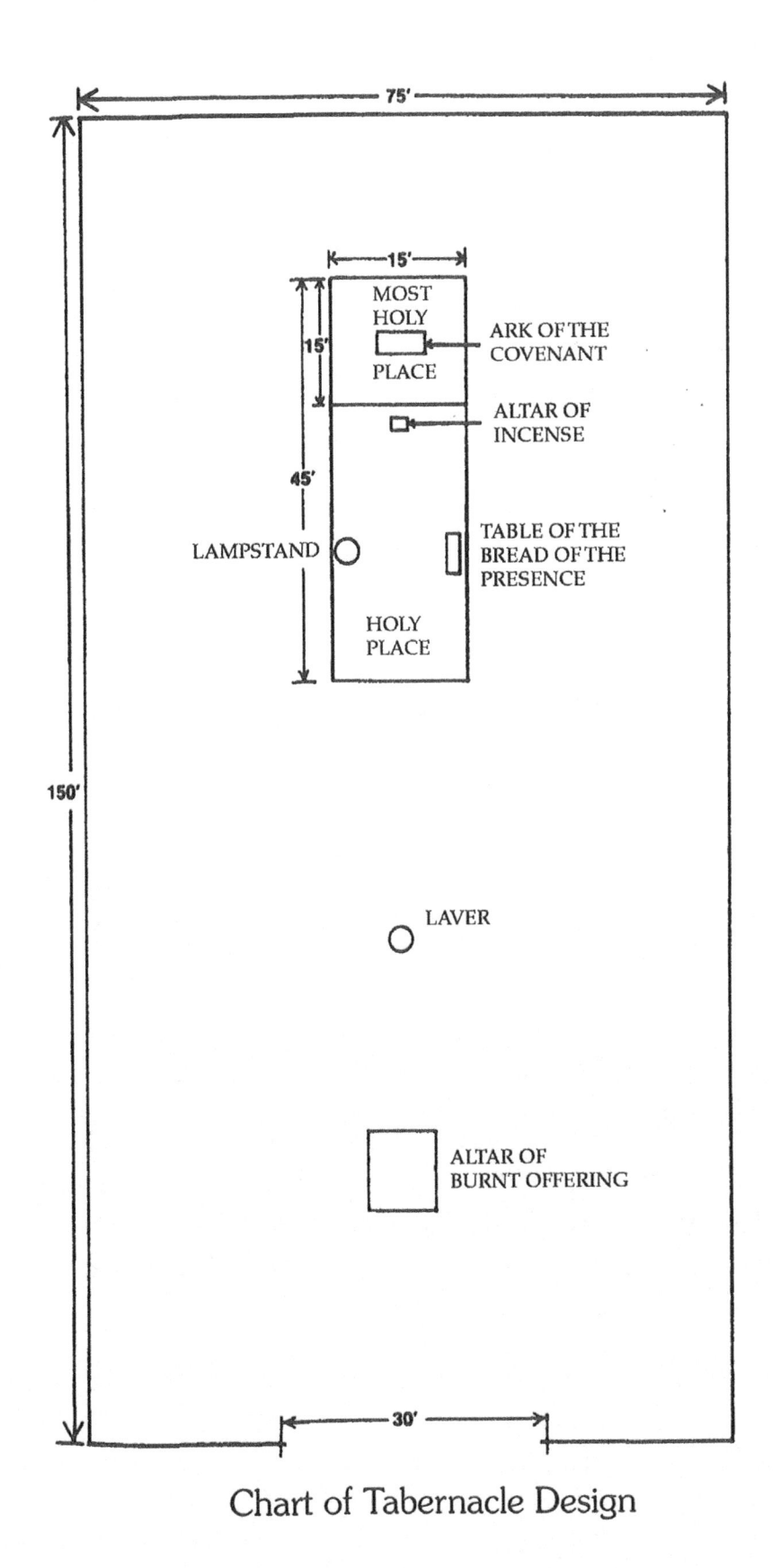

I choose God to be my guide...

Choice	God	me	Result
1. _____			_____
2. _____			_____
3. _____			_____

The Lord will guide us all the time.

P-3

Prayer of Commitment

Lord, I thank you for saving me and giving me eternal life. I am glad to know that you have a purpose for my life. I want to know what your plan for me is.

Please help me to live the way your Word says. With your help, I will obey it and do my best in every responsibility that is given to me so that I will be prepared to carry out your plan for me.

Signed _____

P-4

COURAGE CARD

◆ I believe that God is with me and will not forsake me.

◆ I will trust him to help me speak up for him this week.

Signed _____

Don't be afraid.
God is with you wherever you go.

P–5

My Needs & God's Answers

Need	Date	How God Answered	Date
1.			
2.			
3.			
4.			

P–6

My Choice

I will learn God's rules by studying God's Word.
I choose to live by God's rules, trusting God to help me.

God's Word	God's rule	I'll obey
		✓ here
1. Luke 10:27		
2. Luke 6:31		
3. Colossians 3:13		
4. Colossians 3:20		
5. Colossians 3:23		
6. 1 Thessalonians 5:18		
7. Ephesians 4:29a		

God's Word shows me how to live God's way.

Signed _____

P–7

GOD'S CORRECTION

Accept   Resent

Name _____

Do not resent the Lord's correction.

P–8

My Fellowship with God

Today:

1. I read God's Word and he told me _____

_____

2. I talked to God and

   I praised him for _____

   I confessed _____

   I thanked him for _____

   I shared with him _____

   I asked him _____

P-9

My "Thank You" List

I complained about _____

I thank you, God for

1. _____

2. _____

3. _____

Thank the Lord for everything.

P-10

I will
TRUST GOD
to help me be thankful this week.

_____

Name _____

Thank the Lord for everything.

P–11

My Promise to Jesus

★ Thank you, Jesus, for dying on the cross to take my sin punishment.
★ I love you with all of my heart.
★ I want to please you in all I do and say.
★ I will be quick to confess my sins to God when I do wrong.
★ I will get to know you better as I grow up so I can help others to know you the way I do.

Signed _____ Date _____

God sent Jesus to save us, not judge us.

P–12

GOD

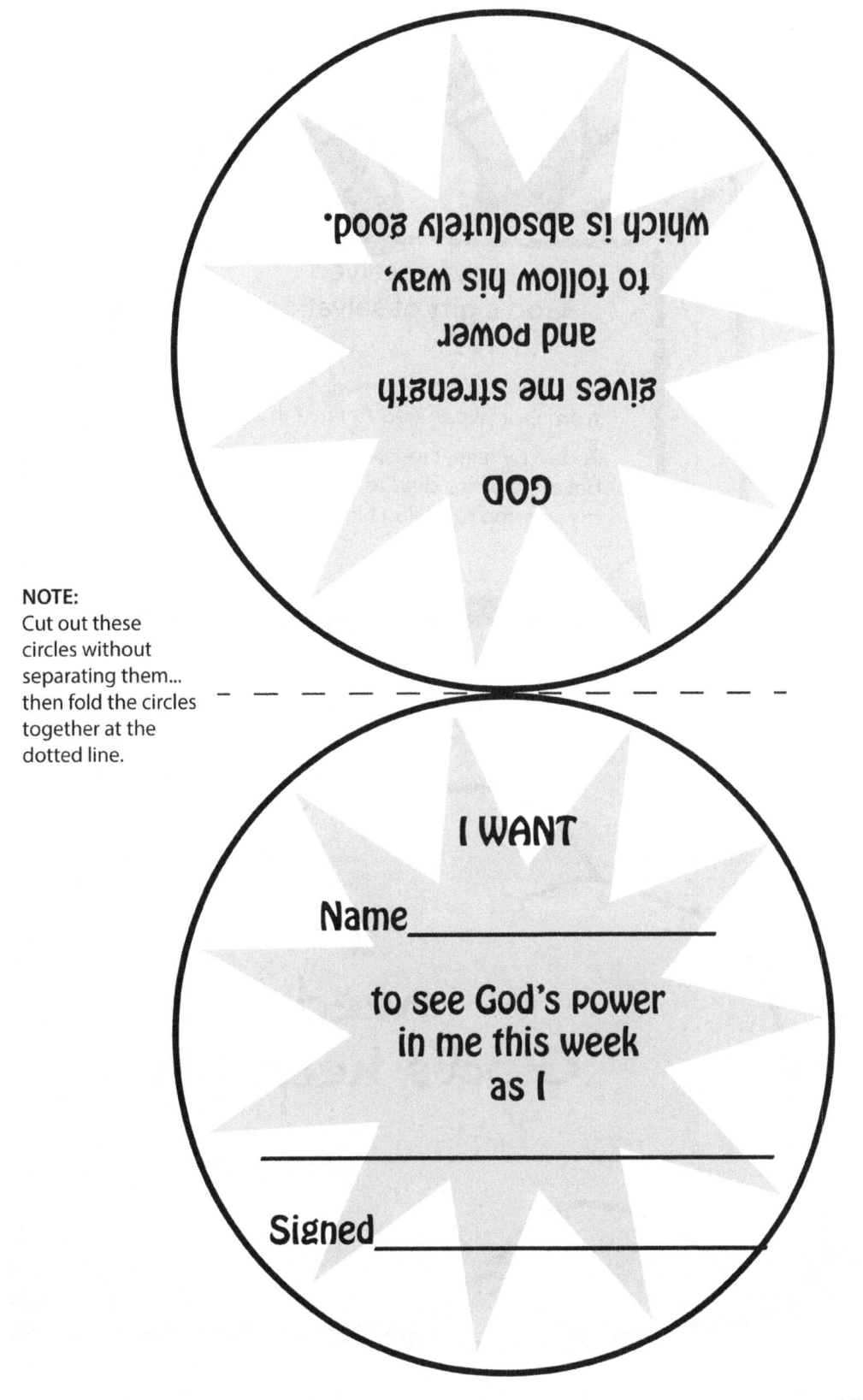

gives me strength
and power
to follow his way,
which is absolutely good.

NOTE:
Cut out these circles without separating them... then fold the circles together at the dotted line.

I WANT

Name_____

to see God's power
in me this week
as I

_____

Signed_____

P-13

**I have received
God's gift of salvation.**
❏ **Yes**   ❏ **No**

You cannot save yourself, salvation is a gift from God when you believe in Jesus.

Today, by faith, I receive God's gift of salvation by believing Jesus died to take the puniushment for my sins and receiving him as my Savior.

Signed _____ Date _____

P–14

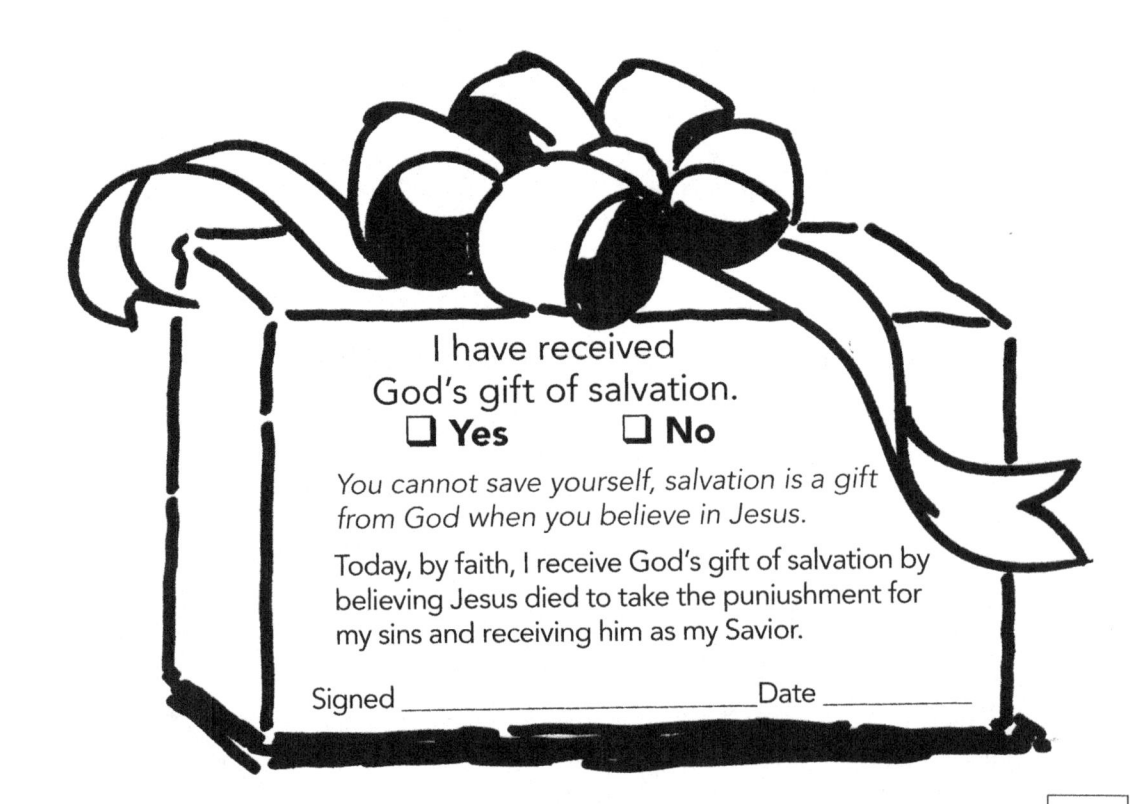

I need God's help for

_____

P–15

The Ten Commandments by God in Exodus 20

1. Do not have any other God.
2. Do not make or worship idols.
3. Do not use the name of God thoughtlessly or carelessly.
4. Do all your work in six days; rest on the seventh as God did.
5. Honor your father and mother that you may have a long life.
6. Do not murder anyone.
7. Do not commit adultery.
8. Do not steal.
9. Do not tell lies about your neighbor.
10. Do not want for yourself what belongs to your neighbor.

God Provides for Us
Name _____
BCM

God Provides for Us
Name _____
BCM

God Provides for Us
Name _____
BCM

God Provides for Us
Name _____
BCM

God Provides for Us
Name _____
BCM

God Provides for Us
Name _____
BCM

Teaching Materials and Supplies
available for
God Provides for Us

FO2T	Teacher's Text	

Contains helpful introductory information, 17 unified lessons that are integrated with the PowerPoint scenes, sidebar options to enhance interactive learning and notes to expand the teacher's understanding, and a Resource Section with take-home items to visually reinforce student response to God's Word.

FO2VCD   Visual CD
Contains PowerPoint visuals in two tracks (KJV and NIV) for Review Chart, Memory Verses and Lessons
Full-colored flashcards can be downloaded to visualize the lessons

FO2RCD   Resource CD
Contains the following:
Creative Idea Menus (program ideas for each lesson)
Visualized Memory Verses (KJV and NIV)
Student Memory Verse Tokens and Token Holders (KJV and NIV)
Student Bible Study Helps

FO2TK   Teaching Kit with computerized visuals
Includes Teacher's text, Visual CD, and Resource CD

FO2F   Felt Figures in full color

FO2R   Felt Review Chart

FB   Felt Backgrounds in full color
See the complete list of backgrounds at our ministry store online.

FBD   Felt Board
A 26-inch x 36-inch folding cardboard, covered with blue polyester felt

FBC   Felt Board Clips
A set of 3 clips to held felt backgrounds on the Felt Board

TGLM   Tract: *God Loves me*
Based on John 3:16; use with children, ages 3-6

TJ316   Tract: *How to Become a Child of God*
Based on John 3:16; use with children, ages 7-11

TCG   Tract: *A Child of God*
Presents salvation and basic teaching for new Christians; use with children, ages 7-11

Order materials online, by phone, or by email.

BCM Publications
https://www.bcmintl.org/ministry-store/
Toll-free: 1-888-226-4685
email: publications@bcmintl.org

Mailbox Bible Club correspondence Bible lessons
Excellent follow-up material. Contact BCM Publications to order or get a sample lesson.

Made in the USA
Middletown, DE
18 September 2021